teenagers

teenagers

AN
AMERICAN
HISTORY

GRACE PALLADINO

BasicBooks
A Division of HarperCollins*Publishers*

Designed by Elliott Beard

Library of Congress Cataloging-in-Publication Data
  Palladino, Grace.
    Teenagers : an American history / Grace Palladino.
      p.   cm.
    Includes index.
    ISBN 0-465-00767-8
    1. Teenagers—United States—History—20th century.
    2. Adolescence—United States—History—20th century.
    3. Teenage consumers—United States—History—20th century.
    4. Popular culture—United States—History—20th century.
    I. Title.
  HQ796.P3115   1996
  305.23'5'0973—dc20   95-49125
                                                           CIP

96 97 98 99 00 ❖/HC 10 9 8 7 6 5 4 3 2 1

In memory of Pfc. Rudolph J. Festa (1925–1944),
a teenage hero of the Second World War

contents

acknowledgments

ALTHOUGH WRITING ITSELF IS THE MOST SOLITARY OF TASKS, producing a book takes outside help. I am pleased to acknowledge the many colleagues, friends, and family who assisted along the way.

My mother, Frances Palladino, kept me well supplied with newspaper clippings, as did Charlotte and Pete Piepmeier. Pete Daniel read an early draft of the manuscript, provided pictures, and (along with friends at the Irish Times) kept my spirits up. Mary Panzer not only provided advice when I needed it but managed to introduce me to Paul McCartney, fulfilling a teenage dream. Estelle Ellis, Kelly Schrum, and Bill Tuttle shared valuable information, Peter Albert and Stuart Kaufman offered crucial encouragement, Jeff Eaby got my computer up and running, Steve Fraser, Karen Klein, and Justin McShea at Basic Books were both enthusiastic and helpful.

Only my family—immediate and extended—can appreciate what finishing this book actually entailed; suffice it to say, we helped each other through the worst of times. Finally, Brad Piepmeier cleared so many paths, so many times, that I am happy to acknowledge that he makes it all possible.

introduction

"They're Getting Older Younger"

"THEY'RE BACK!" THE COVER OF *BUSINESS WEEK* TRUMPETED in 1994. Better yet, there are going to be more of them than ever before, buying pizza, going to concerts, purchasing clothes, cosmetics, CDs, cars, and computer games. They sound like an advertiser's dream—a consumer group with the free time and disposable income to support an affluent life of leisure. Of course, that's exactly what they are—teenagers with more money to spend, more products to choose from, and enough influence in the marketplace to crowd out their baby-boomer parents. After a fifteen-year population decline from 1977 to 1992, teenagers are now riding the crest of a demographic wave that promises big business for years to come. And that almost guarantees them a prominent place in the public spotlight. For no matter what we profess to believe about teenagers and their vital importance to the future, we tend to value them most as consumers.[1]

It's a role that seems oddly suited to their stage in life. "The teen years, after all, are a time of experiment," as *Business Week* puts it. "Trying on new fashions, music, TV shows and movies, products, ideas and attitudes, is what being a teen is all about." Caught in the crosswinds of puberty and inexperience, they are notoriously obsessed with their complexions, their appearance, their social life—typical teenage problems that have spawned a thriving industry of advice givers, guidance counselors, orthodontists, dermatologists. Their legendary need to fit in with the crowd generates healthy profits for a host of businesses from clothing manufacturers to pop music producers—teenagers are almost driven to keep up with the latest products and styles, marketers point out. With a population of 25 million and counting (there should be almost 31 million teenagers by 2006, an all-time high), they constitute a red-hot consumer market worth $89 billion—almost ten times what the market was reportedly worth in 1957, when Elvis Presley was riding high.[2]

That doesn't even begin to count the $200 billion their parents spend on them, either—a healthy figure in anyone's book. In fact, since parents are likely to be at their peak earning power by the time their children are in high school, they are considered a teenager's greatest financial asset. "Parents give teens what teens think of as necessities—a car, a computer, video games," market researchers report. But since teenagers choose the products themselves, companies are advised to court them directly with specialized products, services, and advertising campaigns. "Marketers ignore this group at their peril," a car manufacturer insists, since teenage shoppers are known in the business as "early adopters." Those who develop product loyalties when they are still young and impressionable will carry them through adulthood, marketers promise. And at that point they will have even more money to spend—a tantalizing prospect, given current population trends.[3]

Crass exploitation? Perhaps. A disturbing sign of the times? Hardly. A new corruption of teenage life? Absolutely not. On the contrary, the *Business Week* article is only the latest version of promotional material that has been circulating for decades. Ever since the word "teenager" first came into popular use around the time of the Second World War, the group has been linked to "buying power and influence," a heady combination that promised big business to postwar moviemakers, cosmetic firms, clothes manufacturers, and even grocery stores. At the time, the change was revolutionary—only a decade or so earlier, most teenage children had worked for a living. In fact some had been required to pay back the debts they had incurred in childhood before they were free to leave the family home! They, not their parents, were considered assets to be exploited for a family's good, and they usually had very little to say about this or any other family matter.[4]

Now they were identified as high school students with the time and the inclination to shop for clothes, party goods, records. But in the 1940s retailers found this hard to believe at first. Since nobody knew whether teenagers actually had money to spend, they doubted their value in the marketplace. So fifty years ago promoters launched the idea that teenagers could be counted on to spend their parents' money—after all, they were the family members most likely to demand well-appointed recreation rooms, up-to-date cars, modern appliances, and the latest electronic equipment. And they apparently had no trouble at all getting what they wanted. Now that the war was over, promoters pointed out, parents were willing and able to "play Santa Claus 365 days a year." But if companies wanted a piece of this business, they added, they would have to speak directly to the kids themselves, a proposition that was controversial at the time. Teenagers were still considered children in society's eyes, and that meant they required guidance and protection in the marketplace.[5]

Today those concerns are still raised periodically, but the market itself has settled the controversy. The concept of teenagers as an independent age group with its own interests, attitudes, and spending money is so ingrained that high school students rule their own commercial space—retail chains like Urban Outfitters and the Gap vie for their business; magazine publishers offer *Seventeen*, *Sassy*, *YM*, and *Teen* (among others); and television networks like Fox and MTV program with their demographics in mind. Newspapers from the *Staten Island Advance* to the *Santa Fe New Mexican* feature weekly sections devoted to teenage issues that range from roller blading to body piercing, from prom clothes to mosh pits, to what's hot and what's not. Manufacturers recognize their buying power with specialized lines of "teen spirit" products or makeup specifically formulated to combat teenage "zits."

Indeed, as far as marketers are concerned, teenagers inhabit their own leisure world, one that is dominated by movies, music, fashion, fads, and shopping.[6]

Teenagers rule their own social space, too. As a group, they have come to expect a level of personal freedom that is limited only by their own sense of decorum and discipline—a remarkable shift from the days before the Second World War, when high school students were supposed to put their free time to good use, preparing for adult futures. In the 1990s, they assume they have what the papers call "a right to party" (whether they exercise the right or not), and they take it for granted that their teenage years are prime time to let off steam with their friends. When the National Highway Transportation Board considered setting a curfew for teenagers in 1993, for instance, in hopes of getting drunk drivers off the road, the suggestion did not get very far. "Getting arrested for not being home on time, that's bizarre," one high school student told the *Washington Post*. "That goes against your constitutional rights to . . . freedom." As another teenager put it, "This is America, the land of freedom. So don't restrict ours." They take the same approach when it comes to expressing their personal style, their values, their sexuality. "Nobody should have a say in who I am," a seventeen-year-old puts it plainly.[7]

This determination to establish separate identities and to demonstrate their independence, one way or another, from their parents' world, often brands teenagers as potential troublemakers in the public mind—we tend to expect them to be hostile, indifferent, or messed up, victims of an increasingly complex world that makes them old before their time. We look at their grungy clothes, their nose rings, their tattoos, and we think the worst. We hear snatches of their music and wonder what's the matter with kids today? We pick up the morning paper and assume that the "burnouts" who usually make the news represent the high school crowd. A reporter for the *Dallas Morning News*, for instance, presents a typically bleak picture of the modern teenage world: "Children barely old enough to drive flirt with pregnancy and the possibility of AIDS. Students accosted at knife point give up their jewelry and $100 running shoes. Kids swagger through high school corridors, guns stashed in their belts."[8] Although the reporter acknowledges that the image is overdrawn, the message is nevertheless repeated in countless newspaper and magazine articles, on television shows, in movies—a teenage crisis is at hand. What used to be called juvenile delinquency or deviant behavior now passes for everyday teenage life.[9]

This certainly is not the image that pioneer marketers envisioned back in the 1940s, when they first began to promote teenagers as a group apart. On the contrary, they usually portrayed teenagers as fun-loving, wholesome high school students eager to try out adult freedoms, but willing to live by adult rules. In fact, when they referred to teenagers, they actually had adolescents in mind, a term that dated back to the nineteenth century. According to the experts—psychologists and educators who popularized the idea—adolescents were awkward, vulnerable creatures, the innocent victims of raging hormones, rampant insecurity, and fervent idealism (which often bordered on arrogance), characteristics that were apparently linked to puberty and a lack of experience. Because they were susceptible to worldly temptations (like cigarettes, dance halls, gambling, and liquor), adolescents had to be protected from the adult world, ideally in high school. There they could work through the storm and stress of their teenage years in a disciplined, wholesome, adult-guided environment. In the process, they would discover their talents and goals, develop good work habits, and learn the value of respect for authority—or so the theory went.[10]

The idea that high school guaranteed a healthy adolescence made sense from the experts' point of view. In the nineteenth century, industrialization and specialization had already put a premium on higher education for youth who expected to rise in the world: By the turn of the century, boys who intended to hold "good" professional or white-collar jobs needed a high school diploma just to get started. But at the time, the majority of families could not afford to invest in education. For instance, although the high school population doubled in the 1890s, only 6 percent of the nation's seventeen-year-olds earned diplomas in 1900. Ten years later, when about 15 percent of the age group went to high school, only a fraction stayed long enough to graduate.[11]

But that was not enough, experts insisted. A high school system that ignored the bulk of teenage youth could not produce the literate workforce employers demanded. And a teenage majority left to fend for themselves would not develop the personality, skills, and internal fortitude they needed to survive in a competitive world. Part of the problem could be traced to the schools themselves. High schools offered a classical curriculum designed to serve college-bound students only: Latin, Greek, English literature, history, algebra, geometry, physics, and chemistry.[12] If high schools wanted to attract a broad teenage public, then experts would have to design programs with teenage tastes in mind—a "progressive" philosophy that began to take hold around the 1920s. Emphasizing poise and personality, along with Latin and Greek, high schools began to offer practical courses that students wanted to take, including home economics, stenography, typing, and bookkeeping. The investment paid off in increasing enrollments—by 1930 almost half the teenage population were high school students. Within ten years, a majority of seventeen-year-olds had earned diplomas.[13]

The teenage market that began its spectacular takeoff in the 1940s was the commercial expression of this progressive philosophy. Since high school fashions, fads, and social life apparently kept students interested and involved in school, why not offer students a full array of high school products to choose from? Adolescents would not only learn how to become careful shoppers (a goal that seemed particularly important for girls, who would be raising families soon enough), but they would also have no reason to rush into adult life or adopt what the experts called "precocious" styles—styles that allowed them to look (and often act) much older than they really were. Envisioning the teenage market as an after-school extension of a home economics class, pioneer promoters took it for granted that adults could shape teenage tastes and steer young consumers along appropriate, wholesome paths— a theory known at the time as character building. It was just a matter of finding the right mix of teenage choice and adult guidance to help the next generation find its way in life—and incidentally build up a healthy business in the process.

Consider the model of teenage life promoted by *Seventeen* magazine, the leading proponent of this economic venture. Styles were classic, teenagers were portrayed as wholesome and clean-cut, and advice was tailored to responsible high school students concerned with their futures, their reputations, and their parents' point of view. But since *Seventeen* was also trying to sell advertising space, promoters presented a different picture of teenagers to the business world. In this context, they were enthusiastic, indiscriminate spenders whose highest priority was to fit in with the crowd. High school students were "copycats" promoters promised advertising agencies, "and what a break for you." They "speak the same language, wear the same clothes, eat the same foods. . . . You'll see them shopping together, sipping Cokes at the corner candy store, going to the movies . . . together," traits that were apparently rooted in their adolescent stage of life.[14]

Although these contrasting images made practical sense from a business point of view, they opened a Pandora's box of mixed messages that came to define the conventional version of adolescent culture. On the one hand, character builders like *Seventeen* expected teenagers to take life seriously. In fact, the magazine offered solid advice about preparing for college and future careers and treated young readers as full-fledged citizens with an interest in politics, the United Nations, and issues like democracy and social justice. On the other, *Seventeen* encouraged teenagers to define themselves through their appearance (and their dates) and ensure their status as successful teens by purchasing the products they saw advertised in its pages. At the time, the incongruity of these ideas went unnoticed—since advertisements for household furnishings, hope chests, and classic outfits (complete with hat and gloves, and shoes and bag to match) prevailed in the 1940s and 1950s, no one worried about the magazine's dual message. *Seventeen* targeted strictly white, middle-class teenage customers who intended to follow in their parents' domestic footsteps, and as long as this was the case, the teenage market could be sold as a means of training potential homemakers (and breadwinners) for the future.

By the mid-1950s, however, *Seventeen*'s respectable brand of adolescent culture had real competition—white, middle-class teenagers were not the only high school students with money to spend! Postwar prosperity had opened the door to an entirely different teenage world, one that was populated by working-class and black teenagers who had never participated in high school social life before. This demographic shift changed the nature—and the appeal—of the teenage market. Once a broad group of teenagers had the chance to cast their dollar votes (without benefit of adult guidance), wholesome high school life and domestic dreams lost their power in the marketplace. And once a mixed group of teenagers were encouraged to speak in their own, distinctive voices, they shifted the market's focus to an uncharted world of teenage passion and excitement in the form of rock 'n' roll, leather jackets, fast cars, and drive-in movies.

The change enraged adult critics, who mourned the passing of "vanishing adolescents" and decried the rise of "teenage tyrants." Even well-brought-up teenagers were rejecting their status as adults-in-training. Instead, they embraced a teenage rebel culture of risk, romance, and relaxation—cruising in their cars when they should have been doing homework, hanging out on the streets as if they had nothing better to do, drinking beer and going steady, even though this kind of behavior only led to trouble. Thanks to the rise of rock 'n' roll (the most successful teenage product to date), teenagers had lost their innocence and their direction, critics believed, and juvenile delinquency had taken over the nation!

As the number of teenagers began to soar in the late 1950s, however, these criticisms lost their sting, and by the 1960s the economic value of the teenage market silenced all but the most determined critics. Rebels or not, baby-boom teenagers demonstrated an unprecedented ability to open their parents' wallets, and that made all the difference in the adult world of commerce. Whether they were screaming for the Beatles, protesting an unpopular war, or experimenting with a counterculture of sex, drugs, and rock 'n' roll, teenagers were now the center of commercial attention. "Social change started moving *up* through the age groups," a demographer explained. "Adults started imitating teens."[15] In the process, youth replaced age as the font of social wisdom, and exuberance replaced experience as a key political value, or so it seemed at the time.

From that point forward, teenagers began to shape their own space and chart their own futures without reference to their parents' plans. Rejecting the rigid family roles that had shaped adolescent culture since its nineteenth-century start, they also refused to follow hypocritical social rules that had forced earlier generations to camouflage their real identities (and behavior). After the 1960s, high school students tended to lose their virginity earlier (and in larger numbers) than their predecessors had, and they considered alcohol a rite of teenage passage, not an indication of pathological distress, as adults usually assumed. And after the

1960s, teenagers no longer feigned wholesome innocence for their parents' sake. They knew about divorce, birth control, abortion, homosexuality—subjects that were rarely acknowledged, let alone discussed, in earlier eras. Commenting on the change in 1992, one mother was struck by the candor of modern teenage life. "Condoms! A few years ago you would never hear me say that word. It used to be whispered. . . . Now it's gone prime time."[16]

After the 1960s, teenagers also took their place as a respected and dependable "niche" market—one that would wax and wane along with population trends like any other. Brought up from a very young age to be consumers, not producers, post-1960s teenagers expected to live and dress well. Thirteen-year-olds with a wardrobe of $40 designer jeans were not unusual by the 1980s, and neither were junior high students with their own telephones, televisions, and complete stereo systems. And they did not have to grow up in affluent families either. "Sometimes my mom punishes me by making me go to my room," the adolescent daughter of two hardworking high school dropouts told a reporter in 1993. "But that's o.k.," she said, since the room was equipped with a television, a VCR, Nintendo, books, magazines, a telephone line, "and a bunch of other stuff."[17] Quintessential consumers, today's teenagers take it for granted that they (and their parents) were born to shop.

Ironically, though, they are also the first postwar generation to have serious qualms about their economic future. In an age of automation, plant closings, corporate downsizing, and dual-career families, they are learning the hard way that middle-class comforts are not guaranteed. Indeed, ambitious teenagers who came of age in the 1980s and 1990s were already well aware that they would have to make money (and plenty of it) to live almost as well as their parents did—a sharp contrast to 1960s radicals, who felt no compulsion to find a job and disdained the very idea of joining the "rat race." Those with no taste or talent for schoolwork, or no interest in science and the technical world, face the greatest obstacles. For unlike their predecessors in the 1950s and 1960s, who could at least look forward to good manufacturing jobs, regardless of how they spent their teenage years, teens today cannot expect to support themselves (let alone a family) without a solid education.

This economic wake-up call has fashioned a new public image for teenagers. No longer amusing adolescents eager to ape adult styles or cultural rebels in conflict with society's constraints, in the 1990s teenagers are presumed to be a mixed bag of independent, risk-taking individuals, forced to grow up too fast in a dangerous, demanding world. Today young teenagers are expected to decide for themselves at a very young age how to live their lives and which road to travel to adulthood—a dramatic reversal of the sheltered, wholesome, adult-guided adolescent formula. "They still have the same issues of identity and self-loathing and all that psychological stuff that J. D. Salinger wrote about [in *The Catcher in the Rye*]," a television producer explained in 1994, "but you're dealing with a different playing field."[18]

This book attempts to compare and contrast teenage playing fields over time by tracing the twists and turns in teenage life (and adult attitudes) that transformed allegedly "sheltered adolescents" into today's "pragmatic, precocious kids." It begins with high school, the institution that first set the age group apart and launched the radical notion that teenagers were entitled to enjoy a social life and the personal freedom that went with it—with or without their parents' approval. It follows the concept through the Second World War (when the high school crowd first drew national attention), postwar prosperity (when the teenage market took off), and the baby-boom era (when the combination of economic security and an unpopular war undermined traditional notions of adult authority).

Each of these eras witnessed a significant change in teenage life that altered the concept of growing up for the next generation: the notion of "democratic" family life in the 1930s, which promised teenage children a voice and vote in their own affairs; the emergence of high school social life as a "typical" teenage experience in the 1940s; the vast expansion of the commercial marketplace in the 1950s and early 1960s, which opened the doors of teenage culture to whole new segments of the age group; and the transformation of mainstream middle-class high school students in the late 1960s and early 1970s from adolescents more or less willing to play by society's rules to teenagers determined to escape the social conventions that had trapped their parents.

At the same time, a rapidly changing social structure reshaped teenage visions of the future and influenced their approach to everyday life. The explosion of manufacturing jobs in the 1940s and 1950s, for instance, gave boys with no interest or aptitude for school a solid chance to make a living, whether they finished high school or not—an economic aberration that gave a healthy boost to teenage "rebel" culture. The opening of professional opportunities to college-educated females (coupled with advances in reliable birth control) gave "nice" girls their first real chance to decide for themselves who and what they wanted to be, options that ultimately revolutionized the structure of family life. And the breaking down of racial barriers in the 1950s and 1960s (thanks to efforts of civil rights activists) not only opened crucial educational doors to ambitious black teenagers but also exposed the callous, hypocritical, and unjust structure of "respectable" American life. In fact, it was this exposure—through television, magazines, and especially popular music—that set the stage for the turbulent upheavals that came to define youth culture in the 1960s.

We tend to assume that the rise of independent teenagers (as opposed to dependent adolescents) is really a tale of cultural decline and parental neglect. But in fact, the evolution of teenage culture over the past fifty years is a story of institution building, market expansion, racial desegregation, and family restructuring. Bombarded as we are today with stories of armed teenagers in high school, pregnant teenagers with no plans for the future, and self-destructive teenagers who drink and drive despite the yearly ritual of high school funerals, it is easy to lament the passing of a simpler time when teenagers respected their parents, high schools turned out educated graduates, and sex never reared its ugly head. But that cherished image of a well-functioning past, as this book demonstrates, tells us more about adult fantasies than teenage reality: The order and discipline we usually associate with the good old days had more to do with a lack of opportunities and alternatives than it did with a shared culture of "traditional" family values or teenage respect for adult authority.

Time and time again over the past sixty years, teenagers have proved that they cannot be separated from the "real" adult world or molded according to adult specifications: Ever since the architects of adolescent culture imagined a sheltered, adult-guided world of dependent teenage children, their high school descendants have yearned to breathe free. In the 1930s, they battled their parents over curfews, cigarettes, and swing music; half a century later, the issues were sex, drugs, and rock 'n' roll. But the basic conflict remains the same, regardless of the issue or the era: Who gets to decide how teenagers look, act, and experience life? And who decides what that experience means? Although adults often interpret this conflict as a simple attack on parental authority tempered by hormones and a biological need to stand apart, that is only part of the story. The evolution of modern teenage culture has as much to do with a changing economy, a national culture of consumption and individualism, and the age-graded, adolescent world of high school as it does with inexperience or hostility to adult rule.

Part I

Adolescents

chapter one

High school classroom, Springfield, Missouri, 1929. *Library of Congress, Prints and Photographs Division, FSA Collection [LCUSZ 6284360]*

The High School Age

WHEN ALFRED FONDLER SLAPPED A TEENAGE GIRL WHO WAS sitting behind him in a New York City movie house in 1936, he saw no need to apologize. She had been talking and laughing all through the picture, and then, instead of quieting down when he asked her to, she had started to argue. Even the newspapers agreed that he had only done what everyone else there wanted to do. After all, didn't adults have the right to watch a movie in peace?[1]

The girl and her friends didn't think so. Unwilling to recognize Fondler's authority, as good children might, they had him arrested and hauled before a local magistrate. That their complaint was dismissed was not surprising: Adults had the right, if not the obligation, in the 1930s, to discipline children however they saw fit. But the girls saw the case in a different light. In their estimation they were no longer children and, that being the case, they had some rights of their own, including the right to set their own standards. Like teenage youth all over the country, these outspoken movie-goers were taking a stand: They were old enough to express their opinions and their individual personalities, they believed, and they had no intention of deferring to adult wishes without a fight.

The story was a classic; adolescents had been trying to go their own way ever since Adam and Eve first outgrew the Garden of Eden. And adults had been trying to hold them back. The conflict

3

seemed inevitable, given the natural rivalry between exuberance and experience. For what looked to adults like commonsense standards and valuable advice often seemed hopelessly out of date—or even humiliating—to their offspring. "You can hardly blame us for distrusting most of your standards," a high school group told *Parents* magazine in 1932, "when some of them . . . have proved so obviously foolish."[2]

A sixteen-year-old put it this way: "Most people our age want to grow up as fast as they can [but] their parents don't want them to," she told a radio audience. "They won't let them . . . do things that other students . . . do." Some could not go out on school nights, or stay out as late as their friends. They were not allowed to use the telephone or drive the family car. Their parents picked out their clothes, their friends, their hairstyles—they even wanted to plan their futures! But these students had a startling message for parents determined to keep their children too young too long: Their strategies were doomed to fail. High school students wanted a voice and vote in family affairs, and parents who valued harmony at home would have to take them seriously. They expected to enjoy a measure of personal freedom and privacy, too—grown-up rights that high school students would exercise one way or another. "When parents do not give any responsibility at all, hold their children down and try to keep them young," a boy explained, "the student will go out behind the parents' back."[3]

The fact was, adults had been trying to slow their children down for decades, but so far they had not managed to stop the teenage clock. Even back in the 1870s, Louisa May Alcott had railed against "precocious" behavior in her novel *An Old Fashioned Girl*. Yet this ringing endorsement of a long, slow childhood fell on deaf ears, at least as far as high school students were concerned. "Unhealthy" or not in adult eyes, adolescents would not give up the grown-up clothes, grown-up parties, and "giddy" social life they already enjoyed. Nor would they conform to the adult-approved models of "sheltered" adolescence that psychologist G. Stanley Hall had proposed around the turn of the century. Fully grown as far as their physical development was concerned, they believed that they were capable of judging for themselves just "what they should do or refrain from doing"—an attitude that alarmed educators as early as 1914. Like it or not, these young adolescents intended to enjoy the "parties, receptions, and dances of the grown-up type" that they already associated with the "high school age."[4]

But these high school students were by no means typical. In the nineteenth and early twentieth centuries, adolescents who took education and a private social life for granted were only a tiny elite. Up until the 1930s, most teenagers worked for a living on farms, in factories, or at home, whatever their families required at the time.[5] They were not considered teenagers yet, or even adolescents, for that matter—the term only applied to high school students at the time. They were teenage children who could expect to be seen but not heard within their family circle and ignored, for the most part, outside of it.

By the time the chattering moviegoers tested their rights in court, however, high school was on its way to becoming a typical teenage experience. The Great Depression had finally pushed teenage youth out of the workplace and into the classroom. By 1936, 65 percent were high school students, the highest proportion to date. In the process, adolescents had become an age group and not just a wealthy social class, a shift that helped to create the idea of a separate, teenage generation. When a teenage majority spent the better part of their day in high school, they learned to look to one another and not to adults for advice, information, and approval. And when they got a glimpse of the freedom and social life that the high school "crowd" enjoyed, they revolutionized the very concept of growing up.

This remarkable transformation had as much to do with the high school experience as it did with raging hormones or adolescent insecurity, a social consequence that took the experts by surprise. In fact, ever since G. Stanley Hall popularized the theory of conflicted adolescents, progressive educators had presumed that they could produce the kind of cooperative teenage students they wanted as long as they adopted a sympathetic, open-minded approach in school. Unlike Hall, who believed that adolescent storm and stress fueled the process of teenage self-discovery, these experts preferred the concept of stress-free growth. With the proper help and guidance, they believed, adolescents would conform to adult society's standards without a fight, as long as they believed that they had made the choice to conform on their own.[6] And what better place than high school to learn how to make wise choices? It offered a sheltered, safe environment where students could try their hand at scholarship, athletics, student government, and a host of activities such as debating teams, school newspapers, and dramatic societies. It provided a serious atmosphere of disciplined, productive work. And it set high standards of respectable conduct. Dress and behavior codes prohibited smoking, gum chewing, and excessive cosmetics, for instance, and teachers tolerated only good-natured, respectful, and ambitious students in school. In theory, at least, high school offered a wholesome alternative to precocious behavior and diverted teenage attention away from a frivolous, unhealthy social life.

In practice, though, high schools often produced a very different effect. Upstanding teachers might frown on flirtations, and principals could ban sororities and fraternities from school grounds, but that did not mean they ceased to exist. Demanding taskmasters might require attention and respect in the classroom, but their influence rarely extended beyond a high school's gates. In 1914, for instance, an educator reported that high school students were sniffing chloroform for amusement and shooting heroin and cocaine for a lark! Around the same time, a survey of high school youth workers indicated that 42 percent had direct knowledge of "wrong relations" among high school students, and 52 percent had at least heard rumors of questionable moral behavior![7] If student interviews in the 1930s were any indication, progressive high schools and social education had not reversed (or even controlled) the process.

In fact, by the 1930s high school students seemed more convinced than ever that experimentation was a normal part of growing up. A not-so-innocent high school student stated the case squarely: "I understand myself. I know my weaknesses and I know my assets, too," he said. "Everything I do, right or wrong, I consider part of my education for life." Girls were beginning to adopt the same independent attitude, much to their parents' dismay. "The movies have given me some ideas about the freedom we should have," a sixteen-year-old girl reported in the 1930s, and her notion—to go out and have a good time, but to watch her step—was not so different from what a sixteen-year-old boy might have proposed. Although her attitude would not have alarmed a "new woman" of the 1920s, it was probably light-years away from what her mother had been taught—especially if she had not been fortunate enough to go to high school herself.

Behavior that had once marked adolescents as dangerously unconventional, in their parents' day, was now becoming a standard high school style.[8]

For instance, boys had once hidden away to puff on forbidden cigarettes, but now high school students, boys and girls, often smoked in public. And that was a dangerous sign of the times, according to adult critics. "The youth who uses cigarets, tends to fail in his classes, to quit school, to lose respect for his mother, to have low ideals and ambitions, to commit crimes and to drop all interest in religion," the Anti-Cigaret Alliance warned in 1930. The consequences for girls were even more dire: Those who had a taste for tobacco, the group asserted, were likely to lead "unmoral" lives.[9]

If that was not bad enough, high school boys were developing an unhealthy taste for liquor and scandalizing their parents by staying out late and coming home "tipsy." Their parents could not do much to stop them, either. Harsh discipline and close supervision could not guarantee compliance, a teenage boy explained. Parents who refused to let a boy grow up only pushed him to do "the things that seem to him grown-up—smoking, staying out late, doing things that are slightly shady—just to prove that he is grown-up." Another made a similar point: "You take a lad of seventeen, hold him in and rule him with an iron hand. What will happen?" he asked. "It will not be long before you have a sullen, back-biting stubborn lad, if he is anything like me." Adolescents were still willing to listen to advice on issues like morals and behavior, but if adults tried to issue a command or "an order without any reason," he said, "why, students don't feel like doing it." If parents or teachers really wanted to guide adolescents, "they should present both sides of the problem," a teenage group agreed in 1936, "and then try to let the student make his own decisions."[10]

As high schools claimed a larger proportion of teenage youth during the 1930s, this concept of teenage rights and democratic family life began to take off. Convinced that they were old enough to set their own standards, high school students assumed a measure of personal freedom and generational independence that challenged traditional notions of parental authority and respect. They claimed the right to dress and act they way *they* wanted to, even if it meant battling their parents every step of the way. And they claimed the right to choose their own friends and run their own social lives, based on teenage notions of propriety and style, not on adult rules of appropriate conduct. Where parents had once chaperoned courtships, for instance, deciding what qualities children should seek in a mate, high school students adopted a "dating and rating" system in the 1930s, based on their own ideas of who was suitable to spend time with and who was not. Did a boy have the use of a car, or would a date with him mean riding public transportation? Did a girl dress like everyone else and wear her hair in a stylish cut? Were her parents the modern type who would set reasonable curfews? Or would a boy have to pass muster before he was allowed to take their daughter out? "This new world of youth is not so frightening when we understand it," a journalist reported in 1932. "It wants primarily to be left alone by its elders," she said.[11]

Critics blamed this social revolution on "scientific" education (which weakened church and family ties), scandalous movies (which projected depraved notions of adult life), and "pleasure-seeking" high school students who spent more time with their friends than they did with their families. But they blamed parents most of all, especially those who seemed to be "afraid of their children." If parents had any hope of stemming this teenage tide, critics warned, they would have to exercise some authority at home. Parents had not only the right but the duty to supervise their children's free time, they insisted. Parents also had a duty to insist that their children keep reasonable hours, associate with "worthy" friends, and accept the fact that "father owns the family car and controls the family purse strings."[12] According to this strict, no-nonsense view, parents who lacked the stamina to enforce these basic house rules, or failed to seek moral support from those who did not, had only themselves to blame.

Even if parents had wanted to keep their children close to home (and many parents did not, especially if they had active social lives of their own), high school students already had other plans. By the 1930s, active high school students did little more than eat and sleep at home. "During my entire sophomore year I had some place to go almost every night," one busy student explained. On Monday there was basketball practice, Tuesday the YMCA, Wednesday he went to the movies with friends, Thursday swimming practice, Friday the movies again, and Saturday he learned to dance. He was not always happy that he spent so little time at home, but on the other hand he was a popular and successful student. And that was his priority at the moment; popularity was already the measure of true high school success.[13]

It was also the measure of family rank and social acceptability. In the 1930s, only children of the most prosperous, professional families could afford to enjoy a social life in high school. It took money and family status (measured by a car, a telephone, a spacious house, and an ample allowance) to rate as part of the high school crowd—assets that were rare indeed during the Great Depression, when almost 77 percent of American families earned less than $2,000 a year (which was roughly equivalent to a household income of about $20,000 today, not nearly enough to provide middle-class comforts).[14] At the very least, boys in the popular crowd had to dress well, and that could be expensive. Basic wardrobes usually included white duck pants and at least two suits (gray and blue were popular) with both trousers and more casual slacks to match. Well-dressed boys also needed sports attire (and proper equipment), stylish rain gear, and assorted shirts, sweaters, ties, hats, and shoes.

Clothes were just the starting point, of course. Popular boys needed plenty of spending money to finance three nights a week out with friends—and parents willing to spring for a variety of unbudgeted expenses, such as summer travel (and the luggage that went with it), fees for after-school clubs, and occasional treats for the crowd. If they were dating, their expenses were higher still, since boys had to pay the girl's share for dinner, a movie, and maybe some dancing. They also had to arrange for suitable transportation if they could not come up with a car—popular girls did not ride the bus under any circumstances!

Popular girls had expenses, too, since they needed a range of stylish clothes to rate a date. This required a substantial investment on a parent's part. Many high school girls considered themselves adequately dressed in the 1930s if they owned two sweaters and skirts that could be mixed and matched, or three new blouses (even if they were homemade). But these girls were not part of the popular crowd and did not expect to join it. For a suitable high school wardrobe, according to some well-heeled girls, included "several little school dresses, a pair of sports shoes for school, perhaps a beret and a sport coat," along with "a good dress coat and hat, one or two simple evening dresses," and their list went on and on.[15]

These assorted expenses kept the vast majority of high school students from "running with the crowd," as one boy put it. "Those who don't have the money . . . feel out of it," he said, especially now that they knew just what they were missing.[16] But money alone could not guarantee high school status. Popular high school students also needed "sympathetic" parents who were willing to let their daughters as well as their sons stay out until midnight at least three nights a week for shows, parties, and automobile rides—parents who remembered how they felt when they were young and were willing to change with the times. "How can a girl be pretty and popular," a distraught student wanted to know in 1931, when her mother made her wear "woolen underwear, cotton stockings and flat boyish oxfords?" The simple answer was she could not, no matter what her mother thought. Students who failed to dress according to high school standards had no chance to rate with the crowd. And unsympathetic, old-fashioned parents oblivious to the cruel ways of high school would pay the price, their children warned. For in the end, they would have to deal with the "antisocial" offspring their inflexibility inevitably created.[17]

No wonder more traditional parents, and immigrants in particular, saw no good reason to send teenage children to high school. On the one hand, they often needed their children's wages or help at home to survive. But on the other, they considered high school a needless luxury that only made their children "fresh" and dissatisfied with family life at home. From their point of view, the family functioned best as a dictatorship, not a democracy. These parents expected obedience from their children without any back talk. In a world where times were always tough, Depression or not, they based their concept of family solidarity on economic necessity, not companionship or mutual respect. "There has never been any 'palship' between us that is seen in so many native American homes," the son of a Danish woodworker remarked. Others echoed his complaint. A social worker who studied Italian immigrants was shocked by the "lack of companionship" between parent and child, while a German daughter regretted the fact that her mother was not as "sympathetic" as American mothers seemed to be.[18]

As far as these Old World parents could see, their teenage children were better off working than they were wasting time in high school. The Danish woodworker, for instance, took it for granted that boys found a job when they finished eighth grade. But his son convinced him otherwise; in America, boys had a right to go to school, he said, and his father eventually relented. In time, he even took pride in the fact that he was able to educate his children, first in high school and then college. The German daughter had a rougher time, probably because girls were expected to marry anyway. "My mother was willing to see me go to school until I was fourteen," she said, but "she couldn't get the idea of going for four years. . . . For six months straight we had an argument nearly every night and I was about sick but I finally won out." But this was only the first of a series of struggles. "I never had an allowance; I had very few clothes; I had an argument every time I needed books or had to contribute something at school—my mother thought it was all nonsense," she said.[19]

Her high school experience had nothing in common with the social whirl the wealthy crowd enjoyed. "I didn't make many friends in high school—boys didn't interest me and I didn't interest the boys," she admitted. But popularity had never been her goal—in her estimation, high school was a means to economic independence, a golden opportunity for girls like her to escape their social fate. Graduating at the top of her class, she managed to land a good job as a stenographer—a definite step up at the time. Yet according to her mother she had wasted her days in school. She still could not sew or cook a meal, could she? And how would stenography help her raise a family? She would have gotten a more useful education at home, her mother believed, since at least she would have learned how to do housework.[20]

Traditional Italian parents agreed wholeheartedly, and they did their best to keep their daughters too busy to imagine any life outside the home. From their point of view, a girl became a woman at age thirteen, and that meant she had family responsibilities. "I go to school, and come home and do the dishes," one teenage girl described her daily routine, then she went down to sit on the stoop with a girlfriend until it was time to come up and cook. With her free hours taken up by shopping, scrubbing, or mending, she had little time left to spend with boyfriends, even if her father had allowed her to date. But he did not, and she knew better than to ask to bring a boyfriend home, since her father, as head of the family, would find a husband for her soon enough—

a girl who was not married at age eighteen was an old maid in her neighborhood. In the meantime, her brothers would escort her to any outside activities and "wait on the curb across the street" until it was time to walk her home.[21]

Old World Italian fathers were notorious for trying to evade school attendance laws, and no wonder: Once teenage girls saw how the other half lived—at school, at the movies, on the street— they began to challenge their parents' rigid control of their lives. A girl who could not bring a boyfriend home would meet him elsewhere, the experts warned, and less dutiful Italian daughters proved their point. One teenage girl used her father's love of high culture to win permission to visit a museum regularly—a privilege he was proud to grant. He did not need to know that she met her boyfriend there, any more than other parents needed to know that their daughters rode around in automobiles or attended public dances. "I'm not supposed to go to dance halls," an Italian girl admitted, "but other girls do so why shouldn't I?" Whether traditional parents liked it or not, their bolder daughters envied the middle-class custom of high school dating, and they were willing to risk the wrath of their fathers—and a probable beating if they were caught—to live more independent lives.[22]

She and others like her were fortunate to live in cities that provided high schools for everyone, whether parents believed in education (and teenage freedom) or not. But there were others who were not offered even this small measure of opportunity. Many communities could not—or in some cases would not—support high schools. In the rural, segregated South, for instance, where education was not a high priority, only 11 percent of black teenage youth (3 percent of the age group overall) were high school students in 1930. And this was a distinct improvement over the recent past: The number of black high schools had jumped from 67 in 1916 to 1,860 in 1928, but still almost three hundred counties in fourteen states provided no high schools at all for black students. There was also a serious shortage of instructors—studies estimated that for every black high school teacher in the South, there were 210 potential students (the ratio for whites was 1 to 60). There was a serious shortage of money, too. State governments in the South were never generous with education funds for either race, but they spent more than twice as much to educate a white student ($50) as they did to educate a black student ($20).[23]

However, even when black youth had high schools to go to, they already knew that their skin color—not their talent, effort, or ambition—limited their horizons. For instance, black teenagers who played by society's rules and took education seriously knew that they could never move beyond the bounds of their own, separate communities. "There certainly isn't much inducement to work or study knowing that in competition with a white fellow your chances are slim," a seventeen-year-old college student pointed out. The teenage son of a hardworking janitor agreed. "Well, I want to go to school as long as I can. I'd even like to go to college. But I don't guess it's much use though," he admitted. As one girl put it, she didn't need a high school diploma to do domestic work, and her general resignation to her social fate was echoed over and over again in the 1930s. "Such is life," a disillusioned teenager explained. "If you ain't white, you just ain't right."[24]

Conditions were even bleaker for poor black teenagers clustered in the South—according to the conventional (white) wisdom, book learning only spoiled good field hands. In the South, schools closed during busy seasons: In city schools the term averaged 182 days a year, but in black schools 146 days was the norm.[25] Worse than that, teachers could take lessons only so far if they wanted to keep on teaching. An instructor at a plantation school might be permitted to "teach the art of planting . . . how to build a house or repair steps," a reporter in Mississippi noted in 1935, "but she may not teach either children or adults how to keep a receipt or how to compute their earnings."[26] If she did, black students might figure out for themselves how the tenant-farming system actually worked! As far as white landowners were concerned, it made no practical sense to educate black youth for the kind of independent life they would never live in the South.

Poor white adolescents in rural areas did not fare much better. Clinch Valley, Tennessee, got its first high school in 1937, but the eighty-three students it served had to make do with a "small, four-room building constructed of undressed, unpainted pine boards." There were only thirty-five desks, and these were grade-school size, too small to fit most of the students. However, no one was complaining; on the contrary, students appreciated what little they finally had. "Even a half chance like this is valued," a student explained, since "such an opportunity has never been offered us before."[27]

Compared to what students enjoyed in more prosperous communities, though, the students in Clinch Valley were definitely shortchanged. For even at the height of the Great Depression, high school students in Shaker Heights, Ohio, for instance, spent the school day in a modern brick building (on nineteen landscaped acres) that housed a well-stocked library, a swimming pool, two gymnasiums, and a good-size cafeteria—an impressive environment that symbolized the central importance of higher education to a prosperous future.[28]

A stark contrast, perhaps, but one that illustrated a hard social fact of teenage life—the expansion of the high school population, during the 1930s, did not guarantee teenage youth equal opportunity to succeed and prosper. High schools were funded by property taxes (which dropped precipitously during the Depression), so the students most in need of outside help were the least likely to receive it. Expenditures for students nationwide dropped 25 percent (a figure that masked the Depression's impact on poor communities)—and more than seven hundred schools were forced to close their doors in the 1930s.[29] Thus, in a world that rationed educational opportunity according to a community's ability to pay, innate talent and drive could only take an individual teenager so far, especially when times were tough and jobs hard to come by.

In the 1930s, however, concepts like individual ambition and equal opportunity for teenagers black and white, male and female, had no real meaning. There was only one standard of respectable life, and adolescents had little choice in the matter: Girls were destined to be mothers and homemakers, boys to be fathers and breadwinners. Moreover, the particulars of these family roles were all but determined by a family's social background. For instance, white middle-class sons could expect to go to college and do "clean" office or professional work; their immigrant counterparts could expect to work with their hands; and black and other darkskinned youth could expect to be teachers or preachers, if they came from the upper classes, or low-paid service workers if they did not. The lines of social demarcation were as clear as they were rigid: What you were, in the 1930s, determined who you were and how far or fast you could expect to go in life. An adolescent's future rested squarely on a parent's past.

So did an adolescent's present—it made a great difference to teenage students whether they were part of the established, high school crowd or the first of their family to stay in school. And it made a great difference to teenage students whether they viewed high school as a means to an end (be it social or professional) or as a prison designed to contain and humiliate them. Before the 1930s, no one thought seriously about these differences, since only the most stable families sent their children to high school. But during the Great Depression, when teenagers had no other choice but to go to school, these conspicuous differences in experience, expectations, and preparation could not be ignored. In fact, by the mid-1930s, the federal government was forced to acknowledge that every adolescent needed help to reach the future, whether families could afford to provide it or not.

This was the lesson of the Great Depression where teenage youth were concerned: Once work was no longer an option for the vast majority, high school had to bridge the gap. With the help of progressive educators (or so the theory went), even the lowliest teenage students could learn how to make the most of their assigned positions in life—the girls to manage their future homes efficiently and raise their children intelligently, as the National Council on Education put it, the boys to provide a reliable family income.[30] In the process, the least fortunate would learn the same rules of respectable living and self-discipline that the middle class were supposed to learn at home, through classes, extracurricular activities, and a supervised, high school–based social life. That kind of well-rounded social education would prepare adolescents, whatever their background, "for those important social relations of tomorrow," the experts insisted.[31] And that, after all, was the real goal of adolescence in the 1930s: learning to behave responsibly by keeping the future in mind.

$\mathcal{A}$re You a Girl Who—

Likes to read Exciting Stories?
Likes to make Pretty Things for Herself?
Likes to go on Nature Hikes?
Likes to know how to give a Party?
Likes to Collect Stamps?
Likes to know about World-Wide Interests?
Likes to meet Distinguished Women?
Likes to cook Delightful Foods?
Likes to read about Other Girls?

If you have any one of these desires, you will find them satisfied in reading EVERYGIRLS, the Magazine of the Camp Fire Girls. Or, if you have a friend who likes to do any of these things, she, too, would like EVERYGIRLS. You may subscribe anytime during 1931 for the small sum of 75 cents. Spread the glorious story of the Camp Fire Girls in your community by telling them about EVERYGIRLS.

Send Subscriptions to

EVERYGIRL'S PUBLISHING COMPANY
LYON AT OTTAWA   GRAND RAPIDS, MICHIGAN

Advertisement, *Everygirls,* 1931.

Advise and Consent
Building Adolescent Character

ADOLESCENCE WAS NEVER AN EASY STAGE OF LIFE TO NEGOTIATE, but it seemed particularly hazardous during the 1930s. Sustained economic depression put a very practical spin on the process of growing up. When the margin of error was painfully small, youth's high spirits could prove expensive. "The crucial thing for the working-class youngster was to find a job, any job," according to James Collier, who grew up during the Depression. For a middle-class child, "it was to get that high school diploma that could lead to a white-collar job. Those who could not get regular jobs," he pointed out, "could not marry, could not set up households, could not lead ordinary lives."[1] That was a chilling reality for boys who grew up expecting to head families. Work was the key to a respectable male's identity in the 1930s, a lesson that middle-class boys learned very young.

Marriage was the key for girls. The two went hand in hand. In the 1930s, a respectable middle-class family was an affectionate economic unit—a small business funded by the father and managed by the mother. The spheres of influence were separate but equally demanding. Both required a certain expertise: Boys had to learn how to earn money enough to support a family in style, and girls had to learn how to spend that money wisely on their family's behalf. Both required a certain level of discipline, too. Boys were expected to forgo serious romance until they were safely enrolled in college; girls had to protect their innocence and preserve their good names if they intended to marry well. Delayed gratification and sublimation were the cardinal rules of middle-class adolescence, rules that seemed particularly binding as times grew increasingly hard.

Or at least that was what professional character builders thought. Recreation specialists associated with organizations like the Boy Scouts, the Camp Fire Girls, the YMCA, and the Girl Scouts prepared middle-class youth for their futures as husbands, wives, and responsible community members. As group leaders, character builders supervised teenage leisure, providing a parent-free but adult-guided environment after school. They were trained to serve as partners, not to dominate an organization, and they aimed to keep the lines of generational communication open. Ideally, their presence demonstrated that individuals could share values and ambitions regardless of their age and experience. For the point of character building was not to force adolescents along an adult-approved path in life but to have them choose that path for themselves.[2]

Character builders took it for granted that society worked best when males and females maintained their separate spheres. Boys, for instance, were encouraged to think of themselves as competent, aggressive providers. Exotic subjects like Indian lore and wilderness survival taught them the value of skill, and elaborate camping trips and athletic programs had the added benefit of keeping them busy and out of harm's way, as they learned how to work as a team.[3] The lesson was essential, since family life depended on the give-and-take of individual members—including adolescent children. "Most of you . . . know you are partners with your father and mother in their financial affairs," the *American Boy* explained. This meant that boys needed to act responsibly, not because their parents wanted them to, but because the family prospered that way. Take the case of reckless driving, a bad habit adopted by short-sighted adolescents who never considered the consequences of their actions: "Your mother and father . . . are trying to help you on in the world. . . . So if you put them in a hole with [an automobile] accident that the insurance doesn't cover, you've been a rather poor partner, don't you think?"[4] Obviously, the commonsense answer was "yes."

Boys also had to learn how to make a good living, a subject that character builders took very seriously indeed. Magazines like *American Boy* and *Boys' Life* offered them an amazing range of moneymaking opportunities, from learning how to print cards and circulars ("Print for others, big profit") to buying bicycles that would allow them to deliver papers or take on odd jobs ("Gee Dad, if I get that bike I can make lots of money"). Boys were also encouraged to "invest" their profits in products that would help them discover their true calling in life (and incidentally fill their after-school hours). "Enjoy the thrill of your new skill," an ad for a motorized tool set promised. Another advised boys to become radio experts with the help of a home-study guide. "The advertising pages of this magazine are the highways of commerce," the *American Boy* pointed out, and it urged young readers to study them carefully to get a head start in life.[5]

Odd jobs and moneymaking schemes were only the preliminaries, however. For a real chance at financial security, boys had to prepare themselves for a job or profession, depending on their talents, their disposition, and their family's place in the community. "The easiest possible way to get a job is to have a father who owns the business," the *American Boy* frankly explained, but if that route were closed, then intelligent planning and education would help. With articles spotlighting different kinds of jobs and the skills they required and short stories detailing the challenges inherent in different careers, boys' magazines made the search for future employment a kind of adventure story. Would the boy identify the skills he had and translate them into a paying job? Would he be satisfied with the work and with the money? "Big money, big man, big job—they all went together," a fictional advertising man explained. "Big job meant tough job."[6]

This approach seemed fitting. Adventure was the name of the game in a cutthroat job market. "Every day brings nearer the time when you will be working for a living and fighting for a career in a competition that is as keen, as remorseless, as subtle as you will ever know," warned *Scholastic*, the high school weekly. So it made sense that boys' magazines were littered with inspiring adventure stories, which provided ample opportunity for teenage heroes to show off the benefits of hard-won skills and competence. These fictional heroes could handle a gun (the Daisy Rifle Co. was a frequent advertiser), and they knew how to survive in the wilderness. They were the kind of competent, virile males who could win a war when called on to fight and protect their families at all costs. But they were also responsible males who never took risks lightly. They realized that there was no glory in adventure for its own sake. As an article on aviation made clear, it was one thing for a test pilot to crash for the good of science and quite another for daredevils to risk life and limb for a thrill.[7]

Whether the fictional arena was a battlefield, a deserted camp ground, or even a basketball court, these adventures took place in an all-male world. Mothers and sisters only rarely made an appearance in boys' magazines. Girlfriends (and wives) were never mentioned, except in an occasional advertisement. That boys would grow up to be breadwinners was taken for granted. But it was never discussed in the context of family life. Although the experts were beginning to argue that fathers should assume more responsibility at home, that was not a message boys were likely to hear. On the contrary, they learned that males were required to earn a good living and that boys had a duty to prepare themselves for work or a career, and not much else. After all, the rest of the family business (including romance) belonged strictly to the girls.

And that was fine with the girls' organizations. They relished the responsibility. Character builders firmly believed that women's work was more interesting and significant than men's. What could be more satisfying, they wanted to know, than creating a beautiful home or more challenging than raising healthy, happy, productive children? What could be more fulfilling than domestic life approached with imagination, insight, and affection? If girls wanted to make the most of their futures, groups like the Girl Scouts and the Camp Fire Girls pointed out, they had to nurture their special talents—a mother who was gifted in art, music, sewing, or even theater, for instance, could offer her children a richer introduction to life. They would also have to master a wide range of domestic skills from housework and cooking to nursing and shopping in order to do the job right. But most of all they would need to develop a deep commitment to family life, for it was this that transformed even household drudgery into useful, social work.

A story in *American Girl,* the Girl Scouts' magazine, set the tone for this program. "Peggy hated to think of growing up—she was sure that only young people have a good time," the story began. But before it was over, her best friend's mother had taught her that life went on after age sixteen. And it even got better—especially if you married and had children. "Raising a family is like anything worth doing. . . . You have to like all of it, bitter as well as sweet, hard as well as easy," the mother explained. "To find something bigger than yourself, bigger than any one person, and give yourself to it wholly—that is really living." You would not get everything you wanted, of course, but if you were flexible you just might get "some wonderful surprises."[8]

The trick was to develop broad interests beyond hearth and home—otherwise girls would be "dull at thirty."[9] Like boys, they had some important life choices to make; they needed to discover whether they would pursue fine arts, community service, athletics, or even a career, along with raising a family. Middle-class girls had the same opportunities that boys did to travel or learn camp craft through their organizations, and their magazines offered a wide range of fictional models, from female airline pilots and mountain climbers to more familiar debutantes and homemakers.[10] Domestic "how-to" articles, ranging from how to cook and serve a meal to how to be a bridesmaid, were popular features. But so were articles on how to build a canoe or host a radio program. The girls appreciated the mix. "I don't like to sew," one reader confessed in 1930, and she asked the editor to publish "some articles for those girls who like to handle a saw, hammer, and a keg of nails."[11]

American Girl and *Everygirls* (the Camp Fire Girls' publication) encouraged their readers to earn their own spending money, too. "How many things have you wanted that you couldn't get because you didn't have the money?" asked an advertisement for the Earn-Your-Own Club, which organized girls to sell magazine subscriptions. "Don't you want to be financially happy and free?" another wanted to know.[12] Well, yes, as a matter of fact they did, even more than character builders realized. In fact, a growing number of adolescent girls assumed they would be working in the future—the Great Depression had made it clear that girls, as well as boys, had to be able to support themselves. In 1930, so many readers asked the *American Girl* how to become teachers, doctors, and lawyers that the editors wondered "if you're all planning to have careers?"[13] They did not encourage these inquiries, but neither did they ignore them. The magazine published a few articles on becoming a sculptor (in 1930), a doctor (in 1935), and a lawyer (in 1939), among others. However, the editors made it absolutely clear that the professional world was a man's world that females entered at their own risk: Male artists refused to hire female apprentices, female lawyers had the best chance of acceptance if they clerked in their father's office, and medicine offered one of the few opportunities for a woman to combine home and professional life.[14]

The girls themselves were more encouraging, even though they realized the risks involved. When one wrote in asking whether it was possible for a girl to become a lawyer, for instance, another urged her to follow her heart's desire, no matter the opposition. "Go ahead, Betty, and don't let anyone spoil your hopes," she wrote, for she, too, had wanted to become a lawyer but gave up when people laughed at her choice. "They described me as I would look trying to plead a case. So I decided that I would have to be a stenographer just like almost every girl, and I started a commercial course." Now in her last term of high school, she still had not found work that interested her. "I would willingly start my high school course all over," she admitted, "if I thought that I could resist opposition."[15]

But career concerns (including future motherhood) rarely dominated high school life. For the most part, girls were preoccupied with current questions like dating and popularity. And unlike boys' organizations, which refused to recognize the social side of teenage life (lest aggressive young adventurers discover their sublimated passions), girls' organizations at least acknowledged it. Adolescent girls had to learn the rules of proper behavior and successful dating, character builders agreed, if they hoped to enter satisfying marriages. But that did not mean they got to set the pace. *American Girl* avoided the subject of boys until 1935, and then offered fictional portraits of wholesome friendships between groups of boys and girls. *Everygirls*, on the other hand, published

"Talking It Over with Aunt Cherry," a monthly advice column that ran until the early 1930s (when the magazine folded). It did not include the girls' letters, and it did not dwell on romance, but the column addressed adolescent concerns in a general, affectionate, and eminently sensible way.

"Two or three boy-problem letters of late have ended with the query 'Am I in love with this boy and what shall I do about it,'" Aunt Cherry wrote in 1931. "Now, darlings, let me tell you something. You can be in love with the ice-man . . . or a movie actor on the screen, or the awkward, lanky, postmaster if you just let yourself think about him long enough." These emotional experiences were natural and right, she explained, "for they are nature's way of getting a girl interested in mating, but you can't marry them all . . . so the next time you have this feeling of special delight in a boy's presence . . . just say to yourself 'It isn't time, yet. This is the false dawn they have in India . . . it doesn't mean what it seems to mean.' Then you'll let the false dawn fade away," she added, "and wait for the real one."[16]

While they were waiting, girls wanted to know what to say to boys on a date (get them to talk about themselves, she counseled, since that was any man's favorite subject); whether to accept blind dates (it's not wrong, but "decidedly unwise, like any gamble"); or whether to send a Christmas gift to a "boy friend" ("first, be sure the boy would welcome a gift from you"). They also needed help persuading their mothers to let them dress the way other girls did. "I might answer sensibly that beauty and popularity do not depend on clothes . . . but I know that is not a satisfactory answer," Aunt Cherry admitted. Instead she suggested arranging a mothers' conference so that the conservative mother could see for herself just how far out of step she was. Overall Aunt Cherry advised her girls to avoid depression by determined cheerfulness; to steer clear of crushes (on males and females alike), and to use their leisure time wisely, learning to sew, to play an instrument, to help others. "Just remember, girls, that we mothers have been through the mill," she added, "so we have some reason for the advice we give, and most of us hate nagging just as much as you do—so cure us of nagging, by doing what we ask promptly!"[17]

Character builders took it for granted that adult-approved social standards would prevail as long as they were presented in flexible, commonsense ways. But adolescent group members, who tended to vote with their feet, could not be counted on to cooperate without good reason. Even the most elaborate recreation programs would not stifle their interest in the opposite sex or their efforts to get to know them better. Boys were notorious for dropping out of clubs that had no social program, and girls pushed their organizations to broaden their outlook beyond motherhood and domestic life. After all, it was the girls themselves who forced "Aunt Cherry" to answer their questions on life and love, even though she thought they were far too young to be so interested.

By the mid-1930s, high school educators had also discovered that they could not ignore teenage social life—not if they hoped to have some influence on it, that is. Although many schools still retained an official "hands-offs" policy, *Scholastic* magazine (which was often used in the classroom) began to address after-school issues in 1935: "If you ask for the privilege of coming and going as you please, don't wreck your school work by falling asleep over it repeatedly," an editorial urged. "If you ask for the privilege of running your class dance without adult interference, don't turn it into a rowdy, undignified affair. Be as grown up in handling privileges," *Scholastic* advised, "as you are in demanding them."[18]

A few months later, *Scholastic* confirmed the growing importance of high school social life when it launched a new column, "Boy Dates Girl," in September 1936. Written by Gay Head, soon to be a recognized authority on teenage life, the column concentrated on dating etiquette, not on issues of life or love, standard procedure where teenage social life was concerned. Adults took it for granted that there was a "right" and a "wrong" way to date—and the right way was to play the field, keep things light, and show a cordial respect for adult authority and tastes. Following that line, Gay Head addressed what *Scholastic* deemed the important issues of dating: how to make proper introductions, which fork to use at a dinner party, and whether to wait for a boy to open a car door or not. Boys were encouraged to chat with a date's parents and even invite them along to the movies as a means of "selling yourself" to the older generation (they would not accept the offer, of course, but they would appreciate the thought, Gay Head promised). Girls were reminded more than once not to apply makeup in public (since boys really hated that), not to correct their dates (boys did not appreciate "brainy" girls), and not to become known as "gold diggers" by pushing dates to spend too much money.[19]

Students apparently devoured the information, since "things always go better when you know the rules," as one girl put it.[20] In fact, by 1938 so many students had been moved to write in that *Scholastic* added a question and answer column, although the editors made it clear that not every question deserved an answer. The magazine offered help with proper etiquette, not "advice to the lovesick." In fact, there was only one column, in 1937, that ventured into romantic turf. In "Boy Dates Girl," the issue of necking was raised, but so were many adult eyebrows apparently, even before the column appeared. As the Teacher's Guide gingerly put it, "the more intimate phases of the subject are impossible to discuss in a mixed classroom." Judging from the column itself, so were the most practical phases.[21]

Delicate subject or not, high school Romeos and Juliets apparently needed to know "that dances and parties and dates often lead to more serious and permanent relations." Goodnight kisses and hand holding might seem innocent enough, *Scholastic* pointed out, but they could invite more serious involvement. "It is perfectly possible for young people today to be frank enough with each other to understand reasonable restraint," the column advised in a roundabout fashion. But there was no point in encouraging high school students to test the limits of those restraints. "The sparkle of life is to be found in pleasant companionship, in work and active play, in games, reading, cooking, handicrafts [and] conversation . . . and not in a steady diet of billing and cooing"—or necking, as the phrase implied. High school students who took the time to think about it would have to agree. Young people had serious ambitions, *Scholastic* noted, to be doctors, nurses, scientists, and actresses, ambitions that required "time and study and concentration of energy—things, which do not mix very well with getting absorbed in love making."[22]

But that was as far as the magazine could go. A student who had not experienced passion (or had no idea why the consequences seemed so grave) would not learn anything more from Gay Head. In fact, a totally inexperienced student would probably miss the references entirely, since they were intentionally oblique. And "proper" principals, teachers, and school boards intended to keep it that way. High schools had no business butting into social affairs, they believed, and educators had no choice but to sidestep the central issue of adolescent development: the onset of sexual maturity. Parents, however, could not ignore it, even if they refused to acknowledge it. After all, even the ancient philosopher Aristotle had recognized that the young were "prone to desire" and had a bad habit of exercising "no self-restraint."[23] Parents who thought they could control teenage social life by prohibiting it were whistling in the dark. For instance, one perfectly reasonable and respectable young man wrote to Gay Head with this problem: "I would like to call for my girl at her home when we go to the movies, but her parents won't let her out on dates and we have to meet on a street corner. . . . What do other fellows do when they have this problem?"[24]

If Gay Head was in no position to address the practical aspects of teenage social life, *Parents* magazine was. In fact, it was one of a very few places where the question of teenage sexuality could be raised—although the phrase was certainly never uttered in the 1930s. Serving as a sort of character builder for adults, the magazine encouraged parents to face the social facts of teenage life squarely: Boys would be boys in sexual matters as in any other, and wise parents would raise a son to consider the consequences of *all* his actions—particularly if they wanted to protect him from the "wrong" kind of girl. "The sex magazines and the movies inflame his imagination, girls of his own social group provoke and tantalize him, girls of another class accost him on the street or ogle him at public dances." If parents hoped to steer their sons away from casual experimentation that could have tragic results, then they had to warn them against the dangers of drunken behavior and venereal disease. "An unwillingness to face facts, a desire to hold on to our fairyland of wishes and desires . . . should have no place in the education of the adolescent boy," *Parents* insisted.[25]

Many parents were neither equipped nor willing, however, to discuss the subject of sex frankly with their sons. So it fell to their daughters to regulate male behavior. "The girls of his own social class have always set the pace for the boy," *Parents* admitted. In fact, whether the issue was kissing, smoking, drinking, or driving—all notorious emblems of male adolescence in the 1930s—it was the mark of a "nice" girl to keep her date in line. As one mother put it, a boy's best girl had "a deep and abiding influence," since her "approval keeps a man sober."[26] The *Ladies' Home Journal* agreed. "Girls it's up to you," the magazine noted in an article on reckless male drivers. "Guide the hand that drives you."[27] Since they were potential mothers and preservers of the race, it was their natural inclination, or so it seemed at the time, to keep the future in mind.

Because "nice" girls had the most to lose when boys violated social codes, they were expected to shun those who drank too much or acted in careless or threatening ways. The *American Girl* could only hint at such issues: The boys and girls featured in short stories, for instance, never needed chaperons, since they were much too busy and well mannered to be interested in mischief. But if character builders were not in the business of providing particulars for teenage girls, the *Ladies' Home Journal* seemed interested in the job. In fact, the magazine published a column designed to teach respectable girls the rules of proper socializing. Addressed to sub-debs, the name given to well-to-do teenage girls, the column concentrated on etiquette and general advice, much as Gay Head did. Girls were urged to be considerate of a boy's finances and to remember that "boys love to run the show and be it." In fact, if a girl had brains, according to the sub-deb column, she would figure out just what a boy liked in a date and adjust her personality accordingly![28]

But the magazine also reminded young readers that chastity was a girl's best friend, at least as far as her future was concerned. "There is more value to quality merchandise than to bargains," the sub-deb column noted, a fact that girls ignored at their peril where the marriage market was concerned. Girls were advised to avoid behavior that lowered their "face value." For whatever a boy said when the lights were low, respectable boys never appreciated kisses that came too easily. Girls had an obligation to keep their standards high and to avoid potentially embarrassing situations, like drawing unwanted attention from boys who were hanging out on the street. "It's your fault for walking by," the editors insisted, if the boys began to leer. "Boys . . . are just letting off steam. Don't you get in the way."[29]

The editors were even less sympathetic to girls who wondered why their dates always ended in wrestling matches. "Boys will

make passes at any girl who leads them to it and makes it easy. . . .
Coy remarks, skirts too short, necks too low, are all red flags."
Once a girl agreed to leave the dance floor, or wander off to the
woods with a date, she couldn't be surprised at the outcome.
"You're just asking for it," the editors insisted. And the social consequences of such loose behavior were worth contemplating. Just
ask the sixteen-year-old girl who thought she had to "go the
limit" with her boyfriends in order to be popular. Although she
never crossed the line beyond light petting, she was popular all
right, "but only with a tough bunch of boys." Certainly not the
type you would want to marry, the editors implied.[30]

High school girls were less concerned with marriage than the
here and now prospects of rating a date, though, and they were
not at all convinced that adults had followed the high moral standards they now prescribed for youth. "It was no use to seek my
parents' advice," a high school sophomore wrote to the *Ladies'
Home Journal* in 1932. "They, in repentance of their own youth, no
doubt, were determined that I should be sweet and chaste and
pure." It was easy for parents to act as if sex had no place in polite
society, but it was not so easy for their teenage offspring to decide
where it fit in their lives. "That was my problem," the sophomore
explained, "whether to disregard the counsel of Conscience and
Prudence, the beliefs of my mother and father, and enjoy my youth
while I had it; or whether to turn back on the Road to Popularity, give up smoking and the rest, for staying home every night
gazing fondly and dreamily at the once lively telephone." The girl's
dilemma was a common one, and the question she asked was
becoming a classic: "Does a girl have to pet to be popular?"[31]

As much as the adult world wanted to avoid the question—the
Ladies' Home Journal certainly didn't answer it—concerned parents
knew they could not. Light petting, better known as necking, was
certainly respectable in the adolescent social world, even if the
subject was taboo. Petting was a fact of life that parents had to live
with, the experts maintained. In fact, petting actually served an
important function in the process of growing up: It taught girls
and boys how to fall in love and what to look for in future mates.
As Dr. Winifred Richmond explained it in 1933, petting or "the
tendency of a boy and girl to seek . . . physical contact with each
other is apparently spontaneous and natural" and nature's way of

getting them interested enough "to wish for closer contact."[32] If parents wanted their children to raise families of their own in the future, a mild dose of petting would certainly do no harm.

But that did not mean that parents should look the other way entirely—far from it. In fact, *Parents* magazine urged readers to play an active role in adolescent social life, beginning when a child turned thirteen or so. In this way, boys and girls could get to know each other before the pressure to date set in, and parents could control the invitations, thus limiting their children's access to acceptable companions and shaping the universe of future dates. Inexpensive entertainments like supper parties after dance class, skating parties for the crowd, or impromptu taffy pulls and fudge frolics were a cheap form of social insurance. They were also the least concerned parents could do, the magazine suggested, to protect their children from their own inexperience.[33]

One reader developed her long-range strategy when her fourteen-year-old daughter wanted to attend school functions with a date. Since she was too young, her mother offered a compromise: She would take the girl and her friends, boys included, as a group and then invite them home for popcorn afterward. From that time on, boys visited her daughter as frequently as girls did, but always in groups, never as dates. "It wasn't always convenient to have the boys and girls there," the mother confessed, but the trouble was worth it since her daughter did not go car riding or to other girls' homes to meet friends. "She met her boyfriends in a friendly, natural manner in her own home." Not only had she avoided conflict over the question of dating, but she had done so, the mother proudly added, with a "sympathetic understanding" that encouraged her daughter to confide in her.

Another mother tried the same plan but with a different twist. Her daughter was infatuated with an older man who was, as she put it, "in no way her equal." Determined to nip this "unpleasant" association in the bud, she spruced up her house and then hosted parties that introduced her daughter to the "right" crowd. "At first her suitor attended all the gatherings," her mother reported, "but the relentless intolerance of youth for one who doesn't 'fit' had its effect." She considered her plan a success when her daughter grew ashamed of her unsuitable boyfriend and he became so uncomfortable that he dropped out of the picture entirely.[34]

Pragmatic "modern" parents accepted the fact that they could not control teenage behavior. Like character builders, though, they firmly believed that they could still mold it along acceptable lines, as long as they were flexible. A mother could not stop her daughter from reading sexy novels, as one told *Parents* magazine, but she could at least offer her earthy classics like *Moll Flanders* or *Maggie, a Girl of the Streets*, instead.[35] And although she could not force her daughter to stop smoking, she could quietly sow the seeds. A casual remark about tobacco-stained teeth (which the boys were sure to notice) would prove much more effective than a lecture on health, modern parents agreed.[36] Likewise, they learned to live with their daughters' "cosmetic urge," whether they approved of it or not. Parents could prohibit the use of makeup at home, but they could not stop a daughter from applying it (with a vengeance) when she was out of sight. Instead, modern parents were advised to supply young daughters with light-colored lipsticks and powders and to use the opportunity to teach their children the value of good grooming.[37]

These solutions only appealed to an audience wealthy enough to provide playrooms and entertain the neighborhood kids and educated enough to appreciate the insights of developmental psychology. Prosperous professionals and comfortable middle-class families could afford to take a chance and trust their children. They knew they had the promise of a good marriage and an attractive future to keep them in line. But the more common folk—immigrants, wage workers, divorced, widowed, and unemployed parents—had no such assurances: Character-building groups like the Boy Scouts and the Girl Scouts were not available to their children, and their economic futures had never looked particularly bright, even before the economy collapsed in 1929.

As far as these parents could see, knowledge was the fruit of all evil where teenage children were concerned, and personal freedom only invited disaster. According to the teenage son of immigrant parents, "father and mother did not believe in telling their children about sex," as if his ignorance would then protect him from harm. But dodging the facts of life and prohibiting boy–girl relationships during adolescence could not guarantee innocence. On the contrary, the Old World strategy could just as easily backfire under New World conditions, as one boy attested. "If my folks had lived in a decent neighborhood . . . where I could have known some American boys and girls, and perhaps, had a girl friend, I would not have gone to the burlesque shows as often as I did." As it was, he was "bubbling over with it" and found that he could not restrain himself.[38]

The consequences of sexual ignorance and social repression could prove far more serious for adventuresome girls. A sixteen-year-old unwed mother, the daughter of a mechanic who ruled his home with an iron hand, dramatically illustrated the point. "My family did not tell me anything about the opposite sex," she reported. Up until her own pregnancy, she had believed that babies resulted "from the mixing of blue blood in the veins of the girl with red blood from the arteries of the boy." A girl who valued independent thinking and admired those "who can't be frightened or intimidated in any way," she had been determined from her early teens to achieve freedom with her friends if she could not with her family. "Things happened that I had never expected would happen," she admitted, but she did not blame her fifteen-year-old partner, who knew no more about the facts of life than she did. Her social worker added a revealing note: "The fact that she felt she was doing something of which her parents would not approve satisfied her because of the feeling of independence it gave her."[39]

Daughters who came from more affectionate homes also suffered when parents tried too hard to shield them from the world, though. "My parents thought a girl should be very domestic and act like she was all grown up," reported a fifteen-year-old unwed mother who came from an otherwise happy home. "The hardest thing for me to do is to obey my parents. They love me but they don't understand what girls ought to be doing these days. I guess they forget when they were young. Besides," she added, "things are different now." Totally ignorant about reproduction, she had met the sixteen-year-old father of her child at a secret party arranged by a girlfriend, and it was by way of subsequent trysts that she became pregnant. Not surprisingly, the boy had since disappeared.[40]

Because they got no help at home, many high school students thought their teachers should have guided them through their adolescence. "Children should be taught to choose right companions, to behave themselves properly both inside and outside of school," a sixteen-year-old remarked. They should also learn "something about real life," she believed. A recent high school graduate who found herself pregnant by a man she barely knew agreed. If she had understood how liquor could break down a nice girl's will or could have "pictured the results and dangers of certain kinds of recreation, it might not have happened," she said. But instead of teaching her to think for herself and size up situations, high school had taught her to follow directions, a very inappropriate lesson in this case. "Something is wrong somewhere or it would not have happened," she insisted, since she never intended to do anything wrong. Like other girls who were lonely, unsupervised, rebellious, or just plain unaware, she had not thought carefully about the consequences of her actions or how they might affect her future. But now at least she had the help of social workers who could provide the training—and the sympathetic ear—that her parents and teachers had withheld.[41]

When parents were unwilling or unable to arm their children with the facts of life, teenage youth had very few options. They could turn to friends for information that was usually wrong or incomplete; they could learn from experience, a choice that was personally risky; or they could piece the story together from pulp magazines. No girl could read *True Confessions*, for example, without realizing that sex without marriage could be dangerous. Every month, fictional young women got "in trouble" and had to face up to the ugly prospects of abortion or dishonor. And someone—usually the girl—died at the story's end. But if these magazines encouraged girls to wait until a decent man proposed marriage, young readers did not necessarily know just what they were waiting for.[42] Even the U.S. Children's Bureau would not tell them when they asked. For better or for worse, the most pressing issues of teenage life and personal development were left for the family to resolve—or, in many cases, to ignore—a decision that seemed sensible enough as long as parents were up to the job.

But in the 1930s it was painfully obvious that many were not. In the context of economic depression and social despair, displaced, disaffected, neglected youth were becoming a national tragedy. The distance between adolescent haves and have-nots was visible but manageable in high school. The distance between teenage students and out-of-school youth (as dropouts were called), however, could not be bridged by advice columnists or after-school clubs. These adolescents needed more practical help—in the form of money for clothes, lunch, transportation, medical care—before they could even consider staying in school. Or they needed training and jobs to provide the support that their families could not.

The Great Depression did not create the structure that crippled these young lives, nor did it create the category of "troubled" or delinquent youth. But it did create the crisis that forced these underlying problems into public view and convinced a majority of Americans that it was time to use federal power—and federal money—to bring middle-class values into lower-class lives.

chapter three

High school students in an agricultural class, San Augustine, Texas, 1939. *Library of Congress, Prints and Photographs Division, FSA Collection [LCUSF 3432978D]*

A New Deal for Youth
"Progressive" Education and the National Youth Administration

THE STRUCTURE OF MIDDLE-CLASS FAMILY LIFE RESTED ON THE promise of the future: Ambitious adolescents who followed a disciplined track in and out of high school were aiming for practical rewards. They expected to live a bit better than their parents had, attending college perhaps, or moving up into "clean" white-collar jobs. They also expected to enjoy the rewards of respectable adulthood—marriage, a family, and a place of their own. But the realities of economic depression, severe and unrelenting by the mid-1930s, altered their plans. Between 1929 and 1933, professional incomes dropped 40 percent, and the supply of white-collar workers dangerously exceeded demand.[1] All of a sudden, or so it seemed, college graduates and newly minted professionals had no jobs to move into, and only one out of ten to fifteen high school graduates could expect to find work in 1933.[2] Even when they were lucky enough to get hired, the youngest workers were learning the hard way that Depression wages did not go very far. Sought-after stenographer's jobs, for instance, which were worth $40 a week to commercial high school graduates in 1929, brought

in only $16 in 1933. And a salesman's job (the most likely occu-
pation for unskilled males) did not begin to cover living expenses.
"Here I am, twenty-one years old, and not even a start in the
world," a disappointed young salesman reported. Unable to pay
room and board to his parents, let alone save up for the future, he
had a sinking feeling that he would never be secure enough to settle down and raise a family.[3] But at least his parents could still
afford to keep a roof over his head, which was more than many
his age could count on. "My mother said if I don't get a job soon
she is going to throw me out," another young man frantically
wrote the government. After several unsuccessful trips to the
unemployment bureau, he was beginning to go "crazy" from
uncertainty.[4]

He was far from alone. During the Great Depression there were
4 million young Americans aged sixteen to twenty-four who were
looking for work, and about 40 percent of them—1 million boys
and 750,000 girls—were high school age.[5] With no place to turn
to for relief and no good reason to remain at home (since they
were only a drag on their families), many took to the road in the
1930s. "It wasn't so bad at home until I was sixteen," one young
traveler explained. Since his father was out of work, the county
had paid his mother an allowance for him. "But after I became
sixteen, they cut us that much, and I couldn't get a job for even
one day." Another runaway, just thirteen years old, left his family
after he quit his job (which paid $1.65 a week) since he was afraid
to face his father with the news. "I hated to leave home, because
he ain't so bad otherwise, but I knew what he would say and how
my sister would look, and how my mother would feel, so I thought
I'd better scram."[6] A fellow traveler who hit the road when medical school grew too expensive understood the young runaways'
strategy. "They figure maybe a job is open in some other section
[so] they ride the freight trains, walk, anything to get there." But in
the end, he pointed out, they were usually disappointed.[7]

Many headed west to sunny California—if they could not find
work, at least they would not freeze. But as a Los Angeles probation officer reported, these runaways arrived with no family ties,
no parental controls, and no supervision, a situation that usually
led to "bad associations" and serious trouble. Runaways were des-

perate to raise money for food and shelter, and they would beg, steal, or even prostitute themselves, if that was what it took to survive. But some never intended to work at all, he pointed out. In fact, as he put it, the most troublesome runaways were willing to subsist on soup kitchen offerings "or beg on the streets as a means of living. They sleep in cheap lodging houses paying ten cents for a bed or five cents to share a bed with several other people." If they could not raise the money, the officer added, "they sleep in public parks or back alleys."[8]

Adolescent runaways or transient youth, as they were called, forced adult society to focus on teenage problems. The idea that a generation might have no ties to the past and no faith in the future was frightening. Youth had the energy and the anger to spark a social revolution—or at least a full-fledged explosion in the streets, and some adults were beginning to fear that they had the necessary political organization, too. In Nazi Germany, Hitler was demonstrating the frightening power of disaffected youth, once they found a charismatic leader who inspired them. In the United States, concerned Americans began to fear the influence of street-corner socialists and communists who were busy organizing anyone willing to listen—workers, college students, farmers, the unemployed. Their call for a new social order, based on planning and need rather than competition and greed, seemed particularly compelling at the time. "When a boy has walked the streets for weeks in search of employment; has slept in parks and has lived only by means of soup kitchens and hand-outs on the way," an observer noted in 1931, "he is a very likely subject for any one who might preach a doctrine of revolution or revolt against existing conditions."[9]

Youthful apathy and despair could be just as disturbing, however. Adults were beginning to wonder just what effect the Great Depression would have on the next generation of mothers and fathers and what kind of social order would emerge from citizens with no faith in the American dream of self-help and self-improvement. Social workers reported that unemployed youth described themselves as "discouraged, disgusted, sullen and bitter" much more frequently than they ever had before. Males seemed especially defeated and distraught.[10] "Can't something be done before it is too late?" a transient-turned-prisoner asked Frances Perkins, the U.S. Secretary of Labor. "The people in the Capital seem to forget there are thousands of young men who have to live as well as those that are married. . . . If you want to help," he added, then "outline a program that will include them."[11]

The writer had a point. The patchwork of state and federal programs that was beginning to evolve by 1933—the National Recovery Administration, or NRA, the Civil Works Administration, or CWA, and the state reemployment bureaus—were designed to help full-fledged adults and relief families already dependent on public welfare. Even the New Deal's popular youth program, the Civilian Conservation Corps, or CCC (which put poor, unemployed, unmarried males to work planting trees, clearing camp grounds, and building dams and reservoirs), was not open to boys under age eighteen. Unemployed teenage youth were supposed to remain in high school to wait out the economic storm, but that option was still too expensive for the poorest families and never appealed to boys who needed or wanted a job.[12] In fact, many of the hardest-to-employ teenage youth had left school before finishing eighth grade, and they had no intention of returning to the classroom now.

That being the case, in the fall of 1934 the U.S. Children's Bureau began to investigate state-run training programs to determine what did and did not work when it came to out-of-school youth. But there were no easy answers. The unemployed wanted jobs, pure and simple, but there were no jobs for unskilled, uneducated, inexperienced workers, no matter how great their need or how desperate their condition. Like it or not, out-of-school youth had to develop marketable skills (and a pleasing personality) just to compete for a job. They also had to learn how to navigate the adult world of work—how to find leads, how to interview, how to dress. All this was certainly possible, the experts agreed, as long as teenage youth were willing to put their time to good use (instead of "hanging around the corner with the boys," as many apparently preferred to do). A comprehensive government program that provided the right mix of financial relief, practical training, and adult guidance, they believed, could turn this teenage crisis on its head. If they hoped to succeed, however, teenage youth

would also have to take responsibility for themselves, the experts
added. They had to be willing to learn—and then practice—the
habits of self-discipline, ambition, and work that more prosperous
youth learned at home or in school.

Trumpeting the motto "Youth Must Be Served," President
Franklin D. Roosevelt launched the National Youth Administration, or NYA, in the spring of 1935. "We shall do something for
the nation's unemployed youth," he proudly announced, "for we
can ill afford to lose the skill and energy of these young men and
women. They must have their chance in school, their turn as
apprentices, and their opportunity for jobs—a chance to earn and
work for themselves."[13] With a $50 million appropriation to invest
in "troubled" youth, the NYA pioneered a program of education
through work, the first of its kind at the federal level. Sponsoring
resident training camps and work projects designed to encourage
the poorest youth to become self-sufficient, it also offered short-
term courses in child care, car mechanics, commercial art, and a
host of academic and practical subjects. Likewise the NYA tried
to teach disadvantaged youth what they needed to know to get by
in the world: how to look for a job, what to expect in an interview, and what employers in specific trades actually required in
exchange for a day's pay.

But the NYA was more than a jobs program to its administrators; it was an experiment in character building designed to raise
the standards and aspirations of the most underprivileged teenage
youth. In the South, for instance, NYA residence centers introduced participants to new standards of living that were "likely to
make them discontented with their former lot," an observer
reported. In fact, this was the point. The NYA fully intended to
transmit the values and habits of middle-class families to those
who had never experienced them. In some resident centers, participants stayed for two weeks, returned home for two weeks, and
then came back, a migration that had a purpose. "They constantly
see contrasts in diets, cleanliness, and general household management," an administrator explained. "They often tell me of applying what they have learned here at home."[14]

The center in Conway, Arkansas, for instance, gave girls and
boys a chance to develop their social skills and acquire what the

NYA called "family-life education." Girls cooked for the entire group and did all the household chores—including raising chickens. They managed family-size homes and spent some time working in a nearby nursery school. At dinners—which they planned, cooked, and served—the girls presided over tables of ten to twelve "guests" each evening and got a rare opportunity to practice the middle-class role of gracious hostess. They may have had nothing in common with teenage "sub-debs," who learned the social graces at a very early age, but now at least they had a chance to experience respectable family life, and that in itself seemed worthwhile.

As for the boys, the camps offered them a chance to play team sports for the first time and to mix with groups of young people their own age. They contributed to residential family life by building shelves and equipment for the model homes. Their real goal, though, was to "earn and learn" on jobs in the city power plant, the forestry service, or auto mechanics shops—whatever the community had to offer. Originally, NYA camps had been designed to train rural boys in modern farming techniques and to encourage them to raise animals and mixed crops of fruits and vegetables so that they could make a better living from the soil. However, since the boys themselves were determined to get out of farming, the NYA offered a full range of industrial courses instead, designed to help participants discover their true talents and vocation.

NYA administrators never assumed that the sky was the limit for out-of-school participants. On the contrary, the program trained teenage youth to reach their full potential within the confines of their social place. White boys and girls, for instance, had more varied opportunities for training than blacks and ethnics did; in the 1930s, skin color and "Americanness" all but determined an individual's occupational future. But the NYA did what it could to help less privileged youth negotiate the system. In rural counties, girls were taught how to shampoo their hair, apply makeup, and dress in middle-class style.[15] In ethnic neighborhoods, they learned how to prepare "American" meals and were encouraged to cut their family ties if Old World parents were too demanding. In fact, according to administrators, the most successful NYA participants were those who shed their parents' foreign or poverty-stricken ways and adopted a more "natural" American, middle-class manner.

For some, the strategy paid off. They were able to use the NYA as a critical stepping stone to an independent life. A black partic-ipant from Houston, for instance, parlayed her stay at a residence center (where she trained in domestic work) into a full-time job and a college education. Another black trainee, who worked as a porter in an NYA sewing center, used the experience to get a much better job at an exclusive hotel, where he earned a comfort-able living. Still another, who started out as a timid, self-conscious member of a racially mixed NYA project in New York, emerged as its leader and had plans to open her own dress shop. In her case, NYA administrators reported, "the race question was never a problem. Her immaculate appearance and fine disposition, plus her ability, made her acceptable to the group from the very first."[16]

On one level, the NYA accomplished its mission with out-of-school youth. It broadened their horizons and provided adult supervision and advice to those who needed and wanted help. On the most practical level, however, it failed dismally. Most NYA participants moved up into other government-funded relief pro-jects (like the WPA), not into private sector jobs. Successful NYA participants may have learned how to fit into a middle-class world, but that could not guarantee work in a stagnant economy. Without a high school diploma, teenage youth were just not com-petitive in a very tight job market, NYA training or not, an eco-nomic fact of life that the NYA took very seriously. In fact, as far as administrators were concerned, training programs for out-of-school youth were a last resort, not a model for future policy. The NYA's primary purpose was to keep potential dropouts in high school and avoid "out-of-school" unemployment in the first place.

The agency's strategy was eminently practical. The NYA funded jobs for high school students (age sixteen and over) whose families could not make ends meet; students earned about $6 a month washing windows, delivering messages, grading papers, or clerking in the school office. The money was intended for car fare, books, or clothing—the relatively minor expenses of everyday life that too often kept teenage students out of school. As one girl put it, "When things became so difficult at home that my Mother and I . . . had one pair of shoes between us, I quit school." Her story was hardly unique at the time. "Again and again in many states we heard the word 'shoes' used as an equation for going to school," reporters noted. Underwear could be fashioned from sugar sacks, and clothes could be patched or remade, but shoes seemed to be "the insurmountable obstacle to school attendance in many impoverished families." NYA jobs were specifically designed with this embarrassing problem in mind.[17]

Like the NYA's other projects, though, these jobs had another purpose. They were intended to teach poor students the value of money and to develop a work ethic they did not learn at home. Local high school administrators made absolutely sure that NYA students earned their government paychecks—getting something for nothing was never part of the plan. In Topeka, Kansas, for instance, students who failed to meet high standards of "character, need and logical scholarship" were dropped from the program, no questions asked. In El Paso, Texas, administrators promptly weeded out a small group who proved to be "unworthy of aid."[18] In Atlanta, the principal of Girls' High was so determined to teach relief students the value of self-reliance that she required them to use NYA earnings to pay back funds donated by the PTA months earlier.[19] A superintendent in Bemus, New York, was even more tough-minded. He would not permit his students to apply for NYA jobs, since their families were not on relief. "As long as our students were able to get along without it, even though some could have used a little, we did not believe we had excuse to apply for [NYA funds]," he said.[20]

To political opponents, the NYA was never more than a Democratic scheme to shore up party loyalty and secure future votes, but to educators who dealt with poor students every day, the program worked miracles. "People who can see boys and girls without shoes, textbooks, clothing and food are the only ones who can appreciate what a God send it really is," one teacher reported. Another sang the praises of an NYA student who used the opportunity to support himself and stay in school, even though his parents had left town to look for work. Left to fend for himself, despite his young age, this student regularly rode his horse

seven miles back and forth to school (and his NYA job) no matter how bad the weather.[21]

Teachers were likewise amazed by the West Virginia student
who had lost all ambition and had run with a tough bunch of boys
before the NYA turned his life around. Employed on the high
school program and then assigned to a summer work project, he
was now determined to finish school. "When this young man can
find the money he purchases lumber and in his spare time makes
articles of furniture for the home," including a writing desk, a din-
ing room table, and two cedar chests that the neighbors were
eager to buy. But it wasn't only the money he earned that made
this transformation possible, his teachers added. It was the confidence he gained by participating in the program that persuaded
him that change was possible, after all.[22]

For teachers who worked with high school students, this boost
in self-confidence more than justified the NYA's expense. "Most
eligible students come from a lifetime of poverty," a school superintendent explained. They had been "denied the traditional
amount of clothes that is almost a birthright to a high school boy
or girl." Never included in social activities (since everyone knew
they had no money to spend), these students ran the risk of developing a crippling inferiority complex. But the NYA had gone a
long way toward solving this troublesome problem, he said. Take
the case of the NYA student who had withdrawn so completely
from those around her that she was almost psychopathic—and all
because she felt deeply humiliated by the lack of suitable clothes.
With the money she earned as a clerk in the school office, she was
able to dress in "clean and comfortable attire" for the first time in
her young life. This caused a startling transformation, he said.
Once she was back in touch with the rest of the student body, she
quickly assumed "an air of confidence, and of authority, and a
position of respect among her fellow students."[23]

But it was the poor students themselves who gave the most elo-
quent testimony to the program's worth. Their stories illustrated
how grateful they were for very small but practical favors. "I think
I can get through [high school] if I had glasses," one student wrote
to the NYA. "It's very hard on me to study with a head ache, and
if you will help me that much, it will be greatly appreciated."

Another remarked how the NYA freed the pupil's mind from money worries and gave him a chance "to help his parents as well as himself." Black students seemed particularly grateful that the NYA adopted "non-discriminating" policies that let anyone work who needed to, "regardless of race or color." Although girls tended to complain that boys had more chances to work than they did, most agreed that the NYA "was just swell." "We would all rather work for the money," a girl added, "than receive supplies from school."[24]

An eleventh grader from Des Moines, Iowa, offered the most detailed description of how the program had improved his life: "When I started school in September, I did not know whether I was going to continue to go or not," but the possibility of NYA work settled the question. "When I got my first check I was so tickled I could have shouted. I went to town that very evening and got some bread for my brothers' and sisters' and my own lunches. We had been taking home-made bread. It was good, but I always thought people made fun of it, so sometimes I went to school without a lunch. Next I got some shoes. Even if they weren't high-priced, I was proud of them, because I had bought them with my own money. With next month's pay I had my teeth fixed," and in the months that followed, he had managed to buy "many things that have made life more pleasant," a simple pleasure he had never experienced before.[25]

High school students had their complaints of course. Some wanted to work more hours and earn $25 a month; that way "a boy or girl could buy himself a suit of clothes or a coat, and it would not take three to five months to get it." Others thought that fifteen-year-olds should be eligible to work. After all, they had expenses, too. But overall their comments were positive, and not only because the NYA offered them a chance to be educated. To the students themselves the opportunity to look and dress like other high school students, to have the same supplies and to participate in some small way in high school life, seemed to be the best part of the NYA. If they were going to go to high school, then they wanted to be part of the crowd.[26]

Government programs like the NYA certainly helped to keep a teenage majority in high school during hard economic times, but the schools themselves also had a hand in the change. In the 1930s, practical programs like home economics, vocational training, and industrial arts were finally expanded; in the context of depression and despair, investing in new high school students suddenly seemed prudent indeed. "The hard dollars spent for tools, power shops and expensive, intricate machinery weigh a great deal," educational reformers pointed out, "but they weigh less when they are balanced against arson, theft, kidnapping, and murder. This is not to say that boys in the technical schools are potential jailbirds," they were quick to add. "Rather . . . many jailbirds are potentially honest, ambitious citizens, requiring only training to make them assets to any community." Giving up their exclusive claim to the academic mind, once and for all, high school educators now claimed an obligation to prepare "as many service-station attendants, automobile mechanics, tailors, barbers, manicurists, printers, [and] shoe repairmen" that a community might need.[27]

The combination of government help and vocational classes during the Great Depression finally achieved the progressive educators' goal: By 1939, close to 75 percent of fourteen- to seventeen-year-olds were high school students, and by 1940, half the nation's seventeen-year-olds were bona fide high school graduates—and that was almost twice as many as in 1929, when the economy had collapsed.[28] This accomplishment did not produce the social results progressive educators had in mind, however. For if they were more convinced than ever before that adolescence *should* be a vocational training period, and high school a laboratory for future careers, high school students themselves had other ideas.

In fact, at the very same time that educators and NYA counselors were focusing on teenage futures, adolescents themselves were discovering a much more immediate, exciting world—a world of radio music, dancing, and fun. As the economy began to recover in the late 1930s (largely due to the outbreak of war in Europe), high school students were developing a public identity that had nothing to do with family life or adult responsibilities. The first teenage generation to send a majority to high school, by 1938 they were making a name for themselves as bobby soxers who lived to dance to the swinging beat of big band music. Adults, too, were beginning to take notice of this crazy, swinging crowd, in magazines, movies, radio programs—attention that high school students had rarely drawn before. Although they were not "teenagers" yet in their own or anyone else's mind, the concept of a separate, teenage generation was beginning to gain ground. For once high school students discovered a beat and a language that was all their own, they happily shattered the expert's adolescent mold. And once they had money of their own to spend, and products to spend it on, their world—and that of their parents—would never be quite the same again.

Part II

Bobby Soxers

chapter four

High school students, Visalia, California, 1940. *Library of Congress, Prints and Photographs Division, FSA Collection [LCUSF 3424175]*

Swing Shift
Bobby Soxers Take the Stage

IN THE FALL OF 1941, JUST A FEW WEEKS INTO THE NEW SCHOOL
term, a teenage girls' club from Havre de Grace, Maryland, sponsored a bus trip to Washington, D.C. Adult leaders wanted to
introduce young members to the splendors of great classical art.
They planned a tour of the National Gallery, where the very best
of the Old Masters—Rembrandt, da Vinci, Botticelli—were on
display. Here was a golden opportunity to stimulate young tastes
for the finer things in life and to train young minds to appreciate
enduring values such as beauty, skill, and talent. For the art
museum was monument to high culture and perseverance, just the
kind of inspiration young girls needed to keep their aspirations
high.

Some of the girls had a different cultural odyssey in mind when
they signed up for the trip, however. A new movie starring Glenn
Miller and his big swing band was playing just a few blocks away,
and a small group of jitterbugs, as they were called, quietly slipped
out to see it. Mesmerized by the fascinating rhythm of the big

band sound, the girls lost all track of time. When they found their way back to the venerable museum, their chartered bus was gone. Still energized by the music, they made their way to police head-quarters to wait for their bus fare home. In the meantime, though, they turned the station house into a jumping dance joint. Astounding the officers with their energy, their attitude, and their jive-talking, finger-snapping ways, these girls seemed to be a strange new species of teenage life, with a language and a rhythm all its own.[1]

The officers shouldn't have been so surprised. Swing music had been shaping teenage style since 1937, when Benny Goodman and his band first got high school students to dance in the aisles of New York's Paramount Theater. As the king of swing, Goodman made the music sound easy. He played his clarinet with a cool, natural style that seemed to echo, effortlessly, the basic rhythms of life. His drummer, Gene Krupa, ignited the dancing crowds with frenzied, almost wild solos, and his trumpeter, Harry James, knew how to keep the excitement high. Years later, their performance—and the young audience's wildly enthusiastic response—would be compared to the advent of rock 'n' roll, but the analogy was faulty. Rock 'n' roll was a musical product specifically created with the teenage market in mind; swing, on the other hand, was a teenage discovery that set the market in motion.

More than just a passing fad, swing music reoriented teenage social life and high school style in the early 1940s. Thanks to radio programs that regularly featured the most popular bands in live performance, it was easy enough to join the crowd; even the most sheltered high school students could develop a taste for "hot" musicians like Duke Ellington, Count Basie, Artie Shaw, and Woody Herman. Hepcats and jitterbugs, who took their music seriously (as opposed to squares, who did not), could easily spend two to three hours a night swinging to radio music, especially when a band was really "in the groove."[2] Or they might spend their free time hunting down new records, or finding a place to dance. The most dedicated swing fans read *Down Beat* to keep up with the latest trends. The most inspired started bands of their own to play at high school dances and parties. "At sixteen I was jam-ming with a few sympathetic pals from the high school marching band," a fan remembered. "By the time I graduated from high school, I had, like thousands of other youngsters . . . given myself the start of an education in jazz."[3]

Dancing the Lindy Hop, the Suzie Q, or the Big Apple (and showing a little too much thigh and enthusiasm for adult comfort), high school students gained national fame as "bobby soxers," the popular nickname bestowed on swing-crazed fans who were developing a new teenage style. In their saddle shoes, skirts, and sweaters, they became the new symbol of high school life, one that was identified with music, fads, and fun. Bobby soxers were known to swoon for Frank Sinatra (who sang with Tommy Dorsey's band). They gave each other "skin" when they met in the street. And they riled their parents with a maddening language that only their friends understood. Worse yet, they spent time and money organizing fan clubs and lined the streets for hours on end whenever a band came to town, just to catch a glimpse of their favorite swing musicians.[4]

Parents, teachers, character builders, and even some high school students themselves did not know what to make of the phenomenon. Rambunctious and short-sighted, bobby soxers did not fit adult-approved adolescent molds. Their obvious obsession with crass commercial culture and their deliberate waste of precious leisure time, for instance, did not bode well for the future. At least not according to Dr. Leslie Hohman, a columnist for the *Ladies' Home Journal*. Adolescents would never focus on "real achievement" in the future, he argued, if everything in their young, impressionable lives was "glossed over and made too exciting." Therefore, conscientious parents had a duty to steer youngsters away from addictive time wasters like swing music, radio broadcasts, and movies, he wrote in 1939. If they were smart they would immunize them against the dangerous virus of bobby-soxer culture by elevating teenage tastes for the finer things in life.[5]

The good doctor was fighting a losing battle, though. Cultural elevation was much easier said than done, as the wily young jitterbugs from Havre de Grace demonstrated. With 80 percent of the teenage population now enrolled in high school, the group demonstrated strong and identifiable tastes in music, clothes, and recreation, and they regularly displayed "typical" teenage behavior that skirted the boundaries of respectable life. In 1941, for instance, high school students were already famous for driving "as fast as their little cars could carry them" and for playing reckless driving games such as "crinkle fender," which was popular in Indianapolis.[6] That same year, *Life* magazine offered an intriguing (and amusing) picture of teenage life that was becoming more familiar every day. "They live in a Jolly World of Gangs, Games . . . Movies . . . and Music. . . . They speak a curious lingo . . . adore chocolate milk shakes . . . wear moccasins everywhere . . . and drive like bats out of hell."[7]

The fact that the population of fourteen- to seventeen-year-olds was larger than usual (9,720,419 in 1940) also gave high school students new visibility. Advertisers and merchandisers were beginning to recognize an attractive new market in the making, one that was not necessarily bound by adult standards or tastes.[8] Celebrating the notion of carefree, high school bobby soxers (whose only concern in life was to have a good time and dance), they began to promote a new social type they dubbed "teeners," "teensters," and in 1941, "teenagers." Like bobby soxers, teenagers were tied to the new high school world of dating, driving, music, and enjoyment, and like bobby soxers, they were a commercial cross between authentic high school students and adult projections of what they should be: fun-loving, wholesome, high school conformists whose main goal in life was to be part of the crowd. Although it would take a few years for the term "teenager" to catch on in the popular mind, the concept was spreading rapidly, particularly as a marketing tool.[9]

In fact, the roots of the teenage market reached back to the 1920s, when the high school population first began to grow. By mid-decade *Scholastic* magazine, the national high school weekly, regularly featured a few ads for goods and services that no discerning student could do without: athletic shoes, class rings, even life insurance to protect a student's future should a father meet an untimely demise.[10] Ten years later the variety of products, and the size and frequency of the ads, had grown along with the student body. Now there were pens, typewriters, and books galore for schoolwork and leisure reading; gym clothes, athletic equipment, and shoes for every sport. There was also a growing line of products that promised to improve a student's social life. Planters Peanuts, for instance, would deliver popularity; Fleischmann's yeast could clear up complexion problems that stood in the way of romance; even Postum, a grain beverage substitute for coffee, offered students a path to beauty and social acceptance through good health.

But it took the swing music craze (and the economic revival it heralded) to move the staid and respectable high school market into more volatile teenage turf. The shift in style and tone was startling. In 1930, the editors of Scholastic had boasted a "high opinion of high school students . . . whose tastes are civilized, whose aims are important, and whose ambitions are serious."[11] In 1935, the magazine warned high school students against mindless, extravagant consumption, pointing out that "any nitwit can spend . . . money he hasn't earned for things that tickle his palate . . . without ever asking why."[12] By the 1940s, however, voracious appetites for high school fashions and fads, as well as movies, soft drinks, and popular music, had put teenage consumption—mindless or not—in a brand new, favorable light.

Now advertisers began to address high school students as teenagers on the prowl for a good time, not earnest adolescents in training for adulthood. For instance, when Pepsi Cola asked, "Do You Dig It?" in a series of ads that ran in Scholastic, the company was speaking directly to high school hepcats. "Come on, Gate! The Man Traps are giving groceries at the Rustlebustle," the stylized copy read. "And Pepsi Cola's hitting on eight!" For those not yet initiated into the swinging world of teenage jive, the ad included a translation: "This joy-boy is inviting his roommate over to the dance where the girls are serving refreshments and . . . Pepsi Cola is getting the big rush."[13] Whether the company's jive would pass muster in a juke joint was not the point: Advertisers were beginning to identify and create a specialized teenage market, and they were appealing to the high school student's age-old desire for independence and separation to do so.

In a sense, market builders were following the path of least resistance. It took almost no effort at all to persuade high school students to see themselves as a class apart, as "teenagers," according to popular standards, with their own age-related tastes, styles, and social concerns. After all, these adults did not invent teenagers out of whole cloth or manufacture the adolescent obsession with looks and popularity. These were direct descendants of the traditional high school crowd, which measured social acceptability by appearance, status, and dates.

Market builders, however, took these concepts to a new, commercial level that encouraged financially dependent high school students to proclaim their social independence through their looks and their style. By 1942, "Petiteen" was producing teenage clothes that were "sized to fit your figure, but *styled* to fit your *age*."[14] Teentimers, Inc., a New York dressmaking firm, advertised "junior" clothes specifically designed for the teenage set.[15] Local retailers also joined the campaign, stocking special teenage shops with sloppy Joe sweaters, gadget jewelry, Indian bracelets, and other fad accessories that promised to turn uncertain adolescents into "slick chicks" and "date bait."[16] The post-Depression realization that teenage identity could be packaged and sold in department stores had great appeal for insecure students who thought their lives would change if they only knew how to dress.

But if market builders were tapping into real teenage trends in the 1940s, they were creating them, too. For the teenage leisure world they portrayed as normal in magazines and advertisements still represented a very select slice of American life. The jive-talking, milkshake-chugging bobby soxers featured in *Life* magazine, for instance (who came to represent a national model of teenage life), were not run-of-the mill high school students by any means. They were part of the wealthy sorority set, sub-debs who expected to marry well and join the ranks of high society. Part of the 9 percent of teenagers who could afford to go on to college, they could not understand why anyone might choose that dreary option—not when they could be having fun![17] That these privileged girls had nothing in common with most high school students, either financially or socially, did not matter to image makers, however. On the contrary, their carefree upper-class style set an attractive new standard for teenagers nationwide, who envied their freedom and their casual approach to the future, to say nothing of their clothes, their cars, and their free-spending ways. Age and desire were the building blocks of teenage culture, and

teenage desire—for experience, for independence, and for fun—
was widespread.

Not that there was anything wrong with that, as far as promoters could see. Even the experts at *Parents* magazine applauded
bobby-soxer culture as the easiest way to keep teenagers interested
in high school. At this early stage in the process, the teenage world
was neither hostile nor rebellious: "Teenager" was just another
name for an adolescent or high school student, a step up (but not
away) from childhood. The term evoked a much wackier style
than the earnest portrayal of adolescents in the past, but it was a
style that adults often found entertaining. Popular radio programs
like "The Aldrich Family," "That Brewster Boy," and "A Date with
Judy," for instance, all analyzed life, love, and family harmony from
a teenage point of view. In Hollywood, teenage stars like Mickey
Rooney, Deanna Durbin, Judy Garland, and Shirley Temple were
bringing the ups and downs of teenage life to big screen audiences
all across the nation. In the process, their wholesome image and
respectful style spread the reassuring word that teenagers and
adults shared the same basic values, even if they danced to wildly
different beats.

Family magazines passed the word, too, as they welcomed
teenage readers to the fold. Sub-deb columns gave way to
monthly high school features in the 1940s, and magazines like
Good Housekeeping and *Woman's Home Companion* hired teenage
reporters to keep young readers up to date. "High school's opening again," a typical feature began. "Grab yourself a chocolate
malt. Tootle on your clarinet. . . . Snitch a jacket from your beau.
Go in for giddy plaids, for suits, for peasant skirts and blouses."[18]

The trials and tribulations of teenage social life also gained a
respectful hearing; in fact, editors apparently agreed that a satisfying social life was a worthy teenage goal. Articles on how to conduct a successful date, which covered the initial phone call, the
always awkward introduction to parents, and the triumphant
arrival home, in time for curfew, of course, became regular features.[19] These magazines even gave lessons on how to finesse an
innocent goodnight kiss after a special occasion, like the prom.
"Just make things cozy," a writer advised. "Slow up as you get near
your house. Search reluctantly . . . for your key. . . . Hesitate on

the doorstep . . . he'll just have to kiss you!"[20] This adult–approved version of teenage life enjoyed a major boost in the fall of 1941, when the publishers of *Parents* magazine launched *Calling All Girls*. Sold on newsstands at 10 cents a copy, it was the first magazine to use bobby-soxer culture to attract a teenage audience. Shirley Temple and Judy Garland headed its junior advisory board (and offered tips on life as a "teener"); Benny Goodman authored an article on "Music as You Like It" for the bobby-soxer set; and the magazine featured advice columns, fashion news, and monthly reports of the latest high school fads to let young readers all over the country know what their counterparts were up to.

But the new magazine was less interested in reflecting actual teenage style than it was in setting a good example for teenagers. For instance, readers were regularly reminded to respect their elders, to put their leisure time to good use, and to act their age. They were also urged to maintain a fresh, wholesome style and to go easy on their makeup. "If we could all remember that the natural . . . look is the right one, we'd never wear too much lipstick, powder the wrong shade, nail polish too dark. Because any of these things look cheap," the editors insisted, "and glamour has nothing to do with looking cheap."[21]

Hollywood offered an equally wholesome introduction to teenage life, one that starred Andy Hardy and his friends as proper teenage role models. A happy-go-lucky high school lad, popular with students and teachers alike, Andy was also a vital member of a very democratic family. In heart-to-heart talks with his father, for instance, young Andy had the benefit of adult advice, but he was always permitted to make his own decisions, and his own mistakes, in matters of life and love. Luckily, his biggest problems revolved around catching the eye of the new girl in town, although he always seemed to make his way back to the girl-next-door (who was more his type anyway). Andy was Hollywood's idea of what a teenager should be: adventuresome but innocent, high-spirited but respectful, and chiefly concerned with the high school world of dating, dancing, and drugstore antics after school. There was nothing artificial in this presentation of wholesome, teenage life. It was life as adults wanted it to be lived, and Andy was more than happy to oblige.[22]

In real life, however, teenagers were rarely so tractable. They loved the music, the movies, the clothes, and the language that advertised their separation from adults, but they did not inhabit the wholesome, asexual, yet somehow totally fulfilling teenage world that adults regularly envisioned for them, and they were not always willing to accept the state of suspended animation their elders prescribed. Mickey Rooney, for instance, the star of seventeen Andy Hardy films between 1937 and 1946, may have taught moviegoers how to act like proper teenagers, but his own adolescence was a far cry from the earnest innocence he portrayed on the screen. As a teenager he was sexually active and spent much of his time in the company of adults, drinking and gambling.[23]

Shirley Temple, another child star who grew into teenage roles, lived a more conventional life. Yet even she could not live up to her innocent, teenage image for long. "Shirley's first . . . silk stockings . . . were as exciting as any girl's," *Calling All Girls* reported when she was thirteen. "She's still not allowed to wear them all the time—only when she goes downtown or to a party." Just three years later, however, this well brought up, respectful teenager was sporting an engagement ring at the ripe old age of sweet sixteen. Barely graduated from high school, she was an experienced married woman by seventeen, a pattern that was not so unusual by the mid-1940s.[24]

Hardly precocious deviants, Rooney and Temple were more typical in their desire for "adult" experience and independence than movie-manufactured "teenagers" ever were. After all, there was nothing innocent about the jive culture that first inspired bobby soxers and gave such a lift to teenage style. Hot jazz musicians with a taste for wild abandon and illicit drugs had improvised the language and the beat that electrified jitterbugs, but this influence could not be acknowledged directly; like commercial teenage culture in general, the swing music craze had to pass through the purifying filter of the middle-class world before it could be deemed safe for teenage consumption.

At that point, however, it could be marketed like anything else. For out of the mouths of well-bred teens, jive talk was just an amusing eccentricity that had no darker roots, and in the nicer parts of town, jitterbugging and teenage carousing were just another part of high school life. They might be considered annoying, or even a waste of time, but they were rarely viewed as dangerous or a threat. Just across the tracks, however, teenage culture could look much more ominous. Outside the familiar bounds of the respectable world, it raised the unpleasant and usually unspoken specter of teenage sexuality and "delinquent" behavior, the underside of bobby-soxer culture that adults preferred to ignore.

For instance, Mexican-American "pachucos," the would-be bobby soxers of a less prosperous community, offered a very different image of teenage life, an image rarely seen at the time, outside of social worker reports or professional journals. Like other minority youth, pachucos were just not considered part of the "American" scene. The children of poor immigrants, they displayed none of the fresh-faced innocence *Life* magazine took for granted. Nor did they have any intention of fitting in with the high school crowd; in fact, they usually dropped out of high school at the first opportunity.

Surrounded by elders who longed for the past and ambitious community leaders who urged them to follow middle-class rules, pachucos were determined to go their own way.[25] Like mainstream bobby soxers, they developed their own style of dress and deportment that set them apart from their parents' world, but their style had a defiant edge that challenged the notion of carefree, teenage innocence. For instance, their teenage "lingo" (a dialect called Calo) was derived from the language of the criminal underworld, and it never failed to draw an angry rise from parents and teachers who did not understand it.[26]

Their distinctive clothes reflected the same notorious influence (and inevitably provoked the same angry, adult response). Pachucos dressed in elaborate zoot suits, with tapered drape pants, fingertip jackets, and broad-brimmed hats, a look that was popular with jazz musicians and gangsters alike. Triple-sole shoes completed the controversial ensemble, which pachucos topped off with an equally controversial hairstyle: the long, slicked-back duck tail, or notorious D.A., that adults would later associate with juvenile delinquents.[27]

The girls (or pachuquitas) were equally provocative, in short tight skirts, sheer blouses, dark red lipstick, and black mascara;

indeed, they embodied the tantalizing, seductive style that *Calling All Girls* found so offensive. "We didn't approve of it and we didn't dress that way," a woman from the same community remembered her teenage years. She had to admit, though, that pachuco style proved far more popular than she and her "respectable" friends ever expected. Called "little tornados of sexual stimuli" by their critics, pachuquitas had no trouble at all attracting boys (and men) with their sassy attitude and aggressive style. In fact, they seemed to have discovered the basic key to popularity![28]

Nonetheless, these teenage girls resented the implication that they were morally suspect just because they looked older than they were. No matter how they chose to dress, pachuquitas were never "easy." They knew how to make a boyfriend keep his hands to himself—they had to. In this otherwise traditional community, girls who were known to go too far were banished from their family homes, no questions asked. "Mexican girls are full of fun, they laugh and joke with boys, but there is nothing bad between them just . . . because they sneak out for dates," a pachuquita explained, giving almost a textbook definition of teenage culture. "We ride around and sing and laugh and go . . . someplace where there's new records. So we get some beer and have a lot of fun dancing and talking and singing and stuff. Americans do that too," she said, annoyed that outsiders held pachucos to very different standards.[29]

The clothes, the music, the beer, and the distance from their parents' world marked pachucos as teenagers, like any other, but their poverty, their heritage, and their skin color made their separation seem that much more sinister and dangerous. For some pachucos who were caught up with neighborhood gangs and turf wars, it was. "These kids are full of animal mad. They can't fight the cops or the gabachos, their enemies," a boy explained, "so to get the mad from their blood they fight each other." Knives and pistols were the quickest routes to neighborhood justice. Boys who believed their honor was at stake usually took matters into their own hands. Their girlfriends cheered them on, or stood by them in court if the police got involved. They were proud to be associated with "rugged gatos" (cats) who were not afraid to prove their manhood to the world.[30]

Mexican-American teenagers were not all pachucos, and pachucos were not all delinquents, but the differences were lost on the mainstream world. Outside of their own communities, minority teenagers drew no attention unless they broke the law. For instance, although half this teenage group dropped out of high school every year, nobody seemed interested; this was not the kind of "bobby soxer" story that *Life* magazine was likely to cover. Even their teachers were not alarmed or concerned; many took it for granted that "Mexicans" were inherently slow and not cut out for school anyway. Except for a few sociologists and youth workers, nobody cared that this teenage group felt no connection to the larger, adult world—not until trouble erupted, that is.[31]

Invisible or not, though, these restless, "precocious," out-of-place teenagers had more in common with mainstream youth than popular imagery suggested. After all, it was precocious, adventurous, risk-taking youth, with no interest in high school, who had given rise to the concept of adolescence in the first place, and by the 1940s it was getting harder to camouflage—or ignore—this troublesome truth, particularly after the outbreak of the Second World War. War created exciting (and dangerous) opportunities for teenagers to prove themselves in the adult world. It opened the doors to work, training, and adult independence that had been closed to high school–age youth for years, and it changed national priorities, at least temporarily: All of a sudden the nation needed mature, responsible teenagers, willing and able to work for their country, not mindless bobby soxers with nothing better to do than dance.

War turned the allegedly carefree teenage world on its head, and not only because wartime shortages put a crimp in bobby-soxer culture. There was no gasoline for joyriding, no ice cream for milkshakes, and even cokes were diluted for the duration. More important, though, war raised familiar yet hard to answer questions about the teenager's proper place in the world. In times of economic depression, when jobs were hard to come by, teenagers were obviously children who had to be sheltered from the adult world of work. In times of war, however, they were expected to be capable of victory on the battlefield, production in defense jobs, and self-discipline when left to fend for themselves, regardless of their age or experience. A father who watched his teenage son prepare for war documented the change in 1942: "Here's hoping that these 'kids' do their job quickly and thoroughly," he wrote in a letter, "so that when our victory is won, we'll all enjoy the benefits of a great Democratic country."[32]

chapter five

Sailor kissing mom good-bye, 1943. *Library of Congress, Prints and Photographs Division, FSA Collection [LCUSW 321006E]*

Andy Hardy Goes to War

*Soldiers, Defense Workers, "V-Girls,"
and Zoot Suiters*

ALTHOUGH THE NATION HAD BEEN GEARING UP FOR WAR EVER since the fall of France in 1940, teenagers were barely aware of the conflict. Most had only a hazy idea of the roles they would be asked to play. For instance, when high school students in Florida considered how they might contribute to the nation's defense, their proposals were largely symbolic. "I suggest that we have a more patriotic feeling," one wrote. Whenever the flag was raised or lowered at school, a bugle could be blown and students made to stand at attention. "This may not seem important," he admitted, "but I think it adds a certain feeling that may not be expressed in other ways." Others offered to organize marching bands or knit sweaters for the troops, but saving tin foil seemed to be the most popular wartime suggestion. As a student from Gainesville High put it, that was "something we can do easily and without expense to us."[1]

More patriotic than practical, these suggestions reflected the teenager's station in life. High school students were *supposed* to inhabit a largely symbolic world, and they were *supposed* to find satisfaction in superficial tasks that mimicked adult reality—at least that was what movies, magazines, and radio programs had been telling them for the past few years. By 1941, high school students looked forward to the "fun and enjoyment" that defined their stage in life—after all, that's what being a teener was all about.[2] No one would expect them to play more than a spectator's role when it came to the adult world of war. In fact, viewed in the context of bobby-soxer culture, their heartfelt, enthusiastic, but basically effortless wartime suggestions made sense.

In the context of international crisis, however, they missed the mark. For the harsh realities of world war made serious new demands on teenage youth, demands that turned carefree sixteen-year-olds into valuable citizens overnight. As older brothers, uncles, boyfriends, and sometimes even fathers made their way overseas, teenagers were suddenly required to keep the home fires burning. There may have been no room for "precocious" youth in adult workplaces during peacetime, but during war there was always something for them to do. Factories, farms, and local businesses depended on teenage hands to stay afloat; both the Navy and private industry were hiring sixteen-year-old apprentice mechanics; and the National Youth Administration, the NYA, still in business until 1943, was training sixteen-year-old defense workers (girls as well as boys) to do a man's job.

Before too long, the boys themselves would be engaged in battle: Eight out of ten high school boys could expect to enter the military as soon as they were graduated, and no one could say for sure just when, how, or even whether they would be coming home. These were not fears that people talked about out loud, but they could not be ignored for long either. Soon after the attack on Pearl Harbor, for instance, high school newspapers were running "Gold Star" columns to mark the passing of young soldiers who had been students only months before.[3]

A teenage defense worker stationed in a shipyard in 1942 was struck by how quickly life had changed: "Everything is serious out here," she wrote in a letter. "Every time you pick up the paper you think how it all strikes home; how some day the little sailors training in the yards will be out there among them. Just seventeen- and eighteen-year-old boys. Some look to be fifteen or sixteen," she added, and she could have been right: Calvin Graham, a twelve-year-old, had lied his way into the Navy in 1942 and earned a Purple Heart and a Bronze Star before he was discovered.[4]

In a sense, the nation needed its servicemen to be boys, and not only because they were suited physically to the task. Their boundless energy, dogged loyalty, and eagerness to prove their ability camouflaged the horror of the job they were about to assume. Fresh-faced high school athletes were the prototypical war heroes, Andy Hardys all grown up and ready to do their duty.[5] Recruiting ads played on this image, as if war were just another challenge to young manhood, like learning to drive or going out on a first date. "Okay take 'er up alone," an Air Force ad began. "You gun the engine. . . . You circle around. And all at once you wish Mom and Dad were there in the stage house watching. Somehow it's like the time you made your first touch down. . . . And you felt great because you knew you had to make good—and you did."[6] The image proved compelling, especially to boys in search of excitement and respect. In fact, when it came to building a fighting force, the nation depended on inexperienced boys whose hunger for adventure outweighed their sense of risk—a quality that often marked them as "precocious" or even "delinquent" in civilian life. "I wanted to be a hero, let's face it," explained a veteran who joined the Marines at age seventeen. "I was having trouble in school. I was having trouble with my mother. They didn't know what to do [with me]," he said.[7] Another linked romantic images of war and heroism to his teenage decision to enlist: "At that age, you look forward to the glamour and have no idea of the horrors," he explained. "My gosh, going across the ocean, seeing the armies, the excitement of it." The fear of death was always present, this veteran admitted, but an even greater sense of adventure, pride, and duty motivated teenagers to join the fight.[8]

Once in the service, however, teenage boys faced up to the fact that there was more to soldiering than putting on a uniform and waving goodbye. "We march twenty miles a day with full field packs, gas mask, rifle, bayonet (60 lbs.)," a teenage soldier told his friends. "We work from 6 A.M. to 6 P.M., eighty-four hours a week."[9] A teenage Marine was amazed that he even survived the training. "They humiliate you, they make you do things that you don't feel are physically possible," he said. "But at the same time, they're making you feel you're something. That you're part of something." This shared purpose gave young recruits a reason to fight—they were part of Uncle Sam's gang, ready to defend their country and their buddies to the bitter end. Accepting this dangerous role as their duty, they did their best to calm their family's fears. "I am now a rifle man. It's something new to me," a soldier who had just turned nineteen wrote home. "But what's the difference. I know how to take care of 'me.'. . . I'm in the best of spirits and health [so] there's no need for any of you worrying." Before the year was over, however, this loving son was gone, and there was no way to camouflage the loss.[10]

If they were too young to fight as soldiers, teenage boys often served as defense workers. When even unskilled workers earned respect plus 50 cents an hour (and sometimes more), it was hard to persuade full-grown boys that they were better off staying in high school. In Boston, almost half of the city's sixteen-year-olds quit school between 1940 and 1941, and the trend continued as war raged on. Nationwide, high school enrollments dropped 17 percent between 1940 and 1944, the first decline in decades. The dropout rate reached 35 percent, according to the U.S. Census Bureau, with boys twice as likely as girls to leave school.[11]

Dropping out was one thing, but doing an adult's job was quite another. Defense workers were not soldiers, but they still had to follow the same wartime rules of self-discipline and cooperation: There could be no military victory without skilled, productive workers. There was no room for "sympathetic" guidance or second chances. Teenagers who wanted to become part of the great war machine had to deliver like anyone else. Ready or not, they traded their claim to childhood dependency (and irresponsibility) for an adult's job (and an adult's paycheck), a hard-edged bargain that thousands made without a second thought.

Unlike their Depression-era counterparts, who had no future at all without a high school diploma, these dropouts expected to prosper, especially if they were eligible to join the NYA's comprehensive training course. Part of the national defense effort until 1943, the NYA offered a cross between a traditional apprenticeship and industrial boot camp. NYA administrators still believed that teenagers needed guidance to find their way to adulthood (and a trade), but unlike private employers (who favored a sink-or-swim training method), they also believed that teenagers needed to develop a sense of self-discipline and perseverance before they took on adult responsibilities—qualities that would get them through life or the Army, whichever came first.

Their parents tended to agree. "He needs help now, because he has lost all interest in school and I have lost control over him," wrote a mother who sent her son to Quoddy Village, an NYA project in Maine. "If he is to become useful to this great land of ours he must be guided now." [12] To some parents, of course, guidance actually meant compulsion, and they looked to the NYA to apply the pressure that had so far failed to work at home. "He does not at present know his own mind and it must be made up for him," one mother wrote, while another pleaded with Quoddy's director to change her son's plans to become a welder. "After the war there won't be such a large field for it," she explained. "I would prefer Machine Shop or Aviation Aircraft." [13]

Mothers of hard-to-handle daughters also looked to the NYA to teach their girls the discipline they had failed to learn at home: "I'm asking you to see that she follows [orders] strictly, as she has had her own way a bit too much," a mother wrote in 1942. [14] Another urged the NYA staff to keep close tabs on her daughter. She wasn't really "bad," she said, but she had a dangerous habit of staying out late and then sleeping the day away. "I wouldn't advise she be given a weekend off for a while," this mother added—her teenage child might slip away if given half a chance. [15] Like other wary parents, she knew what she was talking about: Teenagers eager to drop out of high school and get on with their adult lives were not likely to live by Andy Hardy's rules.

There were always NYA participants who used the program, and the promise of war work, to escape their families. On the one hand, the NYA attracted teenagers who wanted to follow their own plans in life, whether their parents approved or not. For instance, a sixteen-year-old applicant who had done well in grammar school but rarely showed up for high school thought he would be much better off if he dropped out of school to learn a trade. "My mother disagrees with me but many folks *agree* with me. No one would speak to my mother about it," he told an NYA administrator, "so I beg of you to help if you could." [16]

On the other hand, there were teenagers who never expected more from the training program than a chance to be off on their own. Some were known to leave NYA camps as soon as they arrived. Others refused to cooperate or ignored camp rules in a brash show of independence. However, they soon discovered that their teenage "freedom" came at a very high price. For if NYA administrators did not supervise nights out on the town or prohibit girls from smoking cigarettes (which they did in a very "vulgar" manner, according to reports), they drew the line at insubordination.[17] Likewise, when participants failed to cooperate, or acted irresponsibly, they were dropped from the program, no questions asked.

That came as quite a shock to those who realized the NYA's value a little too late. "Gee, whenever I think back to that day, that you sent me home, I really feel like shooting myself," a former trainee admitted, "for I think what I missed."[18] Another boy who left Quoddy for no good reason and then tried in vain to return was equally sorry: "I regret this hasty action with all my heart. Because I haven't a trade," he said. "My mother won't speak to me and my father thinks I'm a lazy tramp that I cannot hold a job." But the NYA took its training mission seriously—there was just no room for impulsive teenagers when it came to national defense, as those who stuck the program out learned almost immediately. "You can call Quoddy a prep school for the Army," one satisfied alumnus thanked the staff soon after he was drafted. Another who landed a good job in an aircraft factory agreed: "I think I was one of the problem cases," he truthfully reported. "Well, I think I turned out good. For the past month I averaged about $30 a week."[19]

For girls, the training was even more valuable. The war opened up a whole new world of high-paid opportunities for females who proved they could run complex machines and test-pilot airplanes with the best of them. Now girls who once had no choice but to work as stenographers, nurses, or clerks wanted to get into exciting new fields like radio and aviation. Like teenage boys who wanted to learn a trade, they eagerly packed their bags for Quoddy. "When my brother told me about the care and teaching the boys have there," a young female applicant wrote in 1943, "I thought that now was my chance to learn something I was interested in, and also help out in the war emergency."[20]

Pioneers in an otherwise all-male world, these female trainees needed a tough skin just to break into defense work. Even young Quoddy graduates did not welcome girls into the fold. "I understand that boys are scarce," a former trainee wrote to Quoddy's staff. "I can imagine Senate meetings with feminine voices screeching back and forth, and a female mayor—EEK!"[21]

He wasn't the only one to regret the passing of the old industrial order. Many employers also had trouble believing that girls could handle the work. "I was the first girl to get into the 'Boat Shop,'" wrote an NYA graduate from her post in Bremerton, Washington, "and I had to do some fast talking to do that even. . . . I started as a 'Mechanic Learner' at $4.64 a day with a raise in a month and a half. I get to run machines," she wrote, "and make tool boxes right now."[22] Another defense worker in Baltimore told a similar story: "Tell the girls that it is great and I would not trade places with anybody," she said. "But when they do come they had better have plenty of determination and an iron will."[23]

At a defense plant in Seattle, officials closed their doors to high school girls entirely; apparently employers considered these young trainees more trouble than they were worth. Their age was only part of the problem, however. For instance, when a group of young Hispanic girls, aged sixteen and seventeen, left Seattle in a rage (prompting the company to demand that future trainees be at least eighteen years old), their youth had almost nothing to do with the conflict.

From the start these girls had a very hard time fitting into the defense workers' world. "Tell Mrs. Leonard [the NYA counselor] to send me home just like she send us here," one of the girls wrote to her family. "Gee we are sure going to tell her out because she said it was sure nice out here and it is not because it is sure hard to get rooms. We stay days looking for rooms without anything to eat or sleep, and they don't like Spanish girls and boys. They call us Mexicans," she reported, adding that "all the girls get drunk, the Americans. Gee all the girls are spoiled out here." Homesick, hungry, and convinced she and her friends were not wanted in Seattle, this NYA trainee was going home, war or no war.

The foreman read the situation differently. As far as he could see, the girls were not interested in defense work at all. Left alone on a job they would just stop and talk over their letters, he reported. "I spent a good deal more time with these girls individually than I should have. And I feel the time could have been spent to a greater advantage with some . . . who showed more willingness . . . to learn methods of work as performed in this part of the country."[24] But an NYA counselor questioned his assessment, particularly after she met with him. "His entire attitude led me to believe that he does not know how to handle girls and, indeed, is not interested in girls in the shop."[25] Although the case had as much to do with the foreman's bias as it did with the teenagers themselves, the NYA agreed that girls under age eighteen were just too young to do defense work.[26]

The decision came as quite a blow to younger girls who looked forward to doing something important during the war. "I love America with all my heart," a fourteen-year-old wrote on her NYA application, "and I also want to do something worthwhile to help . . . I know I am probably too young," she admitted, "but honestly if you saw me you would think I was eighteen."[27] Another ambitious fourteen-year-old was in the same underaged boat. She and three friends wanted to apply for a summer program at Quoddy, but she was not quite old enough yet. "I know that I would do my best to give satisfaction," she said, "for I like work and am anxious to get at those machines." Since she was as tall as the older girls and could easily "pass" in the adult world, she saw no reason why she could not get started now. Like it or not, though, individual talent, motivation, even maturity did not matter—high school–aged girls were just too young, in adult eyes, to make a real contribution to the war, and "that was that," as adults often put it.[28]

By this time the point was moot, however. With the war economy in full swing, the NYA was on its way out. Between the armed services and booming defense industries, the idea of training teenagers at taxpayer expense had lost its appeal. The decision did not matter much to older teens, who had no trouble at all finding work if they wanted it, but it left younger teenagers at loose ends. Adults were much too busy with their own wartime opportunities to take time to train teenagers for jobs, and they fully expected the younger crowd to turn their wartime attention to high school.

The idea was not new, of course. Neither was the hope that

teenagers would regard education as their full-time job. But the war put a new spin on the concept. "Your special patriotic duty is to make the most of your opportunity," *Scholastic* magazine pointed out. That meant *"making your education count."*[29] School newspapers expanded the concept, equating good study habits with battlefield victories. "We are at war," an Indianapolis high school paper began. "Did you go to the show last night, or did you stay home and do your lessons?" an editor wanted to know.[30] "Your School Is Your Camp, Don't Go A.W.O.L," another advised. Since a sound education was the "first line of defense," staying in school was the teenage equivalent of joining the service or working in a munitions factory. After all, it was common knowledge that dictators like Hitler depended on an ignorant public to survive![31]

At the same time, the nation needed educated soldiers to lead the troops and defense workers capable of reading blueprints and following technical manuals if it wanted to win the fight. In fact, if the war taught the federal government anything, it was that too many potential draftees were unprepared—both physically and mentally—to withstand the rigors of war. Determined to reverse the trend, the federal government now encouraged teenage boys to stay in school for democracy's sake and load up on accelerated science, math, and technical courses (as well as phys. ed.) while they were at it.[32]

Gay Head, who was still writing for *Scholastic*, was one of many educators who urged boys to stay in school, especially if they wanted to play a glamorous part in the war effort. In a column entitled "On the Assembly Line," for instance, a high school character debated whether to take a defense job or not. Amazed when his father advised him to stay in school, despite the fact that he could make "sixty bucks a week" in an aircraft plant, the student talked his problem over with a young defense worker. He was surprised to learn that his father was right! Only skilled workers earned that kind of money, not high school dropouts, the defense worker said, and since he had learned that fact the hard way, he now wished that he was back in school, too. "For one thing, if I knew more about math, I'd be twice as well off as I am now," the young worker explained. "I gotta cousin in the Army, crazy about airplanes and motors. He washed out in Aviation Mechanics y'know, because he was so rotten in math."[33]

The government's Federal Security Agency was also spreading the word. In 1942 it organized the High School Victory Corps, a preinduction program for voluntary student "reservists." Although the corps was open to all high school students, it was actively seeking male recruits. The FSA wanted to steer them into air, land, or sea divisions that would force them to work harder in high school. The boys-only air division, for instance, required a heavy schedule of classes, including one year of physics, three of math, pre-flight aeronautics, auto mechanics, radio, electricity, physical education, and military drill. Despite the added attraction of jaunty, semi-official uniforms, though, the Victory Corps failed to interest students. Only about 22 percent of those eligible ever enrolled, and almost 90 percent of those who did favored community service programs over classroom instruction. Apparently, high school students had no great interest in preparing endlessly for a future that might never arrive. If they were interested in the war effort, they wanted to do something practical, now.[34]

For instance, one girl, brought up in what she called a "perfectly normal American family," found herself running the household and keeping her family fed, a job she was proud to do—her brother was fighting overseas and her parents both worked at defense jobs. Another girl in junior high was equally satisfied to do her part, no matter how small it seemed. "The war has left a big dent in my life," she explained. Her oldest brother had already left for the Army, and another would be leaving soon. "Now, instead of having fun after school, I take care of children for war workers from 4 to 11 P.M. . . . I really don't mind giving all these things up because it means my brothers and friends will all be home sooner. By taking care of these babies," she said, "it leaves two more mothers available for work."[35]

In fact, when young teenagers were given a chance to participate in war work, they were eager to get the job done. They raised millions of dollars in war bond campaigns, built hundreds of thousands of scale model planes and ships for the Navy (which were used to train recruits), collected salvage by the ton, and tended victory gardens or worked at nearby farms all through the summer. But boys, especially, thought they could be doing more. "I could clean up around factories and release men for bigger jobs," a fourteen-year-old insisted. Fifteen-year-olds asked for the chance to help fight fires, do factory work, or maintain Army roads. "The boys feel that older people do not consider them seriously," a Scout leader pointed out, and he believed they had a point. Some of the boys he worked with could certainly do a better job in fire warden work, for instance, than many adults who held the job. According to a psychologist, this age exclusion frustrated young teenagers, who deeply resented "being treated like babies when there is so much vital work to be done."[36]

Young girls who wanted to make a difference got some support from *Calling All Girls*. Articles like "We 'Took It' in Hawaii," for instance, described Pearl Harbor from a teenage point of view, and "Navy Girl" featured an interview with a thirteen-year-old who had traveled back to the mainland on a blacked out Navy transport. Dozens of how-to articles and features offered wartime suggestions for younger teens that ranged from dressing for victory (by following the rules of the War Production Board), to babysitting, to investing spending money in war bonds. When push came to shove, though, the magazine's advice followed predictable adult lines. "What can you do?" an editorial echoed the familiar wartime question. "You can do *without*. That is probably going to be the hardest thing of all."[37]

To some degree it was—especially for high school students who resented the war for robbing them of their youthful right to enjoy life! Soldiers and sailors crowded them out of movie houses and after-school hangouts. Gasoline shortages meant no cars for dating, no team buses for high school athletic meets, no racing around playing reckless driving games after school. Food shortages meant conserving butter, sugar, meat, and chocolate—even chewing gum was a wartime casualty. "Did you ever stop to think of the changes that have taken place in these past years for the high school age?" a student wanted to know. Thanks to the war, "most boys and girls walk everywhere," she complained, parties had replaced nights out on the town, and formal dresses could no longer be drycleaned! There was also a serious shortage of available boys, a burden that fell hardest on "young teeners," another lamented. Worse yet, she said, "our elders don't seem to realize it."[38]

They also resented their total exclusion from the glamour and excitement of war. Domestic work, victory gardens, and "doing without" might be patriotic gestures, but they could not compare to flying a fighter plane or building a bomb, and young teenagers knew it. Left to their own devices, as so many were during the war, they created their own brand of excitement. Boys skipped school and got caught up in petty crime. Girls went "khaki-wacky," as the newspapers put it, using makeup to look much older than they were and then prowling the streets at night for soldiers. In fact, if they lived in port cities or near military bases, their social lives thrived during the war. And why not? Why shouldn't a girl enjoy wartime opportunities like everybody else? Why shouldn't she have fun with boys in uniform, who had money to spend and a fierce desire to spend it?

Critics called them "V-girls" or "Victory girls"—a name that implied a kind of prostitution, where young teenagers traded favors for a pair of stockings or a night on the town. But that wasn't necessarily the case. These girls could be more patriotic—and more innocent—than they looked. "I knew very little about sex," a former V-girl remembered, and the uniformed boys she picked up around town did not know much more. Fourteen years old and trying for all the world to look like actress Rita Hayworth, she thrived on the excitement of meeting a new boy every day, sometimes two or three. Her mother did not stop her either. On the contrary, she enjoyed the attention, since her husband worked nights at a defense job. "She'd play a honky-tonk, rinky-tink piano, very well really. I sang," she recalled.[39]

The boys seemed to like it, since they kept coming back for more. When they went overseas, each of them thought this four-teen-year-old was waiting just for him. She wrote all the soldiers faithfully, sending a dozen letters or so a week, and cookies when she could get the sugar. "My grades went completely downhill because I was so busy entertaining the troops. I felt that was my contribution to the war. It was my duty," she said. But that was not how it looked to neighborhood mothers, who kept their daughters away from her. "They thought I was fast," she admitted, "because I had those sailors at the house from the time I was thirteen."[40]

Popular opinion was on the neighbors' side. *Life* magazine found evidence of teenage promiscuity in twenty-two cities. *Reader's Digest* published reports that six hundred teenage "pick-up" girls were hanging around bus stations and hotels in Little

Rock, Arkansas.[41] The National Recreation Association painted an alarming picture of young teenagers prancing "down the streets six or seven abreast" and capturing servicemen in a "very flattering" teenage net. In Mobile, Alabama, V-girls brazenly purchased their own condoms, embarrassing drug store clerks and prompting a journalist to report that "the sex delinquency of young girls" was the city's worst problem. In New York City, the discovery of twelve-year-old prostitutes persuaded a reporter who broke the story that these "adolescents and pre-adolescents" were America's greatest failure to date. "We have not taken their restless energies, their eagerness . . . their wayward impulses, and channeled them into something . . . useful and healthy," he noted. "We have no work camps for them, no play camps for summers, no useful work for them to do. We have not built them into the structure of our community living," he said. Now Americans were paying the price.[42]

To be sure, the popular press exaggerated the story—less than 2 percent of the teenage population could be labeled promiscuous in the 1940s. Since this small proportion broke society's rules with wartime soldiers, though, their indiscretions had more impact than numbers alone implied—especially if they were infected with syphilis or gonorrhea. As juvenile rates of venereal disease began to rise during the war years (increasing 120 percent in Los Angeles, for example), V-girls attracted national attention.[43] Apparently, the conventional wisdom that the girl of 1943 was "not content to dance this war away" had a special meaning for the military—even a small number of diseased, promiscuous teenagers posed a significant military threat when they were dating men in uniform.[44]

Although it always took two to tango, V-girls were blamed for the rise of casual sex and venereal disease, as if servicemen were their hapless victims. "Booby Traps Are Dangerous!" warned a popular hygiene pamphlet. "Prostitutes and 'pick-up' girls are the home front traps for boobs only."[45] The idea that war might undermine conventional morality or that predatory soldiers might manipulate—and infect—young teenage girls was never raised in public. Tradition held the girl responsible for whatever happened on a date, regardless of her partner's age or experience. V-girls were portrayed as wily, aggressive tramps who deserved whatever they got, and no one thought to ask what wholesome, young soldiers were doing with such underage, oversexed streetwalkers.

The Office of Community War Services was one of the few government agencies to suggest that soldiers were not the injured party. In fact, it protested what seemed to be an "unwarranted sacrifice of American girls here at home."[46] Now was not the time to debate issues of sexual responsibility, however. Under the circumstances of war, it was far more important to take practical steps to minimize the spread of disease. Young soldiers who could not say no were urged to "take a pro"—a mere 10 cents bought three condoms on military bases, where vending machines offered "protection" twenty-four hours a day. More than 50 million condoms were sold or distributed during the Second World War, an indication, according to some observers, that "promiscuity had been made safe" for the next generation. [47]

If they did nothing else for the country, V-girls made visible some hidden facts of American life. Studies conducted by the Army suggested that sexually active teenage males had their first experience earlier than adults assumed—around age fifteen—and university investigators backed them up.[48] This was more of a sexual revelation, however, than a sexual revolution; the percentage of active teenagers did not shift significantly during the war years. But there was a new acknowledgment that they existed, and not just in the poor parts of town. Indeed, even the PTA was willing to address the issue. "You may knit and purl, you may roll bandages, donate blood, drive an ambulance," a spokeswoman told busy parents during a PTA radio show, "but . . . you better figure out how to tell your son that practically all prostitutes have VD. You better roll up your sleeves and tell your daughter that to have fun with the boy in uniform is one thing; to complicate your lives with sex is another. . . . You better drive yourself," she added, "to see youth's present problems from its point of view" and not from the vantage point of a fantasy world of carefree, innocent, obedient children.[49]

V-girls also lifted the veil of secrecy from some other longstanding problems, if only indirectly: Competition between soldiers and hometown boys for available girls often stirred up ethnic rivalries that had been simmering for years. When white soldiers and sailors stationed in California in 1943, for instance, began dating Mexican-American girls, riots broke out between crewcutted boys in military dress and long-haired pachucos in zoot suits. Since it was a long established fact of life that white women were off limits to dark-skinned men, pachucos believed the rule should work both ways.

Already a symbol of delinquent street culture, pachucos seemed even more threatening—and disrespectful—in the context of war. For instance, Al Capp (a notorious bigot) used his comic strip, *L'il Abner*, to portray zoot suiters as military slackers who thought nothing of wasting the nation's supply of wool to produce their extravagant costumes! The fact that pachucos were under suspicion for a rash of petty crimes further hardened public sentiment against them. According to the newspapers, zoot suiters had been beating and robbing young sailors almost for sport. When they challenged a sailor on a public bus who was trying to catch the eye of one of "their" women, thousands of soldiers and sailors in Los Angeles, Oakland, and Venice, California, decided to fight back.

Hunting down zoot-suited pachucos in theaters, restaurants, buses, and bars, they proceeded to beat and "depants" them—a particularly cruel act of public humiliation for teenage boys who took "machismo" seriously.[50] As crowds cheered the uniformed marauders on, their victims were hauled off to jail for their own protection—the police were not about to interfere with this exuberant effort to "clean up" a delinquent community. "We're not going to pick on kids in the service," one officer explained. As he put it, most people "were against the zootsuiters, the same as most people are against jitterbugs and jam sessions." The newspapers backed him up. In fact, they went so far as to commend young servicemen for ridding "the community of one of its newest evils—those zoot-suited miscreants who have . . . added a very serious side to juvenile delinquency problems."[51]

The pachucos themselves told a different story, one that had more to do with discrimination than disloyalty. The fact that they were citizens when it came to the military draft but social outcasts under any other circumstances enraged them. "We were kids, anxious to be wanted, but we just couldn't make the grade," one of the rioters remembered. "We were openly discriminated against in public swimming pools. There were no recreation facilities to speak of. We could only raise hell in the streets."[52] Even if they were lucky enough to break into defense work, they did not go very far. Like black teenagers, they were usually steered into unskilled service work rather than into "white" jobs in shipbuilding or aircraft factories.[53]

Although state and local authorities dismissed the idea that social injustice had stoked the violent outburst, federal war agencies were not taking chances. Enemy propagandists had a field day whenever conflict tarnished the image of American democracy, and they were kept busier than ever in 1943. In that year alone, riots erupted in Detroit, Philadelphia, San Diego, and Chicago, and in every case, disillusioned teenage youth played prominent roles. If the government wanted to contain and control these explosions, it would have to pay more attention to the next generation—particularly those with too much time on their hands and not enough adult supervision.

Justifiably or not, the war cast new light on disaffected teenagers, elevating juvenile delinquency to a national crisis. Troublesome teenagers distracted parents from war work, threatened the health of potential soldiers, and drew unwanted public attention to the seamier sides of American life. Kids who had never attracted much attention before outside of their own inauspicious communities were now jeopardizing the entire war effort, or so it seemed at the time. For if promiscuous girls and riotous boys represented a tiny slice of teenage life, the publicity they generated during the war and the irreverence they inevitably projected threatened to infect the teenage majority. Suddenly it seemed very important to reach out to alienated groups like the pachucos and weave them into American society. And suddenly war agencies began to ask teenagers just what Uncle Sam could do to help them get through the war.

It was already crystal clear that teenagers would not conform to adult rules unless they wanted to, especially when they were on their own. It was equally clear that teenagers had their own ideas about how they wanted to spend their time. Adults might believe that high school and housework should absorb their full attention while their parents were busy with war work, but teenagers let the government know, one way or another, that they had other plans. "Mostly we wanted a regular place to meet that was our own," a gang leader explained—a simple request that was echoed by teenagers all over the country. And they were amazed when the government actually responded. "They ought to erect a statue in the Plaza to the Unknown Zooter," a pachuco said. "Cause it wasn't until then, until . . . a lot of kids got beat up, that they gave us our clubs."[54] Although he did not know it at the time, the government was just getting started—in a world at war, the price of disaffected, dissatisfied teenagers was just too high to ignore.

chapter six

High school class, Southington, Connecticut, 1942. *Library of Congress, Prints and Photographs Division [LCUSW 342046D]*

Do You Know Where Your Children Are?

Juvenile Delinquency, Teen Canteens, and Democratic Solutions

ADULT FEARS OF JUVENILE DELINQUENCY WERE NOTHING NEW by the 1940s; the haunting specter of street gangs and impoverished teenage vandals had been animating social reformers for decades. In the context of war, though, these fears took on a new urgency. It was one thing for poor urban youth to bully their neighbors, but quite another for unruly kids to impede the war effort. Since battlefield victories depended on a well-ordered, well-integrated, and productive home front, the issue of juvenile delinquency would have to be confronted—and resolved—at once.

By 1943, women's clubs, church groups, PTAs, and community agencies were thrashing out the problem at public forums. Expert witnesses were testifying at congressional hearings. And the popular press was making juvenile delinquency a household concern—during the first six months of 1943 alone, twelve hundred magazine articles appeared on the subject. Radio was not far behind. Programs like "Here's to Youth" offered special segments on "Young America in Crisis," "What Price Violence," and "The Lost Parent" (an especially popular theme). Even Hollywood turned its spotlight on juvenile delinquents, proving that a national crisis could turn a healthy profit, too. "Where is your daughter tonight?" asked a provocative movie advertisement. "In some joint . . . lapping up liquor . . . petting . . . going mad?"[1]

Whether this teenage crisis was more apparent than real hardly mattered. Thanks to the war, younger teenagers were on their own in greater numbers than ever before, and they *were* getting into trouble. Police kept an eye out for boys who hung around seedy taverns where they drank hard liquor and smoked "reefers" (marijuana-laced cigarettes that were already available in rougher neighborhoods). Juvenile court dockets overflowed with complaints of vandalism, auto theft, and teenage petting and drinking parties. These complaints were not confined to lower-class teenagers, either; wartime delinquency was apparently corrupting "good" kids, too. In Indianapolis, for instance, police arrested a group of inebriated teenagers that included some upstanding members of the Junior Council, an elite high school group that was supposed to help supervise community activities during the war![2]

This apparent epidemic of juvenile delinquency had as much to do with adult perceptions of teenage behavior as it did with a rise in crime, however. In some adult eyes, teenage disrespect and insolence were criminal offenses. Some high school teachers railed against "delinquent" students who had the audacity to laugh out loud at school assemblies—even when invited guests were speaking! Outside of school, behavior standards could be equally high. Adults cast suspicions on teenagers who talked too loudly in public places or failed to defer to their elders on the bus. "Their favorite pastime seems to be making remarks about other passengers," a rider complained. But that hardly constituted a crime—so far, at least, no laws were broken when teenagers annoyed adults.[3] Indeed, the wartime hue and cry over juvenile delinquency probably had as much to do with the fact that adults were losing control over teenagers as it did with a rise in criminal behavior.

And irresponsible parents bore the blame for that, according to the conventional wisdom. A wartime movie, *Children of Mars*, made the point explicit: After a patriotic mother took a job in a defense plant, her teenage son was lost to a gang, while her teenage daughter chased soldiers![4] Some critics were even less charitable. It was not patriotism that lured mothers to factory floors, they said, but greed and a selfish desire to get out of the house. Their obvious lack of concern for their children's well-being only underscored the point. "Some parents seem to think that a child of twelve or over does not need supervision," a citizens' group complained. Not surprisingly, these were often the same oblivious parents who failed to recognize that a problem was brewing. In Omaha, Nebraska, for instance, police thought they were doing busy families a favor when they escorted young girls home who were walking the streets with soldiers. They had committed no crime, the officers admitted, but they were not acting like "nice" girls, either. However, they were shocked to discover that parents resented their interference. They knew what their daughters were doing, police reported, and they did not think anything of it at all.[5]

"Sympathetic" parents were just as bad as incompetent ones, according to critics, especially when they followed "crackpot" advice to loosen the reins of discipline at home. "The biggest problem with children these days, is that instead of doing what their parents tell them to do, they tell the parents what to do, and the parents do it," an astonished observer noted. "So what else can you expect but a generation of saucy, independent, reckless youngsters?" Teenage children had too much money, too much leisure, too much coddling, for their own good, and they were never forced to rely on themselves for anything, another complained. Was it any wonder that they were bored with the routine requirements of everyday life and looked for thrills, speed, and excitement instead?[6]

Comic books and movies were also suspect, since they allegedly fanned the flames of delinquent behavior. But swing music was a major culprit. According to the conductor of the New York Philharmonic, the swing music craze had set the pace for wartime "degeneracy." In fact, state officials in the Midwest were so convinced of the music's evil influence that they tried to outlaw juke-boxes. "Some of the most sinful situations existing are in these dimly-lit, smoke-filled taverns where people wiggle around while juke boxes blare," insisted a state legislator from Indiana. It wasn't the liquor that made youngsters feel so peculiar, another pointed out. "It's the music that gets' em," he said. If Americans intended to raise wholesome, productive teenagers, they would have to nip jive culture in the bud, these legislators believed, before the next generation caught the (jitter) bug.[7]

Teenagers rejected the message, especially when local authorities tied their anti-swing efforts to a ten o'clock curfew. Adults thought they were teaching young citizens a lesson in legitimate authority, but teenagers learned about resentment and discrimination instead. As far as they could see, the innocent majority was being punished for the sins of the delinquent few. That being the case, they had no intention of quietly complying with curfew laws. "I'll bet that when the ones on that [city] council were fifteen they stayed out later than ten," an angry student remarked. "Now after they have had their fun, they want to take it away from us."[8] Another blamed the unjust law on unfair stereotypes of teenage life. "High school 'bobby soxers' have been subjected to some of the most cruel and prejudiced criticisms ever heaped upon a group of people. And we ARE people," he insisted, even if "we like to dance . . . wear dirty-saddle shoes, date, drink cokes, and other normal things." A taste for swing music was no indication of potential delinquency, teenagers argued. And it was certainly no reason to curtail teenage rights.[9]

Mark McCloskey, recreation director for the Office of Community War Services (OCWS), agreed. It was his responsibility to solve the teenage crisis, but he had no faith in authoritarian solutions like curfews or music bans. Even if they could be enforced, which was doubtful, they would probably backfire, he believed. A follower of the "sympathetic" approach to teenage guidance, McCloskey accepted the fact that some teenagers would always break society's rules—it was almost a rite of passage. Thus he saw no good reason to dwell on their failings, or to stigmatize adventurous teenagers as delinquents.

He saw no good reason to attack the swing craze either. It wasn't the music that created teenage passions, and it wasn't the music that caused teenagers to act on them. In fact, as far as McCloskey was concerned, there was nothing necessarily delinquent about sexual experimentation—war or no war, it was a normal part of growing up. He likewise believed that sexual energy

was a normal part of life. It could be harnessed, perhaps, and channeled to wholesome ends, but it could not be obliterated or
denied. "I understand perfectly why the kids dance down the
aisles in the Paramount Theater when Harry James blows a great
trumpet," he said. "It's what I call a neo-Dionysian revel . . . the
spirit that has been in all cultures, all life of all time."[10]

Like other youth experts, McCloskey looked to organized
recreation to keep teenagers healthy, happy, and off the street. In
fact, when witnesses testified at the 1943 congressional hearings,
they agreed on one point: Teenagers who participated in recreation programs were not the boys who were breaking into houses
and cars or the girls who walked the streets in search of excitement.[11] They also agreed, however, that recreation facilities for
teenagers were few and far between. Even when federal recreation
funds were available (as they were in military-affected areas, such
as defense industry boom towns), they were usually earmarked for
servicemen or adult war workers, not teenagers with nothing to
do. Local funds were not generally invested in teenage recreation,
either. During the war, many towns cut back on services like
swimming pools and community centers to save essential material and tax money, too.[12]

The resulting lack of alternatives pleased no one, teenagers least
of all. "The boys and girls themselves feel that fun and recreation
are essential and will be obtained at all costs," one witness testified. Whether adults approved of their behavior or not, teenagers
would hang around sleazy drug stores, nightclubs, skating rinks, or
movie houses, if they had no better choices.[13] That was the crux
of the problem, recreation specialists agreed. Didn't decent young
citizens have a right to fun "without fear of temptation," they
wanted to know? Didn't the federal government have an interest
in protecting that right, since the future of the American family
depended on it? "By establishing youth centers *now*," one special-
ist argued, the government could teach boys and girls the value of
wholesome recreation, a lesson they would carry over to a happy
married life.[14]

McCloskey welcomed the support and the funding that
resulted. However, his ideas for teenage recreation did not follow
traditional, adult-directed lines. Ideally, McCloskey thought that
teenagers should be integrated into the larger adult world, not set

apart by themselves. He believed that recreation programs should teach teenagers (and their parents, too) that they were citizens like everyone else, with individual rights and community responsibilities. The war made it impossible to develop the first part of his program, he admitted. But the congressional mandate to do something for teenagers gave the second a boost. With the backing of the OCWS, McCloskey offered teenagers a chance to design recreation programs that reflected their tastes—but he expected them to take the initiative and run them, too. "This world has been full of trying to do all things that kids don't want to do in a way that kids don't want to do it," he said. It was time to clear a new path.[15]

Unorthodox as it seemed to conventional character builders, McCloskey's OCWS team asked teenagers themselves how and where they wanted to spend their time. The response was unequivocal—the high school crowd wanted a place to meet their friends and dance. By 1944 newspapers were spotlighting "teen towns," the neighborhood recreation centers that were popping up all over the country. In fact, before the war was over, more than three thousand teen canteens (with names like the "Jive Hive," the "Boogie Barn," "Swing Haven," and the "Buzz Bucket") were open for business. Most were equipped with jukeboxes and dance floors, ping-pong tables, and coke bars. (Coca Cola and Royal Crown were early corporate supporters, since teen canteens provided a steady market for their wares.) Some canteens were decidedly more elaborate, depending upon community resources and support. In Jacksonville, Florida, for instance, teenagers converted a vacant Army building into a triple-decker teen canteen that offered shuffle board and bowling alleys, lounges, game rooms, and the obligatory dance floor.[16]

Teenagers were not entirely on their own, of course. Adult sponsors were always on hand, behind the scenes; teen canteens would never have gained community support without them. In the most successful clubs, adults served on joint governing boards with elected teenage members and helped to write the constitution and bylaws. They also signed contracts, raised money, and served as unobtrusive chaperons. When it came to planning activities, though, adults were supposed to keep out of the way. The whole point of the enterprise was to give teenagers a real opportunity to learn the ropes of organization and management for themselves.

In New York City, for instance, teenage committees ran the snack bar and jukebox. In Jacksonville, the canteen operated like a model teenage city, with a mayor, a police commissioner, and a city council to manage affairs. Not every governing board was so flexible, however. There were always adults who insisted on dominating club affairs. They appointed teenage board members (rather than letting the group elect them) and set the club's agenda, a combination that usually proved fatal. Finding the right mix of adult sponsorship and teenage management was probably the most important (and elusive) element of a successful teen canteen. For in general, adults tended to favor structured programs and small, neighborhood clubs where they could get to know individual members—just the kind of formality and intrusion teenagers wanted to avoid.[17]

Some clubs, of course, suffered from the opposite problem— they failed for lack of adult support. Many parents disapproved of dancing and card playing, or believed their children were better off spending their free time at home. Others were too busy with their own lives to volunteer any time, and that was definitely shortsighted, the experts agreed. For when teen canteens flourished, as they usually did, they seemed to be an answer to a wartime prayer. "Youth centers have proved that the terrible teens can solve their own problems without 'snoopervision,'" supporters attested. They also demonstrated that the teenage idea of a good time was as "mystifying, as wholesome . . . as the high school boys and girls themselves." At least according to some reports, teen canteens also put a real dent in delinquency rates. "Since Firehouse 13 became the meeting place for the entire high school crowd," a Detroit reporter boasted, "the police have been able to relax in the area that was once called 'the juvenile crime center of the world.'"[18]

That was something of an overstatement, of course. By offering teenagers an alternative to hanging around on the street, teen canteens alleviated adult fears of juvenile delinquency, at least for the duration of the war. And by providing a respectable, supervised place for teenagers to dance, these clubs protected "good" kids from evil influences. For instance, teen canteens took the danger out of swing music, since they lessened the chance that the dancing crowd might grow too wild once the music started. Membership was limited to high school students only, and they had to agree to follow the rules: no drinking, no gambling, no pick-up dates.[19] (In fact, just to be on the safe side, girls who wanted to bring soldiers to a dance usually had to register their plans in advance.) The fact that teen canteens were organized along neighborhood lines also guaranteed that the crowd would not be too mixed. In effect, neighborhood canteens meant that Catholics, Jews, and Protestants, whites, blacks, and Hispanics, tended to join their own separate clubs, essential social insurance, considering that teenagers intended to dance. .

Given the tenor of the times, that was hardly surprising. Adults routinely encouraged teenagers to keep to their own kind, especially when it came to dancing or dating. The high school population might have been more mixed than ever before in the 1940s, but the social structure was still mired in tradition. Like their parents, teenagers tended to form "cliques," groups of friends who shared similar backgrounds and interacted only with each other. "The boys we dated had to meet with each other's approval," a girl explained in the early 1940s. In fact, her clique maintained a list of socially acceptable dates—and those who cared about their social standing paid close attention to it. Just ask Joan, who had the temerity to date outside her crowd. "We do not have anything to do with her *now!*" reported a former friend.[20] Ambitious parents, who recognized the social (and economic) value of an elite circle of friends, tended to back the crowd. "I am disgraced," a mother wailed when her daughter insisted on dating a Jew, even though she would lose her chance to join a high status sorority. "Mabel must be made to see the folly of her foolish actions. She simply must be popular, every girl must be popular," this mother insisted. After all, that was still the key to a "good" marriage and adult success for a middle-class teenage girl.[21]

But if social segregation had a long and practical history, it was getting harder to justify during the Second World War. With the nation embroiled in a fight against fascism, democracy was now in fashion—in theory, at least, if not yet in practice—and teenagers were assigned the task of changing the nation's values. Teen canteens, for instance, were supposed to be an experiment in democracy, one that had not gone far enough, according to promoters. Ideally, the clubs could be used to introduce groups of teenagers to each other so that the next generation would not be handicapped by the kind of social prejudice that had trapped their parents and given rise to the Nazis. The plan seemed to be working in Detroit, where black and white teenagers successfully joined the same canteens and supported a citywide, biracial youth council in 1944.[22] In Queens, New York, a predominantly Italian-American canteen opened its doors to the rest of the neighborhood, and in nearby Brooklyn, teenagers hosted public forums to combat religious and race prejudice. In Iowa and Indiana, meanwhile, teenagers were working with the YMCA and National Association for the Advancement of Colored People to break down traditional barriers between white and black youth.[23]

At the same time, high school educators were using their classrooms to "teach for tolerance"—and not a moment too soon, according to newspaper reports. In Chicago, Cleveland, Gary, Indiana, and New York City, white teenagers were launching hate strikes whenever black teenagers asserted their rights in high school. At the time, though, these bigoted teenagers bore no guilt for their actions. Instead, these ugly episodes were chalked up to ignorant, prejudiced parents, who had poisoned their offsprings' minds. "No kid is by nature intolerant," said Frank Sinatra, the bobby soxers' idol.[24] *Ebony* magazine, the new voice of the black middle class, agreed. Racists were made, not born, the editors pointed out; it was narrow-minded parents who were responsible for passing on the crippling disease.

But that cycle could be stopped. In fact, it would have to be stopped unless the nation planned to fight another war here at home, critics insisted. "The most sensible step would be if children could be segregated from their parents—isolated from the contagion," *Ebony* suggested. Since that plan was undoubtedly unconstitutional, however, the magazine favored social education, confident that teenagers would break with their parents' reactionary past once they understood its significance. "If the teensters can achieve the melting-pot ideal at home," *Ebony* predicted, "they carry happy tidings for a world hungry for final peace." After all, it would be zoot suiters and bobby soxers, not their narrow-minded parents (or "wheezing Washington politicos"), who would be leading the way to the future, a hopeful image of social change as far as *Ebony* was concerned.[25]

As if to confirm the teenagers' new importance in constructing the postwar world, *Seventeen* magazine began publication in September 1944. "What kind of world do you want?" the editors asked young readers. A world ruled by narrow-minded prejudice against Jews, Catholics, Poles, or Chinese? A world that taught innocent children to revile "dirty Wops?" A world in which skin color determined how people were educated, what kind of jobs they could hold, and where (and how well) they were permitted to live? That was the world as it was, *Seventeen* admitted, but that was not the world as it could be. Teenagers had a unique opportunity, the editors believed, to chart a new course for the future. Since they had no stake in their parents' segregated world—or so it seemed at the time—they represented the nation's best hope for a democratic future. "We expect you to run this world a lot more sensibly than we have," *Seventeen* conceded. "No group of adults who have created a civilization which is blackened by a world war can claim to have done a good job."[26]

Like Mark McCloskey and *Ebony* magazine, *Seventeen* rejected the popular teenage stereotype of swing-crazed juvenile delinquents. On the contrary, the editors addressed teenage readers as capable, conscientious citizens with a big job to do. "You're going to have to run this show," the premiere issue noted, "so the sooner you start thinking about it, the better."[27] In fact, during the 1944 presidential election, *Seventeen* urged teenagers to get involved in the campaign. "The only people who are too young to . . . have political opinions are the truly infantile who *can't* read, and the perpetually young who *don't* read," the magazine pointed out. Teenagers had a duty to themselves and their community to learn all they could about the candidates, to make up their minds on the issues, and then to declare their decision—a valuable exercise, even if their votes did not count. "If you don't take your part [in the political process] you're only making the war and the others before it mean too little," the editors warned. "Your grandfathers didn't . . . come to America for the boat trip. Your fathers didn't go to Europe [during World War I] for a student tour. Your brothers, your beaux—they're not away for the lark." Politics mattered, *Seventeen* insisted, and it was up to teenagers to learn how the political system worked.[28]

They also needed to understand how the social system worked and to do all they could to change it. In fact, *Seventeen* offered a crash course in practical democracy: If teenagers were going to build a better world, they would have to combat bigotry wherever they found it. Since that often meant confronting family and friends, the magazine provided some tactful suggestions. Suppose a family was choosing a summer camp and an owner casually mentioned that his was restricted to Protestants only. According to the *Seventeen* scenario, parents would think nothing of his remark, but a democratic daughter would not let it pass. "Mother, I know lots of girls and boys who aren't Protestant, and I haven't found that being Protestant makes me any different from some of my friends. I don't think I'd feel at home at a camp where other nice people couldn't go."[29]

Or suppose a family had strict ideas regarding girls and boys and the work they could do. Parents often took it for granted that daughters would share household chores, while sons did outside work. "If yours is such a family," *Seventeen* advised, "you have a job of education to do." Mother and dad had to learn that family work (preparing food, serving, and washing dishes) were jobs to be shared "by *all* the citizens of your home"—male as well as female. Even if dad were set in his ways, teenagers had a duty to persevere. "Remember, he's just carrying over attitudes that were quite the accepted thing in his youth."[30]

Seventeen had equally strong ideas about teenage rights and responsibilities that were hammered out in articles on more popular issues like grooming, clothes, and appropriate behavior. Through the pages of *Seventeen*, teenagers learned about teen canteens and how to run them ("*Do not* . . . let the control of the project out of your hands"). They learned why they should finish high school and make plans for the future ("A marriage license is no longer a stay-at-home guarantee. Your only real security is what you go out and get for yourself"). They got the lowdown on the dangers of promiscuous kissing ("Men who are burnt out at 40, and women who are . . . pathetically afraid of growing old are the ones who crammed their growing up years with experiences they weren't ready for").[31]

Apparently, teenagers appreciated the advice. And if reader mail was any indication, they relished the attention and the magazine's respectful tone. "For years I have been yearning for a magazine entirely dedicated to me," a satisfied reader wrote. Another thanked the editors "for looking upon us teenagers as future women and Americans, instead of swooning, giggling bobby-soxers."[32] Their parents appreciated the magazine, too, especially if they lacked the time—or the talent—to deal with teenage issues themselves. According to one grateful mother who put in long hours at a defense factory, *Seventeen* provided the "kindly, authentic loving guidance" that "daughters of busy, tired, working women need."[33]

Considered in the light of a war to end fascism and the concerted national effort that victory required, *Seventeen*'s concern with democracy, social equality, and the political process made practical sense. After all, teenagers had a pressing obligation to build a better world than their parents had. Mark McCloskey, the architect of teenage-run canteens, put it this way: "A lot of . . . people are hoping [to return to a] patched up old world, in which *they* happen to be comfortable," he remarked in a 1945 speech. They were in for a rude awakening, though. The next generation would never accept the same level of inequality their parents had. The war had demonstrated the real costs of such bankrupt, intolerant thinking, and the experience of wartime mobilization and national cooperation had opened young minds to new ideas, new aspirations, and new social and spiritual concerns, he said.[34]

This did not mean that the battle was over, though. Not by a long shot, McCloskey implied. It seemed to him that adults were more interested in developing technology than they were in developing teenage character or building strong, harmonious families, and this was an indication, he said, that the adult world intended to sell teenagers short once the war was over. "More money and research are being devoted . . . to the subject of television than to the betterment of family life," McCloskey reported. "What we know about the causes of emotional instability in children is small in comparison with what we know about the mechanism of our car engines."[35]

If McCloskey expected teenagers to rally to his cause, as they had to teen canteens, he was probably disappointed. Even then the vast majority had been far more interested in dancing and having a good time than they were in managing the operation. By the time the war finally came to a close in the summer of 1945, teenagers had their own ideas about their role in the postwar world. In the first place, they were ready—more than ready—to pick up where bobby soxers had left off. There were new records to buy, new clothes to wear, and a whole new world of places to show them off, now that gasoline was available again.

Secondly, they had a brand-new identity as an important social group. As an OCWS report put it, the country had become more "youth conscious" during the war. Teenage boys and girls had definitely become teenagers by the summer of 1945; even the word was now popular. They had their own style of dancing and their own places to dance; their own fads and fashions and new magazines devoted to their interests; and best of all they had their own money to spend, changes that boosted their sense of independence. There would be no going back to the prewar days, when teenagers had to fight for their right to a social life. During the war, they had experienced a level of personal freedom that they did not intend to relinquish now. As adult observers put it, the "entire tempo of teenage social life [had] been changed."[36]

There would be no going back to the days when teenage children were seen but not heard, either. On the contrary, over the next few years, adults would be straining to hear what teenagers had to say about their tastes, their problems, their dates. The teenage market that had started to thrive in the early 1940s was now ready for takeoff. In a postwar world of prosperity and market expansion, teenagers would prove to be ideal consumers who not only had the time and the disposition to try out new products, but the inclination to spend money freely.

Like adults all around them, they were in a national mood to shop. During the war they had worked hard; they had enlisted in the service, worked for the national defense, endured the loss of family and friends, made do, done without. Now that the war was over, they were eager to taste the fruits of victory, and enterprising marketers were more than ready to help them out.

Part III

Teenagers

chapter seven

High school homecoming, Worthington, Ohio, 1944. *Courtesy of Charlotte Piepmeier.*

The Advertising Age

Seventeen, *Eugene Gilbert, and the Rise of the Teenage Market*

FOR JULIE FERGUSON, A SHY, MOTHERLESS FOURTEEN-YEAR-OLD just beginning to navigate high school's rough social waters, an evening dress for an upcoming dance promised to change her luck. It would have to be the right evening dress, of course, one that would identify her as a person worth knowing and transform her into an entirely new girl, the kind of girl who was self-assured, not awkward, who laughed and danced easily with boys, and who always knew what to say and when to say it. A popular girl, sought after and secure, who never had to wonder whether anyone would ask her to dance.

With her entire future tied up in the purchase of such a dress, a girl needed advice. How was she to know which colors and styles best suited her type when she wasn't quite sure what her type should be? Luckily for Julie, an old family friend guided her purchase and taught her the basic rules of good taste and quality. As for the rest of her dress requirements, though, Julie was on her own. Before the school dance was over she would learn the hard way that clothes could not bestow the self-confidence and grown-up personality she craved and that personal transformation came only with experience. It would take experimentation, disappointment, reevaluation, and a strong measure of internal fortitude to see the process through, yet that was a difficult assessment for a fourteen-year-old to make, especially one with no mother to guide her.[1]

Although Julie was a character in a teenage novel—Betty Cavanna's *Going on Sixteen*, which was published in 1946—there was nothing fictional about her adolescent dilemma. In the years immediately following the end of the Second World War, an active social life became the measure of success for more teenagers than ever before. The quest for popularity—for dates, invitations, and a sought-after group of friends—assumed new importance in the postwar world. In fact, it was the driving force behind a new and improved teenage market for clothes, entertainment, and, most important, information and advice, but it was a quest that teenagers pursued on their own, whether their parents were available or not. After all, part of the process of growing up was learning to stand on your own two feet. Determined to prove that they could take care of themselves now that they were in high school, teenagers were far more likely to turn to their friends or to magazine columns for help with their personal problems than they were to involve their parents.

The truth be told, parents were in no position to advise teenagers who felt out of place in high school. In their day only the cream of the social crop enjoyed the kind of social life the postwar generation took for granted. Also in their day, parents had claimed the right to set their children's standards on the basis of family values and social position, not popular standards at school. Times had changed radically in the twenty years or so since an adult's youth, however, for parents as well as their children. As anthropologist Margaret Mead put it, something had happened to the culture as a whole when mothers "cease to say 'When I was a girl, I was not allowed . . . ' and substitute the question, 'What are the other girls doing?' "[2]

Something had happened, indeed. In the years between the start of the Great Depression and the close of the Second World War, American family life had witnessed a basic transformation: Adolescents were no longer children. They were "bobby soxers" and "teenagers" who had a voice and vote in family affairs and who fully expected to enjoy a private social life. What had once been the model of a privileged, upper-class, "carefree" youth now set the standard for "normal" teenage life. The shift must have seemed startling to parents who had had to fight for the right to go to high school! What had once been the province of the family and the family alone (initiating children into the mysteries of adulthood) was now the concern of professional experts, educators, and magazine editors, who had their own ideas about what was best for youth. Dr. Evelyn Duvall, a noted family life educator, underscored the controversial nature of the change when she addressed a radio audience in 1945. Acknowledging the central importance of popularity to a successful teenage life, she suggested that high schools begin teaching girls how to attract and keep a boyfriend, since that would make them feel "adequate" in school![3]

Authors like Betty Cavanna, who could be categorized as more traditional character builders, did not go that far, but they certainly agreed that teenagers needed some kind of life guidance. Studies showed that high school students saw no connection between ability and occupation, or preparation and economic success. That is, they saw no connection between the choices they made as teenagers, and the life they would live as adults.[4] Trying to bridge this gap, teenage novels like *Going on Sixteen* offered the kind of solid advice that only came from experience—adult advice, which teenagers were likely to scorn as a matter of course when it came from their parents.

For instance, Cavanna let her story unfold over the course of a high school career. She carefully guided young readers through Julie Ferguson's tortured freshman year, when her efforts to keep up with the crowd failed miserably and she isolated herself to avoid embarrassment, her more productive sophomore year, when she discovered extracurricular activities and began to carve out her own social space, and up through her triumphant emergence as a self-assured upperclassman who not only earned respect as an editor of the school newspaper but also discovered her adult goal in life—to become a commercial artist.

In the process, Cavanna allowed Julie to demonstrate to young readers that life was what you made it, in or out of school. The trick was to set a grown-up goal and then develop the skills you needed to meet it. By designing and following your own path, you were bound to make real and valuable friends. Your actions and accomplishments—not your clothes or your car—identified you as a person worth knowing. Once you made that all-important philosophical leap, popularity would take care of itself. At that point, however, as young Julie happily discovered, it would not matter anymore. In the long-term scheme of life, high school popularity was fleeting, Cavanna implied, and it was certainly no substitute for a solid hold on the future.

The advice was timeless, but the novel's context was already dated by 1946, as if the author had failed to recognize, or perhaps to appreciate, the evolution of teenage culture since the mid-1930s. In Julie Ferguson's adolescent world, dogs were more important than boys (even at age sixteen), and daydreaming offered the most dramatic, and apparently annoying, sign that a child was growing up. There was no swing music, jitterbugging, necking, or arguing in this well-ordered world, no hot rods, no beer, no staying out late. Instead, Cavanna's high school students were a sturdy, reliable lot who helped out with family chores without being asked, took school work seriously, and put their unsupervised free time to good use.

That was no accident either. At the time, librarians and English teachers had more influence in the world of "young adult" fiction than teenage readers did![5] No matter how grown-up teenagers thought they were at home or in school, they still inhabited a social twilight zone between dependence and autonomy in the commercial marketplace, and as far as many adults were concerned, that was exactly how it should be, since teenagers had neither the wisdom nor the experience to make good choices on their own. They may have identified themselves as a group apart, with separate interests and tastes, but in the 1940s separate did not mean equal, and teenage did not mean adult. On the contrary, high school students were still adolescents in society's eyes, and that meant they still required protection and supervision as they made their way toward the future.

Nonetheless, postwar teenagers had very different expectations of their rights and responsibilities, expectations that were directly linked to the economic prosperity their families now enjoyed. They were coming of age in a world of expanding opportunities and increased leisure time, and they fully intended to make the most of their good fortune. The war had taught them the meaning of sacrifice, to be sure, but it had also stirred their appetites for records, clothes, cars—the "stuff" of teenage life. Thanks to full employment and a buoyant economy, a larger proportion of American families could now afford to support their teenagers in style.[6]

In fact, it seemed as if everyone had more money to spend, once the country got past its immediate postwar jitters. Between 1939 and 1950, managers saw their incomes rise 45 percent; supervisors, 83 percent; and production workers, 106 percent. By the late 1940s, the average family could afford to acquire some middle-class comforts.[7] The number of car registrations jumped from 26 million in 1945 to 40 million in 1950, while the number of single-housing starts grew from 114,000 in 1944, to 937,000 in 1946, to 1,692,000 in 1950—and all of these had to be furnished![8] The combination of pent-up demand, dependable employment, and relatively high wages fueled an expansive cycle of material abundance that came to symbolize the American way of life for adults and teenagers alike. By 1952 almost half of the nation's households boasted a television set, and by 1960 only 15 percent did not.[9]

For teenagers, this economic prosperity was quickly translated into personal freedom and enjoyment. Boys, for instance, now expected to get a driver's license at age sixteen, and they fully intended to use the family car—by now, a household necessity for those who lived outside the city. Better yet, they got an after-school job and purchased a car of their own—usually the kind of rundown jalopy that drove parents crazy. With a little money, effort, and help from *Hot Rod* magazine, which began publication in 1948, boys turned these cars into modern symbols of teenage life. Dual carburetors, super chargers, and oversized pistons, unheard of in high school circles before the war, were now becoming standard equipment for boys who spent more money "souping up" their prized possession than their fathers did maintaining the family car.[10]

This postwar propensity to spend money freely ultimately boosted the teenagers' stock in the commercial world, and by the late 1940s, the teenage market was getting back on track, but with a noticeable difference that would revolutionize the very notion of teenagers in a few short years. Youth-oriented marketers, more concerned with teenage tastes than teenage futures, would now give traditional character builders a real run for their money. In the days before Pearl Harbor, adult marketers had naturally assumed that their job was to tell teenagers who they were and what they wanted to buy. Ten years later, they would be asking teenagers to speak for themselves and presenting the younger generation as bona fide consumers with a right to spend their own (and their parents') money as they pleased. In the process, they would also expand the variety of specialized teenage products, including clothes, cosmetics, shoes, skin care products, movies, records, even record players, thereby increasing the market's—and the teenager's—value to adults.

This shift did not occur overnight. Although the commercial world had embraced bobby soxers enthusiastically before the war, in the immediate postwar years the job of selling teenage consumers was harder than it looked. The teenage market paled in comparison to a broad base of adults on a national buying spree. On the one hand, this reflected population trends—low birthrates during the Great Depression meant fewer teenagers in the late 1940s. On the other, teenagers did not appear to be reliable customers at first. For instance, when a television producer tried to launch a show called "Teen Canteen" in 1946, she got no cooperation from the high school audience. Although the show was built around teenagers and dance music, a formula that was working well on radio, it flopped almost immediately. The boys involved refused to dance on camera, leaving the girls to jitterbug by themselves. "Teen Canteen," had great possibilities, as "American Bandstand" would prove ten years later, but in 1946 both advertisers and television executives thought that teenagers were more trouble than they were worth in the marketplace.[11]

Many retailers agreed. "Stores didn't recognize this age group as a viable consumer group," Estelle Ellis remembered. Promotion director for *Seventeen*, she had a hard time persuading retailers to take teenage buyers seriously. "They didn't want them," she said. "They felt that these kids were getting in the way of serious buying by older people."[12] Determined to counter this negative image, *Seventeen* spearheaded a campaign to measure teenage opinions, tastes, and buying habits and to use that information to promote an alternative view that presented the younger crowd as capable, reliable potential consumers who had a vital interest in learning how to shop.

Each month, the magazine offered mini-courses in home economics, complete with recipes, party plans, and decorating ideas by the dozen—and notes on where teenagers could buy the products they needed to put these plans into action. The magazine provided detailed grooming regimens, diets, and fashion hints that not only took the worry out of teenage life but introduced young readers to products (and manufacturers) that promised to solve their problems. Although parents generally applauded *Seventeen* for the useful advice it provided, at least one mother was worried about this relentless invitation to shop. Concerned that the clothes and products advertised were too expensive to suit a teenager's budget, she reminded the editors that "prices must fit the 'minding baby' salaries and allowances" that most teenagers depended on for spending money.[13]

Apparently, that was what most manufacturers thought, too, which kept them out of the teenage market. How could such a low-wage group sustain profitable business? Cokes, candy, records, and trinkets were bobby soxers' staple products, and many manufacturers did not believe that the market would ever expand beyond those limits, but Helen Valentine, *Seventeen*'s first editor, was determined to prove them wrong. Teenagers represented a million-dollar business opportunity, she told anyone who would listen, one that was being lost for lack of promotion and interest. She knew what she was talking about: As promotion editor of *Mademoiselle* magazine, Valentine had successfully developed the concept of a college market, demonstrating to publishers and advertisers alike the selling power of a well-defined age-generation. She was already proving her point with *Seventeen*. The magazine sold out its first edition of 400,000 copies in only two days, its second of 500,000 in the same short time, and within sixteen months, circulation topped the 1 million mark.[14] "Meet Teena . . . no one thought she could read," an early promotion circular chided. Yet here she was, a girl with a house and a family in her future, and she was buying *Seventeen* in record numbers.[15]

Buying a magazine was one thing, but did teenagers have the means to buy anything else? Valentine thought they did. To make her case, she hired a professional research team, Benson and Benson of Princeton, New Jersey, to survey *Seventeen*'s readers and scrutinize their tastes, their families, and the products they used.[16] According to Estelle Ellis, this kind of research was unheard of at the time, at least in the world of fashion magazines. "Nobody was talking about demographics; nobody even knew the word. They didn't talk statistics," she said, "because that's not what was sold." In the case of *Seventeen*, though, Valentine was selling a brand-new market, and she let her readers do the talking. "Life with Teena," as the market survey was called, demonstrated in no uncertain terms that "Teena . . . has money of her own to spend . . . and what her allowance and pin-money earnings won't buy, her parents can be counted on to supply. For our girl Teena won't take no for an answer when she sees what she wants in *Seventeen*."[17]

The survey provided a statistical base for the motto "Teena Means Business, Don't Pass Her By!" Promoters emphasized the fact that 66 percent of *Seventeen*'s readers expected to be full-time homemakers—the advertisers' favored target—which meant that the items on their shopping list today would be the ones they'd automatically buy tomorrow: "*Seventeeners* want to get married, eventually . . . naturally! They're dreaming of linens, silver, china— a home of their own."[18] Promoters heralded the fact that 77 percent already influenced their parents' decisions on household purchases, from groceries and furniture to radios and phonographs. "Mother clings to her comfortable old coffee pot until her teenage daughter sells her on a new drip model," one circular read. "Daddy is attached to his smoking chair, but he gives it up when his teenage daughter insists the living room needs its face lifted! Ask the parents," as *Seventeen* had, "and they will tell you that . . . it's their children who usually get them to make a change."[19]

But Teena had her own purchases to make, and the survey made it clear that 65 percent had a strong interest in clothes, and 87 percent helped their friends make selections.[20] "Count on her to convince her parents she needs a new hat, a new dress, a complete spring wardrobe—before anyone else in her family. Watch her go into the nation's stores surrounded by her friends . . . Hear her tell the saleslady exactly what she wants. Suspect her influence when father says she's old enough for black, mother says she's big enough to shop on her own." Young Teena was an advertiser's dream, promoters insisted. She had an open mind, a persuasive manner, and best of all, she wanted to be part of the crowd, to "look, act, and be just like the girl next door. . . . For Teena and her teenmates come in bunches, like bananas. . . . Sell one," promoters promised, "and the chances are you'll sell them all."[21]

If advertisers hoped to reach them, however, they would have to keep teenage tastes in mind. In fact, in the early days, it was Ellis's job to persuade ad agencies to produce specialized teenage copy, never an easy task. In the first place, the advertising industry was still a man's world, and men had no particular insight into the world of teenage girls. In the second, specialized copy cut into advertising profits; agencies made their money by producing a basic ad and then reproducing it in various publications. What made economic sense from an advertiser's point of view, however, would not pay off with teenagers. An ad that worked in *Vogue*, for instance, would not suit the wholesome, fresh-faced girls who read *Seventeen*.[22] Young readers were clear on this point. "Puleez, *Seventeen*, always stay seventeen," advised a girl from Detroit. "That is, some of these so-called magazines for the high school crowd . . . either have us in . . . pigtails . . . or seated at a bar in some swanky night club, fluttering false eyelashes at some Navy lieutenant. . . . What I'm getting at is this," she instructed: "Please stick strictly to high school stuff."[23]

In order to capitalize on this growing market, *Seventeen*'s promoters worked with clothing manufacturers to encourage the design of fashions that not only fit the adolescent body but reflected "the way of life, the style of life, the time of life that teenagers represented."[24] They persuaded department stores to set up special shops to carry new merchandise like Pert and Pretty Teenage Hats, Hi-Girl Campus Caper Sweaters, and Kickerino Boots and then sponsored teenage boards that worked with buyers, ran fashion shows, and generally provided a window on the teenage point of view. The promotion staff also took pains to link department stores to products advertised in *Seventeen*. For example, they devised an elaborate "Tie-Up Kit" to showcase sewing patterns that were featured monthly. "Use . . . this kit to make your department and window display models," the instructions read. "Set one of the 'You saw it in *Seventeen*'s display cards [enclosed] at the base of the mannequin. . . . build a Teen Sewing Center . . . and merchandise teen patterns, young prints, and youthful fabrics, notions, and trimmings in one section of the department." The kit also advised sewing instructors to publicize classes through local home economics teachers and ads in high school newspapers.[25]

Promoters met with corporations like Revlon to persuade them to start thinking about the age-group more seriously. "There are eight million young girls in America who are just coming of age, cosmetically speaking," the health and beauty editor reported. "They have been liberated from the authority of adult control and they want very much to be adults themselves." Instead of offering makeup that suited high school tastes, though, the cosmetics industry favored a sophisticated "painted-lady" look that "nice" teenagers identified as "fast." Flame-glo lipstick, for instance, which advertised in *Seventeen*, offered a sultry promise to keep lips kissable, while a perfume called "Beaux Catcher" billed itself as "the saucy scent that won't take 'no' for an answer." An ad for Chen-nu nail polish spotlighted excessively long, blood-red "talons" that were decidedly out of place in high school. Why would an industry want to snub 8 million customers, *Seventeen* wondered. Didn't companies realize that teenage girls were just as determined as their elders were to spend good money on products they liked?[26]

The industry resisted these appeals at first because an earlier campaign to market juvenile products had failed miserably. But teenagers were not children, *Seventeen* responded. They wanted "grown-up" cosmetics that suited their needs, not bubble bath tied up in a pink bow! Manufacturers that made an effort to court them would be rewarded handsomely, promoters promised: High school social life stimulated teenage demand for cosmetics, making "puppy love" a very serious business, indeed. "A girl meets a boy and she reaches for lipstick, she pressures her parents for mascara, for perfume, for a dressing table of her own." These arguments slowly began to sink in, and by the early 1950s, Ponds was advertising "Angel Face" powder as "the perfect girl-to-girl" Christmas gift, and Woodbury offered "Dream Stuff" for girls who wanted to dance on a star.[27]

High school social life meant big business for the movie industry, too. As *Seventeen* reminded advertisers, "the movie Teena wants to see is the movie her boyfriend takes her to see." In fact, whether they were dating or not, teenage girls had an enormous influence on industry profits. After all, who else had the time and the inclination to keep up with new releases? "We're talking about 8 million teenage girls . . . who spot stars in the making, . . . who spark fan clubs . . . who drag their parents to the movies. . . . We're talking about girls who can afford to spend $170,000,000 a year on movies —outspoken girls whose opinion can make or break a picture."[28]

When those girls brought the gang home after the movies, or planned a Friday night get-together with the crowd, they also boosted the grocery industry. A simple *Seventeen* feature on double-decker sandwiches, for example, could net $17 in purchases, promoters explained, "based on the minimum quantity a girl would buy when she decides to tackle one of these magazine-suggested recipes." Since *Seventeen* published at least three food columns a month, grocery executives had good reason to appeal to teenage customers, and by 1950, chains like A&P and Grand Union were buying space in *Seventeen*, Sure-Jell was hawking homemade jelly as the key to a boy's heart, and Pillsbury had launched the Junior Grand National Recipe and Baking Contest.[29]

While *Seventeen* promoters were busy selling teenagers to advertisers, the editors were carefully shaping teenage tastes along conventional, middle-class lines. Both campaigns were part of the same process, and although the staff referred to building the teenage market, *Seventeen* was a classic example of adolescent culture at work. After all, Helen Valentine was fifty-one and a grandmother when she launched the magazine. She took it for granted that teenagers were family members first and foremost; her editorial voice was that of a friendly (yet concerned) older sister. As an editor, she championed the teenage desire for personal freedom, but always in the context of personal responsibility. Like Aunt Cherry in *Everygirls* and Gay Head in *Scholastic*, Helen Valentine promoted an image of well-informed, well-rounded, and ultimately rational teenagers, adults-in-training who could see for themselves that personal discipline and respectable behavior were the quickest routes to teenage independence. Following her lead, *Seventeen* perfected the breezy "take-it-from me, I-know-from-experience" tone that was the hallmark of successful character builders.

For instance, in a monthly column called "Why Don't Parents Grow Up?" *Seventeen* analyzed the thinking behind some parental rules (like curfews) that seemed to impinge on teenage rights. "Heigh-ho," the column began, "parents sometimes seem to have the knack of taking all the fun out of a date, don't they?" But once teenagers took a closer look, they could see that curfews were not worth fighting over. Who needed to stay up until all hours to prove their independence anyway? "People with a talent for enjoyment, no matter how old they are, always start [for] home while they're still having a good time. You aren't leaving much fun undone when you get home at a reasonable hour—and the aftermath with your family is a whole lot pleasanter," the column pointed out. Of course, there were still teenagers fighting for the right to date, let alone stay out past midnight, but by following the same family-oriented strategy, *Seventeen* promised, they would bring old-fashioned parents around. "The way to break all dads down is to invite more of your beaux to your house," the column advised, since "home is the perfect place to start a friendship anyway." Sneaking out, however, was "really old stuff" and not a solution for up-to-date teens.[30]

These lessons had widespread applications. Teenagers who got along with their parents always enjoyed more freedom, according to *Seventeen*. They were often the same teenagers who showed initiative at home and at school and took responsibility for themselves: They got up and out of bed in plenty of time for school without being nagged, kept their rooms tidy, and avoided health risks like smoking, drinking, and staying out late. They also had sympathy for their parents and respected their point of view; they understood that it took both generations to achieve "a happy parental relationship." Domestic harmony was the easiest way for teenagers to get what they wanted, the magazine pointed out. "Once you've learned to live with your parents in . . . an atmosphere of freedom and friendliness, the world will be yours." Teenagers who proved that they could take care of themselves (by avoiding risky behavior, taking high school seriously, and spending money wisely) were teenagers who had earned the right to exercise the adult privilege of individual choice, according to *Seventeen*.[31]

That was where *Seventeen*'s teenage market fit in. It was part of a balanced apprenticeship for family life that would benefit adults and teenagers alike. On one level, the magazine would translate teenage tastes and buying habits for advertisers and manufacturers. On another, it would teach inexperienced consumers the fine points of intelligent buying: how to devise a budget and live within it; how to evaluate quality and price; and how to distinguish the important differences between short-term style and long-term satisfaction.

As long as participants played their assigned roles responsibly, there was money to be made on every side of the transaction.

Parents who were tired of seeing their daughters wear oversized shirts and rolled up jeans would gladly finance new wardrobes once stores made an effort to stock the kind of clothes that teenagers wanted to wear. Manufacturers who followed *Seventeen's* advice to woo teenage customers would enjoy healthy profits now and in the future because as potential wives and mothers, teenage girls would be doing the nation's shopping in just a few short years, a key consideration. In the meantime, *Seventeen* would serve as a responsible commercial conduit, safely shepherding impressionable adolescents into the adult world of commerce.

Helen Valentine and her enterprising staff were steering teenagers toward productive, domestic futures, complete with college educations, diamond engagement rings, silver tea services, and hope chests, but they did not control the territory for long. A younger generation of market builders was also hard at work, and they were far more willing to follow teenagers wherever they wanted to go. Eugene Gilbert, a young entrepreneur from Chicago, was still a youth himself when he realized the economic potential of the youth market. Some twenty years younger than Valentine, he knew the market from the bottom up. As a high school student during the Second World War, Gilbert had been part of the swing music crowd. A charter member of the bobby-soxer generation, he dropped out of college the minute he realized that teenagers were a moneymaking proposition, and he never looked back.[32]

Just nineteen years old in 1945, Gilbert was working as a shoe store clerk when he noticed how few teenagers shopped in the store, even though it stocked the latest styles. When he persuaded his boss to try advertising directly to the younger crowd, sales took off and so did his career. "Stores and manufacturers were losing a lot of money because they were largely blind to my contemporaries' real tastes and habits," Gilbert remembered. "I started then to become a market researcher in a virtually unexplored field."[33]

Like *Seventeen*, Gilbert realized that teenagers themselves were the key to market expansion, and he hired a group of surveyors to interview students and identify their tastes. Since teenagers apparently loved to pull the legs of adult snoopers, though, he began to hire popular students to do the job, and his business boomed. Within a year, Gilbert had three hundred surveyors working for him and accounts with Quaker Oats, Maybelline, Studebaker,

United Airlines, and *Coronet,* a popular magazine.[34] His research study of the youth market, "The Age of Decision," which dealt with consumers aged eight to twenty, was based on ten thousand completed questionnaires. He also produced two monthly newspaper columns, "The Boys' Outfitter" and "Girls and Teen Merchandise."[35]

Hitting the big time in 1947, Gilbert moved his Youth Marketing Co. to New York City. Within a few years he was being profiled by national magazines like *Newsweek.* "Our salient discovery," he reported, "is that within the past decade teenagers have become a separate and distinct group in our society," consuming 190 million candy bars, 130 million soft drinks, 230 million sticks of gum, and 13 million ice cream bars a week.[36] Industry was beginning to get the message. Spending for juvenile radio shows had increased from $600,000 to $7 million between 1941 and 1951, and weekly shows like "Teen Town," "Teen Timers Club," and "Teenage Party," which were "beamed to the bobby soxers" every Saturday morning, were becoming regular features. Even the Ford Motor Company made a bid for what *Variety* called "juve appeal" by sponsoring the radio show, "Bob Crosby and His Hepcats."[37]

Traditional character builders were taking a lesson from Gilbert, too. Writers of teenage fiction were definitely updating their approach. They were still setting high standards for teenage readers; given society's conventions, and their readers' young age, they could not have done anything else at the time. But instead of focusing on an adolescent's future, they began concentrating on the teenager's everyday life. By the early 1950s, the social world of dating, popularity, and the never-ending search for a boyfriend had replaced more long-term, adult goals like discovering talents and choosing a career.

In fact, the idea that teenagers *should* have an active social life, and that they *could* be taught how to enjoy one, had become commonplace in the world of young adult fiction. In Rosamond du Jardin's novel *Double Date,* shy Penny Howard found her personality, and a boyfriend, too, when she joined the staff of the school newspaper. In *The Seagulls Woke Me,* by Mary Stolz, Jean Campbell used a summer job away from home to achieve the same happy ends. Although she was a social misfit at school (thanks to an overbearing mother who refused to let her grow up), she not only learned how to dance and kiss a boy but wangled two invitations to college football weekends in the process—the very definition of teenage success in the prosperous postwar world.[38]

Anne Emery took the process a few steps farther in her novel *Sorority Girl*, in which she examined popularity from a teenage point of view. When high school junior Jean Burnaby earned a bid to an elite social club, she slowly discovered the real price of teenage success: necking with boys she did not care for, just because they wore fraternity pins; going along when the crowd drank beer; and never having enough time to do the things *she* wanted to do, since she tended to follow the crowd. Eventually striking out on her own, Jean based her decision on personal experiences and values, not adult advice. Even high school society could be boring, she discovered, when your only friends were sorority girls! Unlike adult-oriented Julie Ferguson, who had tied her fate to the future to get through adolescence back in 1946, Jean was concerned with the here-and-now problems of teenage social life.[39]

Even the *Ladies' Home Journal* jumped on the teenage band-wagon. In the late 1940s and early 1950s the magazine's staff interviewed a wide range of high school students about their real life experiences, instead of following the usual path of asking adult experts to explain the younger generation. "It's the kids telling us, instead of us telling them," marveled Maureen Daly, the editor of the series, which was published as a book, *Profile of Youth*, in 1951. The fact that working-class and minority high school students were included in the pool as regular teenagers (and not as delinquent specimens, for a change) was amazing in itself. "I'm proud to be interviewed," a black teenager noted. "It's the first time I ever knew that anyone cared what a colored boy thought."[40]

Once given a national forum, teenagers punctured some popular myths that did not fit *Seventeen*'s or even Eugene Gilbert's model of the teenage world. For instance, high school girls dated years earlier than adults generally approved of—thirteen for movie dates and fourteen for "car dates." They did not seem to follow adult advice about dating etiquette, either. A popular teenager from a small town, for instance, described a typical midnight movie date "where everybody sits in the balcony eating popcorn, whistling, and shooting paper airplanes, and no one would think of getting home before three."[41] Likewise, teenagers did not share respectable adult qualms about going steady. On the contrary, "normal" girls expected to have two or three steady boyfriends before they settled down for good. They even had rituals to mark the relationship: Steady couples exchanged class rings, wore identical plaid shirts, or peroxided matching blond streaks in their hair and necked heavily as proof of their affection—the one aspect of going steady that adults apparently understood! Overall, teenagers interviewed were amazed by their parents' unrealistic expectations about their behavior. "You'd think families would be able to catch on to what kids are like and what really goes on," a teenager casually observed.[42]

The fact was, though, that nobody really wanted to know. Teenagers might have had a more exciting private life than *Seventeen* or young adult fiction writers suggested, but they also had a social obligation to keep that to themselves, unless they wanted to be labeled delinquents. The image of teenagers as wholesome bobby soxers content to dance their free time away was still very powerful in the adult world, and the notion that innocent adolescents had to be sheltered from adult reality still held sway. For instance, in 1947, members of the National Association of Broadcasters agreed never to air shows or commercials that might undermine "juvenile respect for parents, the home or moral conduct." They also pledged never to air salacious material, a pledge NBC kept in 1949 when it refused to play the provocative song "Six Times a Week and Twice on Sundays."[43]

The pledge also meant that television producers and advertisers had to tread very carefully when it came to portraying teenagers for a national audience. When the Peter Hand Brewery arranged to sponsor "Meet Corliss Archer," a 1954 program that featured teenage characters, all hell broke loose long before the show even aired! Although producers insisted that "Corliss" was aimed at a middle-aged audience, the point was moot. Teenagers could not share the television screen with beer commercials, and a less controversial sponsor had to pick up the show.[44] That some teenagers had been drinking beer for years was beside the point. National broadcasters could not acknowledge this behavior or appear to condone it, and they certainly could not profit from it without seriously damaging the industry's reputation.

Postwar character builders took a similar approach. Although fiction writers were willing to acknowledge that teenagers often necked or drank beer, they also made it clear that "nice" teenagers did not. In *Seventeenth Summer*, the first novel of its kind to speak in a frankly teenage voice, the author drew a distinct social line between kids who "did" and kids who "didn't": The beer-drinking crowd was clearly working-class, and the girls who necked casually had nothing in common with the college-bound narrator, Angie. "We had never had beer at our house," she noted when she found herself at a drinking party, "and I always felt that there was something disgraceful about it."[45] Even after she finally agreed to taste the offensive brew, a few weeks later (at a bar that featured a "colored" piano player and rollicking swing music), she did not change her mind.[46] Likewise in *Sorority Girl*, the teenage drinkers were never the ambitious, hardworking students who were involved with school activities or read *Seventeen*. Instead, they were superficial socialites who could think of nothing better to do with their time than date, dance, and drink! Rich or poor, these beer drinkers were just not worth knowing, the authors suggested.[47]

In a sense, this very strict notion of acceptable teenage behavior threatened to limit the growth of the teenage market. Many advertisers considered youth too hot to handle from a commercial point of view, an attitude that probably influenced Eugene Gilbert's complaint, in 1951, that "everybody talks about youth advertising, but only a few do anything about it." In fact as late as 1954, just a year before the first batch of war babies was scheduled to enter their teens, Joan Kapp Philips, the president of Teenage Public Relations Inc., was still echoing Eugene Gilbert's original insight. "Teenagers with characteristics and outlooks unique to their age groups, cannot be effectively impressed with the same kind of advertising created for adults," she insisted, as if the idea were new. "Nor can they be sold through ads which talk down or employ phony teenage jargon," points that *Seventeen* had argued ten years earlier.[48]

On the surface, it looked as if nothing much had changed since *Seventeen* and Eugene Gilbert developed the adolescent high school market that *Scholastic* had pioneered in the 1930s, but surface appraisals could be deceiving. While adults were debating the value and propriety of expanding the teenage market, teenagers themselves were quietly changing the rules of the game. The surprisingly frank comments in the *Ladies' Home Journal* series had given a hint of where teenage culture was headed. By the mid-1950s the transformation was well under way: *Seventeen's* middle-class audience may have constituted the most visible segment of the teenage market in the immediate postwar years, but there was also a growing underworld of working-class teenage "cats" who had no intention of following adolescent rules.

Teenage cats were the high school students who never played the lead in teenage novels. They were kids like Elvis Presley, the son of a ne'er-do-well truck driver and a part-time waitress in Memphis, Tennessee, who did not fit into the "right" high school crowd and did not try to. Both black and white, teenage cats dressed in dazzling shirts with oversized collars and flashy drape pants in eye-catching color combinations like pink and black. They wore their hair long and swirled it back with greasy pomade, a cool, hipster look that mocked the classic, collegiate style of wholesome, high school bobby soxers.

Their unconventional dress was directly linked to the unconventional music they listened to by artists like B. B. King (the Beale Street Blues Boy), Ma Rainey (the Mother of the Blues), Arthur (Big Boy) Crudup, and the brash, hard-driving Wynonie Harris. This was not the kind of music that *Seventeen* reviewed in its record columns. It was the kind of music that black and white teenagers heard on obscure radio programs like "Tan Town Jamboree," the "Heebee Jeebee Show," "Sepia Swing Club," and "Hoot 'n' Holler."[49]

These teenagers had discovered the passionate world of rhythm and blues—"race music," in industry parlance—music that was never played over national airwaves. Relegated to independent record labels and local black-oriented radio shows, rhythm and blues had an authenticity and urgent sensuality that spoke directly to teenagers hungry for experience and honest, unadulterated communication. Echoing the vitality and separateness that animated teenage life, it was music of and for the streets, the uninhibited sound of cool, hip bluesmen, of smoky juke joints, of tough women "Rockin at Midnight."

And strange as it may have seemed to adults who only wanted what was best for their offspring, rhythm and blues opened the teenage market's floodgates. As it developed into rock 'n' roll, the musical anthem of teenage independence, it demonstrated the economic vitality of this new generation and its brash determination to challenge the limits of adult-dominated, adult-approved, adolescent culture. In the process, it broadened the teenage market beyond its affluent middle-class base, bringing working-class teenagers, both black and white, into the mix. The experience would prove to be as volatile and exciting as the music was, for it challenged the social segregation that shaped the respectable middle-class world. By the mid-1950s, teenage cats and high school rebels, not carefree bobby soxers, would symbolize teenage culture. And Elvis Presley and rock 'n' roll, not *Seventeen* and character builders, would be showing high school students the way.

chapter eight

Elvis fans autographing movie poster, 1956. *Library of Congress, Prints and Photographs Division, NYWT&S Collection.*

Great Balls of Fire
Rhythm and Blues, Rock 'n' Roll, and the Devil's Music

BLACK MUSIC HAD INTRIGUED WHITE TEENAGERS SINCE THE DAYS of swing, although they did not always recognize its influence. Benny Goodman, "The King of Swing," was Jewish, for instance, but he developed his style playing with black musicians at after-hours clubs. When his band brought bobby soxers to their feet in 1937, it was a black musician, Fletcher Henderson, who did the arrangements, and when Gene Krupa set the audience on fire with his "savage" drum solos, he was interpreting (some would say caricaturing) more exciting black rhythms that teenagers would claim for their own in the 1940s. Cab Calloway, Lionel Hampton, and Duke Ellington were as popular as Harry James and Glenn Miller with high school hipsters of either race who prided themselves on their esoteric knowledge of black jazz.

The music had an energy that matched their own vitality. Malcolm Little (later known as Malcolm X), a teenager in Boston in the early 1940s, "just about went wild" when Lionel Hampton's band got the crowd dancing. "I was whirling girls so fast their skirts were snapping," he remembered. "Black girls, brownskins . . . even a couple of white girls there. Boosting them over my hips, my shoulders, into the air. . . . Circling, tap dancing, I was underneath

them when they landed—doing the 'flapping eagle,' 'the kangaroo'
and the 'split.' "[1] Just the type of frenzied dance scene that chilled
the blood of respectable parents of any race.

Rhythm and blues shared the same disreputable aura, although
the term was more a category than a particular style of music
when it was coined in the 1940s. Generally speaking, it meant that
a singer was black and the recording intended for the "ebony,"
"sepia," or "race" market—the last a classification that proved too
thorny to use for long in the world of postwar democracy.
Although rhythm and blues technically covered a variety of styles
from gospel to jazz, it best described the fusion of prewar blues
with wartime dance beats: Louis Jordan's up-tempo jump music,
with its strong boogie rhythm, or the rougher jump style of blues-
man Roy Milton, who developed a true rock 'n' roll beat as early
as 1945.[2]

Whatever the term meant to the industry or to musicians,
rhythm and blues meant excitement for young listeners, the same
kind of excitement Malcolm Little had described. Since the music
was never intended to reach a wide audience, black or white, it
made no accommodation to mainstream tastes, and that was a
large part of its allure. The singing style was harsh, the words too
explicit for respectable listeners, and the rhythm strong and puls-
ing, obviously designed to stir a dancing crowd. The raucous mix
of saxophones, piano, guitars, and drums was always louder than it
should have been for comfortable listening since the music was
designed to excite the audience and heighten tensions, not calm
listeners down.[3]

"It Jumps, It's Made, It Rocks, It Rolls," a rhythm and blues
record company boasted in 1948, making no effort to disguise the
music's passion; "rock 'n' roll" was a familiar blues reference to
sex.[4] On the contrary, rhythm and blues artists and fans reveled in
it. With unabashedly frank songs like "Don't Want No Skinny
Woman," "Gotta Give Me What-cha Got," "Sixty Minute Man,"
and "I Want a Bowlegged Woman," it was obvious that this was
not the kind of music that respectable teenagers were likely to
hear at home.

At least not when parents were listening. By the early 1950s,
though, teenagers could discover the heady, forbidden world of
race music through the random turn of a radio dial; in fact, it was
getting easier all the time. During the war, black migration to

cities like Los Angeles and Detroit had broadened the network of black radio shows. The rise of independent record labels—Savoy in 1942, Atlantic and Chess in 1947, Sun and Vee Jay in 1952—had boosted the power of these radio shows and widened the audience for black music.[5]

Although mainstream broadcasters still thought Saturday mornings were the best time to catch teenage listeners, fans of rhythm and blues knew they had to tune in late at night to hear the kind of music they craved. If the weather was right for good radio reception, teenagers might pick up Jockey Jack Gibson, on Louisville's WLOU, who blasted a bugle when he started his show with the words "My father wasn't a jockey, but he sure taught me how to ride. He said in the middle, then from side to side. Ride, Jockey Jack, ride." Or "Daddy" Gene Nobles, and "John R" Richbourg, in Nashville, Tennessee, who played Southern blues and jumpband jazz at night, when station WLAC switched from country to rhythm and blues. If they were lucky, they might pick up the signal of wild Hunter Hancock, a fast-talking Los Angeles disk jockey whose show was transcribed for stations all over the country. Although he was white, he did not advertise the fact, and his audience did not necessarily know it. He programmed the right mix of jazz, blues, and spirituals—"the latest and greatest Negro performers," as he put it—to satisfy his demanding black audience.[6]

Or perhaps they would listen to "Moondog" Alan Freed, from Cleveland, Ohio. Like Hancock, Freed could howl and growl with the best of the late-night deejays. He was known for drumming along on a telephone book while he shouted "Go! Go! Go!" into an open mic whenever the rhythm got particularly hot. Once he realized the strength of the teenage market for rhythm and blues, he branched out into concert promotion and eventually teenage movies and television shows. In the process, he brought what some called "the devil's music" out of the shadows and into the mainstream as rock 'n' roll.[7]

Freed's critics would later persecute him as a corrupt Pied Piper who cynically manipulated teenage tastes, but there was nothing particularly diabolical about him. He was an entrepreneur in the proud American tradition of business who saw his opportunity in the 1950s and took it. Like Helen Valentine and Eugene Gilbert before him, Alan Freed recognized the enormous economic

potential of giving teenagers what they wanted. Like his fellow
disk jockeys, he understood the provocative power of music—
Freed had danced away his teenage years listening to Benny
Goodman and Tommy Dorsey. He had even led his own high
school dance band, the Sultans of Swing, named in honor of a hot
jazz combo from Harlem.[8]

Although Freed spent two years studying journalism and
mechanical engineering at Ohio State University before joining
the Army (he was discharged within a year since he had flat feet),
his first love was radio broadcasting. In 1942 he took a job at a
one-man station in New Castle, Pennsylvania, doing everything
from announcing a classical music show to sweeping the floor—
all for $17 a week. But lowly as that first job was, he used it to get
a better one in Youngstown, Ohio; he was never shy about exag-
gerating his professional experience or fudging an application if
that was what a job required. As a staff announcer serving a wider
market he was now making $42 a week and trying to make a
name for himself. Freed was never too busy to show interested
high school students around the studio, and when he was promoted to sports announcer in 1943, he enjoyed rubbing elbows
with Youngstown's business elite. By 1945, Freed was working as
a full-fledged deejay for WAKR in Akron, Ohio, hosting "Request
Revue," a jazz and pop listener call-in show that established him
as a bona fide radio personality. With the station actively promoting him, Freed appeared at local school functions, interviewed
band leaders like Count Basie and Woody Herman whenever they
came to town, and even gave autographs to listeners who made
his the top-rated show in the market.[9] When he tried to get a raise
in 1949, though, his employers were not impressed by his argument that he generated more money for the station than his
$10,000 salary reflected. As far as they were concerned, Freed was
already too big for his britches: The twenty-six-year-old disk
jockey was never respectful enough to employers and repeatedly
disregarded explicit instructions on what songs he should play and
when he should play them. When Freed threatened to take his
show to a rival station, WAKR did not blink, because his contract
made that impossible. Invoking a clause that prohibited its most
popular deejay from working on any radio station within a seventy-
five–mile radius, WAKR effectively silenced Freed's well-modulated
radio voice until 1951.[10]

Although he worked on television in the meantime, Freed was anxious to return to radio, and he finally got a job hosting a classical music show on Cleveland's WJW, thanks to Leo Mintz, a drinking buddy who also owned a record store that catered to Cleveland's sizable black community. Teenagers—black, for the most part, but a few whites, too—were buying rhythm and blues dance records like they had never bought before, and Mintz saw a chance to boost his profits and Freed's career at the same time. If Freed could convince WJW to turn the classical show over to rhythm and blues, Mintz would pay all the expenses, including Freed's salary.

At first glance, the move seemed much too risky to the commercially minded Freed. Black music was too raw and earthy to draw a large enough audience, and anyhow, radio was on its way out. But Mintz brought Freed down to the store to see for himself how teenagers responded to the music: They wanted to dance, and rhythm and blues was the only game in town. Mainstream pop music was a veritable desert for teenage listeners. Even though they bought more records than their parents did (a habit made easier by the introduction of affordable 45 rpm disks in 1949, and portable record players), no danceable pop music was being produced in the early 1950s. Music publishers had a vested interest in sheet music and established pop artists, which left teenagers out of the running where musical tastes were concerned. In 1950, the Weavers' "Good Night Irene" led the pop charts, and in 1951 it was Patti Page's "Tennessee Waltz"—nice enough tunes to hum in the shower, perhaps, songs the whole family could enjoy, but not the kind of raucous music that got people dancing, and not the kind of distinctive sound that teenagers could claim as their own.

Once Freed listened to the teenagers and their music, he knew Mintz was right. "I heard the tenor saxophones of Red Prysock and Big Al Sears," he remembered. "I heard the blues-singing, piano-playing Ivory Joe Hunter. I wondered. I wondered for about a week. Then I went to the station manager and talked him into permitting me to follow my classical program with a rock 'n' roll party."[11] In July 1951, Freed opened the show with a wailing sax solo—"Blues for the Red Boy," by Todd Rhodes (which Freed insisted on calling "Blues for Moondog"). He set out to build a mass teenage audience for the late-night show. "Boy, there's a real rockin' thing to get us off and rollin' Moondoggers," he said, as he introduced a new record, "Wild Bill Moore, the Moondog show, Savoy Records and Rock and Roll."[12] If teenagers had any doubt about whether they would be welcome in "Moondog's House," Freed put them at their ease. Within a few weeks, white teenagers from Shaker Heights and Cleveland Heights were calling in requests, along with the black listeners who made up the bulk of Moondog's original audience.[13]

Confident that he had listeners enough to stage a teenage concert, Freed booked the Cleveland Arena for "Moondog's Coronation Ball," a rhythm and blues dance scheduled for March 1952. But even Freed had underestimated his audience: The crowd turned out to be twice the size of the Arena's 10,000 capacity, and the dance had to be canceled when people without tickets crashed the gates. Although local black journalists criticized Freed for exploiting "Negro teensters" with "low-brow, cheap entertainment," trade papers like *Billboard* and *Cashbox* covered the story, too, generating national publicity for the Cleveland deejay and his underground brand of teenage music.[14]

Making the most of this unexpected exposure, Freed called on his listeners to stand up and be counted as true fans of rhythm and blues. "If enough of you can show your faith tonight through your phone calls, through your telegrams, through your cards and letters over the weekend, we will continue the show. If not," he promised, "the 'Moondog' program will leave the radio!" The response was overwhelming, winning Freed six more hours of air time a week from WJW.[15] "Moondog's Coronation Ball" may have been a fiasco in Cleveland, but it was a public relations coup for Freed. It put teenage rhythm and blues on the national map as a potential moneymaker and raised his public profile as the original promoter of rock 'n' roll.

By 1953, Freed was digging into all aspects of the business. He was promoting concerts throughout Ohio and regularly delivering the biggest box office receipts in his home base of Cleveland; he was managing two rhythm and blues groups, the Moonglows and the Coronets (and taking writing credits on their records); and he got involved in record distribution, too. At the same time, he was developing a broader audience. Artists like Fats Domino, the Orioles, and Faye Adams began showing up on mainstream pop charts, and radio stations were taking black music much more seriously.

For instance, 25 percent of radio stations surveyed by *Billboard* in 1953 programmed at least a few hours of rhythm and blues: Bettelou Purvis hosted "Spinner Sanctum" in New York City; Doug "Jocko" Henderson launched his nightly "Rocket Ship" in Philadelphia; "Jack the Cat" Elliot and "Poppa Stoppa" Haman held court in New Orleans; and "Big Daddy" Zenas Sears kept listeners hopping in Atlanta.[16] After New Jersey's WNJR started rebroadcasting Freed's radio show, listeners in the influential New York–New Jersey market could hear "Moondog" six nights a week from 10 P.M. to midnight.[17] Rhythm and blues sales still comprised only a small fraction of total record sales (5 percent, or 15 million records), but the growing popularity of these shows generated mass teenage appeal for the music. Alan Freed's springtime show at the Newark (New Jersey) Armory attracted an audience that was 20 percent white, although all the performers were black, and a few weeks later he hosted a show in Akron that played to a crowd that was one-third white.[18]

Freed's efforts to build a racially mixed, mass teenage audience for rock 'n' roll earned him some fatal enemies. Yet record producers and radio broadcasters could not ignore his uncanny ability to give a broad group of teenagers what they wanted. In the summer of 1954, WINS in New York City publicly acknowledged Freed's influence when it hired him at a reported salary of $75,000. A few months later, *Variety* also tipped its hat when the paper proclaimed that rhythm and blues was no longer limited to a Negro audience. It "had crossed all color lines into the general pop market."[19]

At that point the teenage market for rock 'n' roll became big business. *Variety* began covering Alan Freed's concerts in detail because rock 'n' roll was now considered news. "The kids were jumping like crazy in a pandemonium of honking and stomping," the trade paper reported in January 1955, when Freed hosted a show at the St. Nicholas boxing arena. In fact, it seemed just like the good old days when Benny Goodman and his band had played the Paramount and "the kids were lindy hopping in the aisles." Like the swing bands of old, all the acts at the St. Nicks show "were characterized by an insistent, unmistakable beat. Whether instrumental or vocal," the paper pointed out, "the combos based their arrangements on a bedrock of repetitive rhythm that seemed to hypnotize the kids into one swinging, screaming mass."[20]

A few months later, when "Dr. Jive" (alias Tommie Small, a black deejay from Long Island's WWRL) hosted a rhythm and blues show at Harlem's famed Apollo Theater, *Variety* was still fascinated by the swing music parallel. The lines of young ticket-buyers snaking around the theater, the throbbing pulse of the music, and the kids dancing in the aisles all brought back memories of a vibrant music business. There was no doubt about it, rock 'n' roll was just as potent as the swing music craze, and it generated the "kind of business often dreamed of by theater operators and performers."[21] Rock 'n' roll also generated a kind of audience enthusiasm that seemed almost electric. When Bo Diddley took the stage, *Variety* was thrilled that the crowd picked up the chorus between verses, without any prompting. As he sang, the entire house clapped in unison—three beats normally and two over-head—all the while bouncing wildly in their seats.

In the days of swing, Benny Goodman and Frank Sinatra had faced very different audiences. Kids had been a major part of the crowd at the Paramount, like the kids who now urged Bo Diddley on, but adults had participated, too, a generational mix that had insured a certain civility on stage. Back in 1945, when *Variety* covered Frank Sinatra's performance, the trade paper pointed out that Frankie "deliberately set the kids down front to squealing" and then turned around and told " 'em to keep quiet, there are other folks in the house."[22] But if stars like Bo Diddley, Joe Turner, Lavern Baker, or Fats Domino played to racially mixed houses that would have surprised swing musicians, they only had one generation to please. According to *Variety*, rock 'n' roll shows attracted the thirteen- to nineteen-year-old crowd, and girls under age sixteen tended to dominate—a fact that radically altered the tone of public performances, since the young audience "shrieked at virtually anything as though everything . . . has hidden meanings that they alone understand."[23]

As rock 'n' roll, teenage rhythm and blues became a marketing category in its own right, a category based on age, not race, a demographic shift that would change the very nature of pop music. All of a sudden, it was the beat, not the melody, that drove record sales: Teenagers accounted for 80 percent of the market by 1955, according to one industry spokesman, and if the beat they wanted was rhythm and blues, "there's no reason not to give it to them."[24] But even as Alan Freed broke box-office records at the

Brooklyn Paramount in the spring of 1955, and *Variety* enthusiastically counted the houses for rhythm and blues shows, the trade paper had to admit that there was something a touch unsavory about this moneymaking teenage spectacle: "Swing never had the moral threat of rock 'n' roll which is founded on an unabashed pitch for sex. Every note and vocal nuance is aimed in that direction." If that was not bad enough, the sexual direction sometimes veered way off course. At Dr. Jive's Apollo show, for instance, one young female sang about prostitution, while another act, the popular duo Charlie and Ray, apparently appealed to the "AC-DC" homosexual set, camping it up a bit too much for *Variety's* tastes.

To the trade paper's adult eyes, rock 'n' roll was crossing the narrow line that separated sophistication from exploitation, a risky commercial proposition where teenagers were concerned. Rhythm and blues artists used too much "jelly roll" terminology (another familiar code phrase for sex), and innocent young listeners were being corrupted every day. "We're talking about 'rock and roll' about 'hug' and 'squeeze' and kindred euphemisms which are attempting a total breakdown of all reticence about sex," *Variety* reported with alarm. The paper feared that the government would soon step in to regulate the industry if performers failed to clean up provocative stage shows and abandon what it called suggestive "leer-ics."[25] That would be a tragedy from the business point of view: Rock 'n' roll was breathing welcome new life into the popular music business. With a little adult guidance, the paper insisted, teenage music could be domesticated and before too long "the essential good in the kids" would come to the fore. After all, rock 'n' roll was just the latest teenage shock to the adult nervous system. Adults had not liked jitterbugging either![26]

Variety's concern had more to do with competing business interests than moral decline. The independent record producers who launched rock 'n' roll were challenging *Variety's* best customers. But that did not change the paper's larger point: Before rock 'n' roll could reach a national teenage audience—including middle-class teenagers—performers would have to "whiten" their acts and rein in the music's sexuality. In 1955, Bill Haley devised a formula that seemed to fit the bill. Mixing country swing with rhythm and blues in a song called "Rock Around the Clock," the band leader (who was also a radio disk jockey) broadened the music's appeal well beyond late-night radio listeners. In fact, after the song was featured in the movie *The Blackboard Jungle*, it became a national hit.

Just the kind of white rock 'n' rollers the industry needed to expand the market, Bill Haley and His Comets had no trouble at all upholding conventional standards. The group had no intention of shocking young audiences, except with an aggressive beat. When they recorded "Shake, Rattle and Roll," for instance, the song was already well known. Big Joe Turner, a black blues shouter, had a major rhythm and blues hit when he belted it out in 1954, but where Turner sang about low-cut dresses and made subtle (and not so subtle) references to sex, Haley offered more wholesome lyrics. "We steer completely clear of anything suggestive," the new star explained. "We take a lot of care with lyrics because we don't want to offend anybody."[27]

Purists would later argue that white cover artists like Haley sapped the spirit of rock 'n' roll when they strained away the grit. On one level, they were right. In order for the music to reach a mass teenage audience, authentic rhythm and blues songs, like the Midnighters' "Work with Me, Annie" (which was followed up by "Annie Had a Baby"), gave way to Georgia Gibbs's more conventional version, "Dance with Me, Henry." But teenagers, who were often hearing the music for the first time in 1955, were not concerned with the differences, or even aware of them. As far as they could tell, Bill Haley's "Rock Around the Clock" was a radical break with serene, parent-approved pop music, and they were thrilled to adopt him as one of their own.[28]

For sheltered, mainstream adolescents across the nation, "Rock Around the Clock" was more than a musical breakthrough; it marked the official inception of teenage rebel culture. To country boys on a field trip to Memphis, for instance, who first heard the song at a movie house, it served as a rite of passage into an exclusive teenage club, a club they had not known existed.[29] To urban teens in Buffalo, New York, it celebrated a cocky, confrontational teenage style that adults equated with juvenile delinquency. A popular deejay underscored the point when he urged teenagers to honk their horns if they wanted to hear "Rock Around the Clock." That the deejay made his plea from a perch on top of a billboard (an illegal perch, at that) added to the fun. According to the newspapers, the stunt caused an "ear-shattering traffic jam" that went on all afternoon and landed the deejay in jail![30]

This public demonstration exhilarated teenage rebels, who thoroughly enjoyed defying their elders. Their willingness to break the rules, however, and their obvious pleasure in causing a spectacle only hardened adult hearts against the music. Rock 'n' roll was the musical expression of a delinquent street culture, critics charged, which had to be nipped in the bud. It celebrated the wrong kind of values (and the wrong kind of people) and promoted a hedonistic view of life that mocked the very notion of wholesome adolescence. When lower-class teenagers set popular styles, teenage culture began in the streets, and that could only distract "nice" kids from the hard work of growing up. The most rabid critics made the case more bluntly: Rock 'n' roll was "nigger" music, part of a communist plot to drag white teenagers down to the level of blacks![31]

That was enough, in some adult eyes, to condemn rock 'n' roll as the devil's music and to denounce teenage fans as delinquents. In Bridgeport, Connecticut, authorities banned rock 'n' roll dances. In Boston, they organized boycotts against rock 'n' roll shows. And in the Deep South they tried to keep the music off the air entirely. Newspapers drew links between rock 'n' roll and juvenile crime. Radio stations agreed to ban certain suggestive songs, and church groups encouraged teenage members to speak out against this musical immorality.[32] The fact that *The Blackboard Jungle* focused on teenage gangs and high school violence added fuel to the anti–rock 'n' roll fire, and not only because the movie's delinquent characters jitterbugged to "Rock Around the Clock." According to newspaper reports, teenagers here and abroad were "rioting" in movie houses, proof positive of rock 'n' roll's nefarious power.[33]

But if the music represented a political threat and a social disaster to contentious critics, it was an economic miracle from the music industry's point of view, and this fact changed the climate completely, at least as far as the corporate world was concerned. Late in 1955, RCA Victor signed a contract that promised to deliver the mass teenage audience that had inspired Alan Freed in 1951 and terrified his opponents ever since: The blue chip corporation paid an estimated $40,000 to record Elvis Presley, a teenage rebel from Memphis, Tennessee, whose (white) good looks and (black) singing style promised to cross over every record market that mattered. Like Freed, corporate America saw a chance to make money from rock 'n' roll, and money, as American teenagers were learning every day, changed everything. National broadcasters may have been moved to protect young listeners in 1947 when they banned "provocative" music from the airwaves, but eight years later they had a strong financial reason to change along with the times. Former champions of the fight against teenage rhythm and blues and suggestive "leer-ics," they were now trying to package the music to attract mainstream, teenage record buyers!

Elvis Presley was the man for the job. He could sing everything from gospel and blues to country and pop with the same raw energy and potent sexuality that thrilled rhythm and blues audiences and kept teenagers buying records. He also had an advantage that equally thrilling, dynamic performers like Little Richard and Chuck Berry just could not match: It took a white face to sell rock 'n' roll coast to coast in the 1950s. "The colored folks been singin' and playin' it just like I'm doing now," Presley told a reporter. "I got it from them. I used to hear Arthur Crudup bang his box the way I do now, and I said if I ever got to the place where I could feel all old Arthur felt, I'd be a music man like nobody ever saw."[34]

Bill Haley may have beaten Elvis Presley to a national audience with his rockabilly music, but he was certainly no match for the good-looking singer on stage. Haley had a moon-faced grin and loopy forehead curl that made him look more like a polka-band leader than a rock 'n' roller. Presley, on the other hand, looked exactly like the cat he was with dark good looks, hipster clothes, and daring sideburns. A fan of James Dean and Marlon Brando, whose movies celebrated teenage rebel culture, Elvis had developed his winning look in high school. He bought his clothes at Lansky's, a Beale Street store that specialized in pegged pants, zoot suits, and wildly colored shirts. He wore his collars up, learned to pomade his hair into a startling wave, and favored white suede shoes when everyone else was wearing black leather loafers.[35] As a teenager, Elvis was never popular or secure; he thought he was too short, and his classmates thought he was too odd. Over time, though, he used his clothes and his guitar to carve out an identity, developing a distinctive style in the process. As Sam Phillips, his first record producer, put it, "Man he could wail the heck out of a guitar."[36]

By the time he was graduated in 1953, and making the rounds of county fairs and local dances, Elvis had learned how to sell himself to a crowd. As he told the story, he happened upon the secret of his success—wildly gyrating hips that moved with the music—quite naturally: "Everybody was hollering; I didn't know

what they were screaming at," he remembered an early performance in Memphis. After his manager told him that the girls liked
it when he wiggled his legs, he kept it in the show. "I did a little
more, and the more I did the louder they went."[37] Like any good
businessman, Elvis knew that the customer was always right. His
stage performance may have shocked critics, who would not buy
his records anyway, but his teenage fans loved it. "He isn't afraid to
express himself," a fifteen-year-old told *Life* magazine. "When he
does that . . . I get down on the floor and scream."[38]

Presley was probably lucky that his television debut in 1956 on
the Dorsey Brothers' show did not attract many viewers. His version of "Shake, Rattle and Roll," for instance, was much closer to
Joe Turner's earthy performance than Bill Haley's "whitened"
cover. In his black shirt and light tie, the rock 'n' roller looked too
much like a gangster to suit adult tastes. On Milton Berle's show
later that year, Presley had obviously toned down his appearance.
He seemed a bit more country, despite the same dark shirt and
light tie, but he gave himself away when he started to dance. There
was just no getting around his sexuality on stage. The *New York
Times* panned him as the "virtuoso of the hootchy kootchy," and
the *Journal American* complained that he "wiggled and wriggled
with such abdominal gyrations" that he seemed to be doing "an
aboriginal mating dance."[39] *Life* magazine told readers that "he
does not just bounce to accent his heavy beat. He uses a bump and
grind routine seen only in burlesque." Newspapers spread rumors
that his rock 'n' roll frenzy was fueled by marijuana, and a
Catholic cardinal condemned the singer for encouraging a "creed
of dishonesty, violence, lust and degeneration," a charge that
deeply disturbed his mother.[40]

Whatever his critics thought about his looks, his hips, or his
hold over teenage audiences, they could not deny his appeal. In
1956 alone Elvis Presley sold 10 million records (out of an industry total of 90 million) and claimed 50 percent of RCA's pop
music sales. Girls were wearing Elvis Presley skirts. Boys were
practicing his moves in record stores. Fans were ripping off his
clothes at any opportunity and covering his pink Cadillac with
lipstick mash notes. His performances caused such hysteria that a
judge in Florida threatened to have him arrested if he repeated the
"torso-tossing spectacle" that almost caused a riot the first time he
appeared. Clergymen from the same distraught town denounced

Presley's influence in sermons that linked "Hotrods, Reefers, and Rock 'n' Roll." His fans, of course, paid no attention, and tickets for six upcoming shows sold out in record time.[41]

This did not silence his critics, however, who tried to weaken Presley's appeal one way or another. In the fall of 1956, *Collier's* magazine reported the rise of a Presley rival. A new rock 'n' roll star, Pat Boone, was gaining on Elvis and taking his place with the fickle teenage crowd. And not a moment too soon, either. Boone was everything that Elvis was not: A happily married college student and the father of three, he appealed to adults as well as teenagers, and he was so concerned with his public image that he refused to kiss another woman on screen, lest his children doubt his loyalty to their mother. "Where Elvis has been widely criticized for the emphasis his style places on 'the roll,' " *Collier's* explained, "Pat's reputation is as solid as a rock."[42]

There was only one problem: Teenagers weren't buying it. For every letter that came in praising Boone's boyish good looks, charm, and common sense, there were three supporting Elvis. "The teenage set in Philadelphia just laughed at your article," one writer responded. "There isn't any battle at all . . . Elvis is the best." "Pat Boone is a wishy-washy goody-goody," noted another. She favored Elvis since "at least he's a man." Even a grandmother took Presley's side, dismissing Pat Boone as a "pale replica" who lacked "the terrific masculine appeal of Elvis."[43] Whatever Presley was really selling, there was a market for his wares, and he easily topped Pat Boone in the records charts. He had five "Top Fifty" hits in 1956 (including number one, "Don't Be Cruel," and number two, "Heartbreak Hotel") to Boone's single entry ("I Almost Lost My Mind" at number twenty-two). The following year, Boone reached number five with "Love Letters in the Sand," but Elvis held the number one spot with "All Shook Up."[44]

Even Elvis's critics could not ignore his commercial success. Television's conservative kingmaker, Ed Sullivan, had vowed to keep Elvis Presley off his hit-making show, "Toast of the Town," but after his rival, Steve Allen, booked the rock 'n' roll star (and topped Sullivan in the ratings), he suddenly changed his mind. Now Sullivan offered Elvis Presley $50,000 for three appearances in 1956. The offer virtually redeemed the young performer whom *Billboard* magazine had called "the most controversial entertainer since Liberace."[45]

Making the most of his chance to perform on this highly rated, respectable show, Elvis did what he could to sell himself to mainstream America. He abandoned his gangster look, subdued his dancing (although the censors insisted that he be photographed from the waist up anyway, on his third time out), and delivered a more controlled, self-conscious performance than usual. This was a small price to pay to bring rock 'n' roll to a national audience, though, and the payoff was substantial. Sullivan, who prided himself on his reputation for high standards and integrity, now confirmed what those who loved Elvis already knew: that he was basically a hard-working singer who loved his parents. "This is a real decent fine boy," he told his audience. "We've never had a pleasanter experience with a big name than we've had with you."[46] With these few words, he cleared the way for Elvis to deliver rock 'n' roll to a popular market. Almost overnight, teenage desire became a respectable marketing tool, and teenage rebellion a popular high school style.

With Sullivan's blessing, the rock 'n' roll business moved into high gear. Three Presley hits, "Hound Dog," "Don't Be Cruel," and "Love Me Tender" (from the movie of the same name) traded off the number one spot throughout the fall of 1956. Elvis Presley merchandise was also flooding the market, as a front page story in the *Wall Street Journal* attested.[47] There were t-shirts, hats, black denim trousers, magazines, mittens, stationery, and charm bracelets, all properly licensed and bearing a picture of the newly crowned king of rock 'n' roll. There were lipsticks (Hound Dog Orange, Heartbreak Pink, and Tutti Frutti Red) and glow-in-the dark portraits. There were bookends, guitars, and cologne, and there was even talk of an Elvis Presley soft drink, although that never materialized. Even without it, though, Elvis generated about $22 million worth of business, not counting his records: He sold 4 million charm bracelets, 120,000 pairs of jeans, and 240,000 t-shirts, and that was just the beginning![48] Eugene Gilbert, the guru of teenage marketing, was impressed, but he was not surprised that "fast-moving merchandisers have been able to use the Presley name as an active salesman" by equating it, in the teenage mind, with " 'must have,' 'possess,' and 'can't be without' "—words that still propelled the high school crowd.[49]

Elvis was only part of the story, though. By 1957, the potent combination of his breakthrough success, Alan Freed's methodical market-building, and the teenager's own sense of generational difference was primed for a commercial explosion.[50] Now teenagers were the acknowledged stars of pop music, and their everyday experiences like dating, dancing, driving, and partying dominated the airwaves. Rock 'n' roll standards celebrated teenage style ("Blue Suede Shoes," "Black Denim Trousers," and "Dungaree Doll"), teenage slang ("Be Bop a Lula" and "See You Later Alligator"), and teenage disdain for adult authority ("Yakety Yak [Don't Talk Back]"). Most often, though, they celebrated teenage love ("Earth Angel," "In the Still of the Night," "Tonight You Belong to Me") in innocent and not-so-innocent ways. As journalist Jeff Greenfield, who grew up with the music, remembered, the teenage world of rock 'n' roll was "a world of unbearable sexuality and celebration: a world of citizens under sixteen, in a constant state of joy or sweet sorrow."[51]

There were songs for dancing, songs for necking, songs for just hanging around, and songs that drove parents crazy. There were songs that captured the crazy mixed-up emotional spirit of adolescence: the energy expressed through a wailing sax, the yearning of doo-wop street corner harmonies, the aggressive self-promotion of tricky guitar riffs and powerful piano playing. Although some songwriters shamelessly crafted "teenage" songs to appeal to the youngest adolescents (who, coincidentally, bought the most records), others came by their subjects honestly. Jerry Lieber and Mike Stoller, for instance, were only seventeen when they began to write a string of rock 'n' roll hits ("Hound Dog" was one of their earliest successes). "If we were amused, if we really liked what we did," Stoller explained, "we had a pretty good shot at having a hit, because we were our audience, and we were . . . typical of the people who bought our records. . . . There was something universal about the humor, or the emotional content, that caught the teens."[52]

That universal something—the beat, sex, rebellion, fun—was reaching a larger audience every day as movie producers jumped on the rock 'n' roll band wagon. In 1954, rock 'n' roll fans were still scanning radio dials to find the music. Unless they lived near a good-size city, they were not likely to see performers on stage. Within two years, Columbia Pictures had backed Alan Freed and Bill Haley in *Rock Around the Clock* and teenage movies pitching rock 'n' roll stars were soon the rage. *Don't Knock the Rock, Shake, Rattle, and Rock, Rock, Pretty Baby,* and *Mr. Rock and Roll* were all formula movies that spotlighted daring black performers like Little Richard, Chuck Berry, Fats Domino, and Joe Turner at their provocative best—but presented them in a wholesome, non-threatening context. In *Mr. Rock and Roll*, for instance, Alan Freed tells the story of how he discovered rhythm and blues (flashing back to an all-white version of Leo Mintz's record shop). He goes on to show how he had been fighting ever since to defend the good name of rock 'n' rollers, who were, after all, good-hearted, responsible kids who really just wanted to dance.

Television got in on the bonanza, too. Prime time was still reserved for adult audiences, but on afternoons after school, or on Saturday mornings, shows like "Teenage Dance Party" (in Denver), "Top Ten Dance Party" (in Richmond), and "Bandstand" (in Philadelphia) were drawing reliable teenage audiences at the studios and at home. Once the American Broadcasting Company realized that records played on these shows soon became block-buster hits, the network decided to go national in 1957, first with Alan Freed's "The Big Beat," in July and then with Dick Clark's "American Bandstand," the following month.

Although Freed did his best to smooth the rough edges of his chosen brand of rock 'n' roll, he was no match for the twenty-seven-year-old Clark, whose clean-cut good looks and respectable earnest manner could rival Pat Boone any day. The hippest teenagers may have scorned Clark's "safe" approach to rock 'n' roll, but they were never his target audience anyway. Dick Clark reached 20 million viewers (including a fair number of parents and children) on sixty-seven stations nationwide with "American Bandstand," and he was not about to jeopardize that exposure by inviting criticism. Alan Freed lost his show when a cameraman inadvertently showed Frankie Lymon, a black teenage singer, dancing with a white partner, a painful lesson in the social economics of network television that was not lost on the ambitious Clark.[53]

From the beginning, "American Bandstand" embodied a whole-some image of teenage life, from its swing-oriented theme song, "Bandstand Boogie," and its record-hop set to the "Bandstand Kids," who soon became teenage celebrities: Joanne and Carmen Montecarlo, Betty Romantini, Justine Carelli, and Frankie Lobis, neighborhood high school kids who made the phrase "It's got a good beat and you can dance to it" a national motto. The Bandstand Kids knew how to dance, how to dress, and how to behave in public, and Dick Clark saw to it that they set a good example for their teenage fans. "American Bandstand" had a dress code: coats and ties for boys and no slacks, tight sweaters, or low-cut blouses for girls, and the show had a behavior code, too. Betty Romantini remembered the day when someone in the audience broke the code by tossing a penny at the stage in the middle of a performance. "Dick was just *livid*, but all he said to that poor kid—who must have been wetting his pants!—was, 'How *dare* you do that to someone who is serious about what they are doing.' I'll never forget that," she added, "the one time I saw Dick Clark come close to losing his cool."[54]

By now a standard practice in the commercial world, the wholesomeness cultivated by the Bandstand crew was the key to mass-marketing teenage culture. Like Andy Hardy in the bobby soxers' heyday, the Bandstand Kids taught high school students (and junior high and grade school students, too) how to be teenagers. They embodied the values of good clean fun (like dancing to records that were available for purchase), an attractive appearance (that could be attained through products advertised on the show), and fitting in with the crowd (the real essence of the teenage market). In the process, the Bandstand Kids took the worry out of teenage life for insecure students and the danger out of rock 'n' roll for worried parents. In fact, "American Bandstand" was such a success with adults and young viewers alike that Dick Clark was able to sell himself as a trusted advisor, publishing books and articles (in *Seventeen*, for instance) that offered teenagers a blueprint for living a wholesome, respectable life.

Whether they took his advice seriously was another question. And whether they shared his bobby-soxer vision of high school life remained to be seen. For no matter what kind of spin network broadcasters put on rock 'n' roll to garner a mainstream audience, the fact remained that the music and the style did not mesh with middle-class life—not yet at least. The teenagers who made Elvis Presley a star or went wild for Little Richard in the mid-1950s did not look like the teenagers Dick Clark showcased. They might have come from the same neighborhoods, but they adopted a different approach to life. Rock 'n' rollers wore leather jackets and jeans (or tight skirts and too much makeup), and they tended to make adults nervous when they hung out together on the street. They smoked too much, talked too loud, and got too involved with their steadies to qualify as "nice" kids. They were the kind of tough, risk-taking teenagers that middle-class youngsters were taught to avoid.

The kids who made the music did not look like Bandstand Kids, either, except when they appeared on the show. Coats and ties and party dresses could cover a multitude of teenage sins! Teenage performers were usually kids who did not have the kind of money or family background that it took to enjoy *Seventeen*'s version of teenage life, and they were usually kids who were bored to tears in high school. They were eager to take their chances and see what they could accomplish in the real, adult world. These teenagers were as interested in the business of teenage culture as Dick Clark was. As music, rock 'n' roll may have encouraged run-of-the-mill teenagers to be the stars of their own lives, but as an industry, it inspired poor but ambitious teenagers to become the stars of teenage life—and make some real money while they were at it. Rock 'n' roll singers may have looked for all the world like nice, amusing kids who followed the rules when they appeared on television, but in real life they were playing an entirely different game.

Wholesomeness was just a prop to get past adult censors, a fact of life that came as no surprise to teenagers. They were learning every day that appearance was nine-tenths of the law in the respectable adult world. For instance, Dick Clark's ultimate victory over rival Alan Freed illustrated this practical truth. Both promoters made a very good living out of rock 'n' roll, and both emerged as faithful defenders of teenage virtue. Both were also accused of profiting from questionable business practices that Congress investigated in the early 1960s. But there the similarities ended. Freed, who never learned how to control his aggressive personality, was thrown to the wolves. In 1962 he pleaded guilty to two counts of commercial bribery.[55] The more appealing, cooperative Clark, on the other hand, got a chance to mend his ways and grew up to be the world's oldest teenager.

If teenagers had been asked to judge the case, they might have been more loyal to Freed than Clark. It was the Cleveland deejay, after all, who had recognized the vitality and gritty reality of their everyday lives. No matter how carefully promoters like Dick Clark managed to package commercial teenage culture, two things were already clear: Rock 'n' roll was a business, like any other. And teenagers weren't bobby soxers anymore.

chapter nine

Black and white high school students, Washington, D.C. *Library of Congress, Prints and Photographs Division, U.S. News and World Report Magazine Collection [LCU9 1033A]*

Stairway to Heaven
The Real Life Business of Rock 'n' Roll

ROCK 'N' ROLL AND THE EXPANSION OF THE TEENAGE MARKET may have meant the end of civilization to some adults and the beginning of prosperity to others, but to teenagers hoping to escape the drudgery of a routine life, it promised endless opportunity. Or at least so it seemed to countless high school students from the wrong side of town who wanted more from life than a paycheck but had no real interest in school or the professions. If unremarkable street kids like Dion Di Mucci and his group, the Belmonts, who hailed from the Bronx, could make it on "American Bandstand," they reasoned, then anyone with talent and determination had the same chance to succeed.

Dion, after all, would go on to a lucrative career, despite a resumé that was unimpressive by adult standards. The Belmonts were high school graduates working toward conventional futures, but the lead singer had passed through five different high schools in New York and New Jersey before dropping out in 1957. He was not ashamed of it either and made no effort to disguise his contempt for high school life, as his comments in a national magazine made clear. "Just seeing the same people and making the same scene every day got to be a drag, you know?"[1]

Phil Spector, another overnight success, confirmed the fact that you did not have to go to college to make a fistful of dollars, no matter what adults said. Just seventeen when he penned the hit song, "To Know Him Is to Love Him," Spector had intended to become a court reporter, a job he did not look forward to, by any means. In fact, he dropped out of college at the first opportunity, around the time his group, the Teddy Bears, was a hit on "American Bandstand." Now he was tooling around Los Angeles in a metallic blue Corvette, courtesy of his first royalty payment.[2] Not bad for a teenager with no particular skills, outside of playing a little guitar, that is.

There was also Lavern Baker, the black high priestess of rock 'n' roll, according to *Ebony* magazine. Thanks to her hit record, "Tweedle Dee," she was making $75,000 a year. She had come up the hard way, singing the blues as "Little Miss Sharecropper" back in 1951, before rock 'n' roll opened up a wider space for her kind of music.[3] But it was Frankie Lymon who really inspired young hopefuls. Thirteen years old with a clear falsetto voice and an earnest stage presence, he was the leader of the Teenagers, a mixed group of black and Puerto Rican singers from Harlem. When their song "Why Do Fools Fall in Love" became an international hit in 1956, Frankie Lymon proved that even the youngest teenagers from very humble backgrounds had every reason to reach for the stars.

Industry spokesmen were quick to point out that appearances could be deceiving; only two out of every hundred teenage "stars" ever recorded a second hit. But these odds seemed as good as any, especially to deprived but ambitious minority teenagers whose chances in life were already restricted. The luckiest could expect to fill clerical and manufacturing jobs that were just beginning to open up to "colored" high school graduates in the 1950s. That hardly seemed like a golden opportunity to teenagers hungry for success and recognition, though. They were not interested in conventional dreams of upward mobility that started with a low-prestige job in one generation and paid off decades later when a grandchild entered medical school. They wanted to enjoy the life they had, not embark on a long and tedious family journey. From their vantage point, rock 'n' roll offered more promising opportunities than bootstrap jobs ever could. Risky or not, the budding industry provided the kind of incentive that eluded them in the workaday world: a future that was, in their estimation, well worth working for.

In fact, once would-be teenage stars made up their minds to enter show business, they were eager to get started. Ronnie Bennett, who grew up in Spanish Harlem, was only twelve when Frankie Lymon opened her eyes and ears to the glamorous possibilities of rock 'n' roll. "I couldn't tell if he was black or white, or what," the future singing star (and leader of the Ronettes) remembered. "I just knew that I loved the boy who was singing that song." That was important in itself, for as the daughter of a mixed mother (black and Cherokee) and a white father, Ronnie was beginning to wonder just where she fit in a color-conscious world. "The blacks never really accepted me as one of them. The white kids knew I wasn't white. And the Spanish kids didn't talk to me because I didn't speak Spanish. . . . I used to sit in front of the mirror, trying to decide just what I was," she recalled.[4] Discovering rock 'n' roll took the edge off her adolescent identity crisis. On the radio, she realized, the only thing that counted was performance.

Although sociologists tended to make dire predictions about kids like Ronnie, whose mothers were poor and uneducated and whose fathers had long since departed, the young "half-breed," as she called herself, was convinced she could be a star. After all, Frankie Lymon was just a year older, and he even ate lunch at the coffee shop where her mother worked! Determined to spend her life in the limelight, she worked up a routine complete with songs, dance steps, dedications, and stage patter and began rehearsing every day after school. "I took my career very seriously, even then," she explained. "And why not? I knew my time was coming, and I wanted to be ready when it did." By the time she entered high school in 1957, there was no question in her mind that show business would be her life. She put a trio together, invested in professional singing lessons, and then spent weekends performing at bar mitzvahs and sock hops. The group, "Ronnie and the Relatives," kept her in spending money, but the work was too ordinary to satisfy her cravings. "What we really wanted was to be recognized for the stars we knew we were and that meant making records," she said.[5]

Her confidence may have seemed naive in the competitive business climate of New York City, but in Detroit, where the black teenage music industry was beginning to thrive, Ronnie Bennett would have been just one of a very determined crowd. Teenage rock 'n' roll groups were a dime a dozen in the Motor City, rehearsing in basements, playing at school dances and low-life nightclubs, and waiting for the day when they would cut their first record and wave hard times goodbye. Fifteen-year-old Smokey Robinson regularly practiced harmonies and dance steps with high school friends on his front porch, mesmerizing his young next-door neighbor, Diana Ross, who was already singing (and passing a hat) at neighborhood parties at age eleven.[6] By the time Robinson was eighteen, he and his friends would be recording as the "Miracles." And by the time Ross was fourteen, she would be a member of the "Primettes" (with Florence Ballard, Mary Wilson, and Betty McGlown), a group that changed its name to the Supremes in 1960, just a few months after the teenagers won their first talent contest.[7]

Raynoma Mayberry, another neighborhood kid with big musical dreams, was writing songs by the time she was twelve and recording them in a makeshift studio she set up in her basement. She took it for granted that she and her siblings would produce hit songs, and she thought nothing of sending off their very first efforts to RCA Victor in New York City. "We had high expectations," she remembered, and an early rejection letter did nothing to dampen her spirits. Raynoma kept writing songs, devising dance routines to go with them, and worked up an act with her sister called "Alice and Ray" that she tried out at a local nightclub. Stardom was just around the corner, she felt sure. It was merely a matter of making the right connections.[8]

By the late 1950s and early 1960s, those connections were getting easier to make, at least in Detroit. Berry Gordy, a songwriter turned record producer, was convinced that the Detroit street-sound could sell rock 'n' roll records, and he was determined to discover a singing sensation who could reverse Elvis Presley's winning formula: a black artist who could cross over from rhythm and blues into the more lucrative pop market. Building a strong network of family and friends, each of whom wore an amazing number of professional hats in the early days—backup singer, administrator, songwriter, floor sweeper—Berry Gordy and his associates took teenage dreams of stardom seriously. "Give them all an opportunity and see which ones hit," was Gordy's motto. He and co-workers were willing to sign almost any group that showed a spark of talent or demonstrated their willingness to work hard and succeed.

Gordy knew where these teenagers were coming from. He had dropped out of high school in 1945 with plans of becoming a boxer, but he turned his attention to music once he realized how hard and unrewarding a boxer's life could be. He had also done some time on a Detroit assembly line when an early business venture failed. So he knew from experience that this was no life for free and creative spirits, even when wages were good. He understood what motivated star-struck teenagers and shared their optimistic hopes. The connection was natural: He wanted to find a major moneymaking star as much as they wanted to become one. The company they built together, Motown, or Hitsville as it was locally known, was a fortuitous match of desire and opportunity for everyone involved, creating career ladders for black teenagers who were serious about success.[9]

Berry Gordy came from a family of entrepreneurs, who provided his start-up capital, but he was also surrounded by an ambitious group of teenagers and very young adults who kept the fledgling company going. Janie Bradford, a teenage receptionist, co-authored Berry's first profitable hit, "Money (That's What I Want)," a song that not only captured the company's spirit but bolstered its finances in the early days.[10] Raynoma Mayberry sang vocals, polished lyrics, wrote chord charts, and taught basic music theory to the group. The Supremes were too young to participate, or so Gordy thought at first, but the high school students refused to take no for an answer. They camped out in Motown's reception area every day after school until they were finally hired to do handclaps and background vocals, earning a few dollars a week. In the meantime, eighteen-year-old Smokey Robinson became Gordy's righthand man, writing songs, singing with the Miracles, and bringing in the first number one crossover hit with "Shop Around," recorded on Gordy's Tamla label. In fact, it was Robinson who had persuaded Gordy to go into business for himself. "Why work for the man?" the teenage Robinson wanted to know. "Why don't you *be* the man? You're a cat who knows music and people. *You* be the man!"[11]

Willing to work long hours for low pay just to be part of the industry, Motown's teenage crew was getting in on the ground floor of a business that was just as young and freewheeling as they were. And this was an incredible advantage. They were on the scene when crucial decisions were being made and were ready to pounce at any opportunity to show their elders just what they could do. Billie Jean Brown was still in high school when she was hired to write liner notes, and she caught Berry Gordy's attention with a well-turned phrase that got her a job as his assistant and led to an executive position. Seventeen-year-old Norman Whitfield took a job in quality control that eventually launched his career as a record producer. Martha Reeves was just out of high school when she went to Motown as a secretary, but before too long she and the Vandellas, a group she started singing with in high school, were doing backups and then taking the lead, with hit songs like "Heat Wave" and "Dancin' in the Street." Even would-be teenage stars like the Marvelettes, the Supremes, and Little Stevie Wonder got a chance to develop their style with homegrown record producers, something that was not possible before Motown took off.[12]

Rock 'n' roll offered teenagers opportunities, but it did not provide protection or guarantee success. As countless would-be stars learned the hard way, desire and ambition counted for very little unless teenagers had the discipline to work hard and learn the industry's ropes, something they were rarely willing to do when visions of easy money and celebrity danced in their heads. But there was nothing easy about success, even in the unconventional world of rock 'n' roll. Business was business, whatever the product or the age of its producers. As Ronnie Bennett discovered at her first recording session, making a record was hard, tedious work, especially for someone with no training in music. "We'd be in the middle of a chorus that we thought was perfect," she remembered, when all of a sudden the technician would shout, "Hold it, girls. Somebody in that modulation is still hitting one note and then changing to another note in the middle of the chord." Dumbfounded, the Ronettes would do another take, and then another, and another. But even all that work could not guarantee a hit. Good product or not, disk jockeys rarely played new records unless producers gave them a strong financial reason to do so. Just ask Alan Freed how the business worked!

As the Ronettes and others eventually learned, teenage stars needed the help of adult promoters to push the product and invest in their long-term careers. They also learned, however, usually from hard experience, that adults could not be trusted to protect their interests. In the adult world of work it was every man (and woman) for him- or herself. Record producers could afford to be generous with initial opportunities. They tossed out teenage groups like bait to hungry audiences just to see what worked and what did not. They took almost no financial risks, although they claimed the lion's share of the profits if a group happened to hit. Standard contracts paid no royalties on records sold until all production costs were recovered, and the best producers regularly took a songwriting credit (and the royalties that went with it) whether they authored a song or not. Thus teenage stars were more likely to gain celebrity than riches from their early efforts, especially since they tended to confuse the two. When the Ronettes took home $100 apiece for a ten-day run (playing three shows a day and spending ten hours straight at the theater), the high school group thought they were making a fortune![13]

However, given their age and lack of experience, that was usually the cost of doing business. "We were just three more rock and roll singers. And in those days that didn't earn you much respect," as Ronnie Bennett put it.[14] Young performers usually had no choice but to take the deal offered, and if they were not very careful or sophisticated, they could end up working for free. For instance, Little Richard sold the rights to his song "Tutti Frutti" for $50 before the million-seller was released. In fact, he sold the rights to all his music for a mere $10,000—and then spent years in court trying to recover money that he believed he was owed. "I didn't know anything about the business," he explained, "I was very dumb. . . . I was like a sheep among a bunch of wolves that would devour me at any moment." That did not matter, though since the transactions were legal; he was over twenty-one at the time. As a producer calmly explained, when you sign away your rights, you sign away your rights, a legal truth that escaped some would-be stars. Rock 'n' roll was a business, not a character-building program, and teenagers had to learn to look out for their own best interests if they hoped to have any future at all.[15]

They had to develop staying power, too, an elusive mix of popular appeal, professionalism, and self-discipline that distinguished serious candidates from less viable competitors. The teenage market was a fickle one. Even stars had only three years or so to prove they could appeal to a wider audience (like Pat Boone did) or move into motion pictures (like Elvis) and generate real money over time. There was little margin for professional or personal error in this cutthroat business but plenty of room for failure since entry-level requirements were so low. Raynoma Mayberry, for instance, may have had big teenage dreams for her musical future, but she had a baby, too, a year out of high school, a definite obstacle to stardom, especially after her brief marriage broke up. Frankie Lymon, who sold so many records in 1956, was drinking heavily by 1961, and he had lost his audience, too. By the time he was twenty-five, the onetime star was dead, the victim of a drug overdose.

Given the risky nature of the business and the one-in-a-million chance for celebrity, concerned parents tried to steer star-struck children away from the industry. They preferred more conventional life choices, like college and the professions, or marriage and a traditional job. They overlooked the fact that conventional choices could be just as risky or disappointing, especially in a world that rationed opportunities according to skin color. Would-be professionals had no guarantee that their years of training would pay off, any more than young married couples could count on living happily ever after. Young apprentices in any line of work—show business, the building trades, medicine—had to pay their dues. As far as optimistic, energetic teenagers could see, rock 'n' roll was as realistic a choice as any other. Even if stardom did not work out, as it usually didn't, the young industry still offered exciting ground-floor opportunities to teenagers who pined for the glamorous life.

Parents and teachers assumed they knew better, of course. In fact many believed they could predict a teenager's future based on their own experiences in the past. They also believed that they had a duty, as well as a right, to direct a teenager's choices. As far as they could see, education offered the most direct route to social advancement, especially now that middle-class respectability seemed well within a hardworking black teenager's reach. With job opportunities opening every day, at least for blacks in the North, the time was ripe for ambitious teenagers to buckle down, take school seriously, and prepare for the ordinary future that undoubtedly awaited them.[16] To be sure, this advice was not always wrong. Plenty of would-be stars gave no practical thought to their future, although they certainly should have. But it wasn't always right, either. There were always teenagers who knew exactly what they wanted from life at a very early age, whether adults thought they were capable of making realistic choices or not.

Diana Ross was a case in point. Neither her father, her teachers, nor her friends thought she would succeed. In fact, she and her father almost came to blows over the question of school versus career. Fred Ross had put himself though college while he worked as a boxer, and he had high ambitions for all his children. When his oldest daughter, Barbara Jean, planned to become a doctor, he applauded her choice, but he closed his mind to Diana's less conventional scheme. According to Fred Ross's law, a college degree was the only sensible path to the future. The fact that college had not saved him from low-paying, exhaustive work did not change his argument. Like so many others who had been robbed of their chance to succeed in life, he wanted his daughter to take advantage of opportunities that had not existed in his day. And like other well-meaning and concerned parents whose vivid memories of economic depression never really faded, he believed that financial security was the only career goal worth pursuing.

But Diana was just as stubborn as he was, and she had no intention of altering her plans. When she got a chance to join the Primettes at age fourteen (rehearsing afternoons in a dingy hotel room), she grabbed it, despite her father's well-known objections. On nights that the group performed in their pleated skirts, bobby sox, and letter sweaters (for $15 a show), Fred Ross would wait up for her, brandishing a leather strap he did not need to use to make his point. He could not change her mind, however, even when he tried to stop her from signing a contract with Berry Gordy's "fly-by-night" enterprise. "I felt she was wasting time with this singing," he explained. "But she never understood. She felt I was trying to screw up her life."[17]

No matter how hard parents like Fred Ross pushed higher education, it was just not a priority for teenagers like Diana who set
their goals early and were bored by classwork that had nothing to
do with their plans. She was not lazy or unconcerned with her
future: Ross took evening classes at a beauty school and worked
part time busing tables at an upscale department store, the first
black to work outside of the kitchen there. But school never held
her interest. "She wasn't a very good student because she was so
certain she would find success in show business," a teacher
remembered. "I had her in my English class . . . and many times
she would . . . hide behind a book while she painted her finger-
nails bright colors." Another recalled Diana's impatient response
when the teenager was caught daydreaming in class. "You *know*
I'm going to be a singer *don't you?*" she asked. "Oh you poor
child," the teacher remembered thinking. "You'll never make it."[18]
These adults dismissed Diana's dreams as unrealistic and then
wondered why she would not take advice. Whether they realized
it or not, though, she took advice, and took it gladly, when it came
from people who had earned her respect. Her teachers and her
father thought her plans were crazy, but Berry Gordy thought she
had a chance. At age thirty-three, Gordy was an adult by all counts
except, perhaps, his appearance. The teenage Diana looked up to
him as a mentor who had made his own unrealistic dreams come
true. "Berry was the most amazing man I, as a kid, had ever seen,"
she explained. "So cool, so confident and with such purpose." As
far as the teenage singer was concerned, Gordy was patient, kind,
and wonderful, the kind of adult a teenager could respect. Unlike
her skeptical, critical father, she said at the time, "*he* knows I'm
going to be successful."[19]

Ross did not let criticism from her peers deter her, either. Her
classmates at Cass Technical High may have labeled her a snob, or
laughed behind her back when she announced intentions to sing
on "American Bandstand" some day, but their opinions barely registered with her. She was popular enough, thanks to her good
showing on the swim team and her recording contract. She even
won the Best Dressed title her senior year. But these were unim-
portant victories: Diana Ross wanted to excel, to be somebody,
but her sights were set on higher goals than a successful high
school life. "She didn't really mix that much with the other

youngsters," a teacher remarked. "She didn't seem to want to spend her time chattering, gossiping, and giggling. She simply wasn't frivolous in that way," she said.[20] Her approach to life was probably not so different from other students who took their futures seriously, like those who expected to become doctors, or lawyers, or engineers. They all needed a certain level of competence to succeed, but they also needed a disciplined determination to reach their goal, and that was much harder to come by.

Especially in cities like Detroit, which housed a large number of impoverished black families. Teenagers had to avoid the pitfalls of street life (violence, alcohol abuse, teenage pregnancies) just to take the first faltering steps up and out of poverty. That was not as easy as it might have seemed in an increasingly prosperous world. Often the first in their families to attend more than two years of high school, these teenagers had a hard time coping with teenage culture when they did not have the money to enjoy it. If their parents could afford it, they followed the experts' advice to fix up party rooms to keep young teenagers safe at home. Raynoma Mayberry, for instance, remembered the "teenage pleasure palace" her mother constructed in the basement, complete with a television set, stereo, soft drink bar, and plenty of room for dancing.

This solution was not an option for those who lived in the projects, like Diana did, however. In these neighborhoods, teenagers gathered on street corners to dance or made their way to sleazy nightclubs that rarely enforced liquor laws or noticed the age of young patrons. Unbeknownst to their parents, underage singing groups like the Supremes often performed (illegally) at these venues and socialized with drunken customers who threw change at the stage when they sang. Yet teenagers often paid a high price for the freedom the streets allegedly offered. Sociologists were already reporting that teenage residents of "scanty" environments tended to fight to get what they wanted and were known to carry knives and pistols to pave the way.[21]

Flo Ballard, Diana's partner in the Supremes, could attest to the truth of these studies. She had been raped, at age seventeen, by a knife-wielding acquaintance she met at a dance. Although the episode left deep scars that blighted her life, she and Mary Wilson (the third Supreme) continued to travel with a very rough neighborhood crowd during their teenage years that Diana Ross deemed too dangerous to associate with. Although all three girls lived in the same housing project, their families—and their approach to life—were completely different. One of thirteen children, Flo barely knew her father, a transient who died when she was fifteen. Mary grew up in a middle-class family that she thought was her own until her natural mother reclaimed her at age nine. Neither Supreme could count on her parents for financial support or educational guidance.

Diana, on the other hand, was brought up in a stable family with a father who worked regularly and a mother who took great pride in raising her family well. Diana may have fought with her father to achieve her independence, but nevertheless she internalized his faith in the future and her family's determination to succeed. Her willingness to break with the teenage crowd to protect her interests reflected a homegrown tendency to put her future first. Ross was no puritan, by any means; at Motown, in fact, she was known as a party girl. But she decided early on to party with those who could help her move forward and abandon those who might drag her down. She may have been totally focused on her own advancement, as her friends complained, but if this tenacity failed to win popularity contests, it kept her career on track and allowed her to move beyond the neighborhood streets that trapped so many others. It was her vision of the future and her expectations of success that prodded her to make the most of her teenage opportunities, qualities she shared with successful teenagers of any class or race.[22]

Learning to keep the big picture in mind was never easy in an industry that catered to teenage tastes and short-term desires, however. Professionalism may have been the key to survival in show business, but sensationalism often opened doors for teenage rock 'n' rollers who had to rely on their hips and their sexuality to catch a producer's eye. Ross was probably lucky that she was too young and skinny to play this role. The Supremes were always "the girls" to Berry Gordy, who promoted them as young ladies. That was fine with the lead Supreme, who considered the group a launching pad for a more serious, solo career. Ross had already convinced Gordy that she had the makings of the mainstream star he was looking for, the black Doris Day who could persuade a variety of audiences to spend good money on performances, records, movies, whatever. With Gordy on her side, she could grow into her sexuality while she developed her talents and perfected her stage presence, a rare advantage that strengthened her chances for long-term success.

The Ronettes, on the other hand, were more or less on their own when they started out. Even when producer Phil Spector took Ronnie under his wing, he was always more interested in her personal charm than her career. Probably the first "slutty" girl group to capture public attention, the Ronettes were a prime example of the contradiction between commercial teenage culture and the qualities a teenager needed to succeed in life. As high school students, they managed to land their first job as dancers by stuffing their bras, teasing their hair, and squeezing into tight, eye-catching dresses—with their mothers' help no less! But that was the business they were getting into, and they played the role for all it was worth. "Every eye in the place was on us," Ronnie remembered. "They noticed our looks right away, just like I knew they would. With everyone staring at me, it didn't take much effort to get charged up and dancing. . . . [I] started shaking everything I had."[23]

Although Ronnie and the group led fairly sheltered lives up through high school, they presented a very different image on stage. "If we copied anything," Ronnie explained, "it was the look of the . . . Spanish and half-breed girls who walked around with thick eyeliner and teased hair." Their audience enthusiastically approved. The girls loved it "because we were different—we followed our own style and didn't care what anybody thought. And the boys liked us for obvious reasons. The Ronettes were what the girls wanted to be and what the guys dreamed about," she said. The vast distance between their stage image and reality almost induced Ronnie to drop out of school, however, after the group started working nights at the Peppermint Lounge in Manhattan. On stage she was Ronnie, a grown-up with high teased hair, exotic makeup, and short, tight skirts that kept the audience howling; at school she was Veronica, the cheerleader, a role that seemed superfluous now. Her mother forced her to finish high school and earn her diploma, but not without a fight. "I have to admit that after I got it, I saw how much sense it made to stay in school," she said. "But I still hated my mother for making me go through that."[24]

Playing the role of oversexed teenagers may have worked well at teenage-only rock 'n' roll shows, but it could not deliver the mainstream audience the Ronettes craved. The fact that their racial identity was not exactly clear did not help matters. As the rise of Elvis Presley and the demise of Alan Freed suggested, mass audiences were not ready for black sexuality on stage, and they would not tolerate even the slightest suggestion of interracial sex. In fact, when the Ronettes were offered parts in a rock 'n' roll movie called *Hey Let's Twist* that starred Joey Dee and the Starliters, they learned how particular audiences could be about race. Although they thought their future was made, their plans came to nothing once the producer met them face to face: The Ronettes were too light to play black girls and too dark to be white, thus they would only confuse the big-screen audience. "We still went down to watch the filming," Ronnie remembered, "but it killed us to see the white actresses they hired. . . . The closest we got to being in the movie was when we played dancers in a crowd scene. And that's where we stayed—in the crowd."[25]

On one level, rock 'n' roll opened popular culture to dark-skinned teenagers who had not been part of the mainstream teenage scene before. For instance, *Seventeen* would not feature a black model until 1963, and in the 1950s the only blacks to surface with any regularity were domestic workers in short stories. If the teenage music industry opened economic doors for minority teenagers, though, it offered no protection from the racial realities of the larger world. Once they went on tour, teenage rock 'n' rollers often learned more than they wanted to know about the dangerous world outside their neighborhoods. Used to coming and going more or less as they pleased in cities like Detroit and New York, minority teenagers got a real education whenever they performed in the South.

Soon after they lost their movie roles, for instance, the Ronettes traveled to Florida, where they came face to face with a routine kind of racial discrimination that was totally foreign to them. A counterman at a hot dog stand, who assumed the girls were white, readily took their order. But he refused to serve their mothers, who came in a little later, since they were obviously "colored." Not used to such outrageous treatment, the girls shouted that he could keep his hot dogs, they would not eat them under any circumstances. They realized, however, that their comeback did not sound quite as militant as they meant it to be, and they dissolved into laughter as soon as they were back on the boardwalk.[26]

When a Motown tour of the segregated South encountered a more virulent strain of racism, the young performers were not laughing. Groups like the Supremes and the Miracles may have presented a respectable image on stage, but that was not enough to overcome longstanding racial strictures in the South. As the group traveled through North and South Carolina, Georgia, Alabama, Mississippi, and Florida, they discovered an America they did not know existed. Diana Ross had spent some time in Alabama during her childhood, but she had never paid much attention to the "customs" there because she was just too young to understand them. In Detroit, race had not mattered much when she was growing up. "My first school was all black and so I thought the world was like that," she remembered. "And then I had a racial mix in high school, and that didn't register because I just thought all people were the same." It was on the tour in 1962 that she began to realize "that being black somehow made you different."[27]

On the tour the Motown troupe discovered that white mechanics would refuse to service a broken-down bus if the passengers were black. They learned that white merchants were willing to shoot guns if that was what it took to keep blacks in their place. It was a real shock to learn that some Americans recognized no common bonds of humanity with black people. Or that they could be cruel enough to deny young travelers the use of the bathroom in restaurants. "We all needed to go, *bad*," Florence Ballard remembered. But when a few members of the Miracles tried to persuade a white gas station owner to accommodate the group, he chased them away with a shotgun. Eventually the owner agreed to provide a water hose and a bucket, an experience that caused Ballard to wonder whether she really wanted to be a star at all. "I grew up with white people living right next door," she explained, "and I never saw anything like this before. These damn whites in the South were *crazy*." Diana Ross echoed her astonishment. "What makes them think they're better than us?"[28]

What, indeed. It was a question black people had been asking for decades. The answer had more to do with white perceptions of race and class than it did with blacks themselves. The truth be told, "respectable" white society rarely came in contact with blacks—except as servants—and that was the way the vast majority apparently preferred to keep it. Conventional wisdom took it for granted that black people were by nature low-class, shiftless, and prone to violence. That being the case, there was no good reason to mix socially in neighborhoods or schools where children could be easily infected by these traits.

The rise of rock 'n' roll and teenage rebel culture challenged the social boundaries that had traditionally insulated the white middle class. In the South, racial segregation had long been considered the law of the land, but rock 'n' roll shows were slowly undermining this "custom." When white teenage cats (who later admitted that they wanted to be black, at least on Saturday nights) attended black rock 'n' roll dances as spectators, they sat up in the balcony, with their own kind. If they were forced to share the dance floor, as they often were in smaller venues, the groups were carefully separated by a rope barrier. Once the music got them going, however, the ropes inevitably came tumbling down, a frightening symbol of rock 'n' roll's subversive power. Although officials doggedly stopped the music until the barrier was back in place, the symbol had already lost its meaning in the crowd.[29]

The casual mix of races and styles that was a hallmark of rock 'n' roll music convinced adult critics that it was a breeding ground for bad taste, low standards, and juvenile delinquency. But race was not the only issue, especially outside the South. In fact, in Northern cities white working-class teenagers posed the same kind of threat to middle-class conventions as black teenage cats did to racial customs in the South. Although Northern critics were rarely so candid about their fears, they blamed rock 'n' roll and teenage rebel culture for a host of social problems that ranged from street gangs and teenage drinking to tight blue jeans and disrespect for authority.

They were just as determined to protect their kids from the social virus that the music represented, whether that meant moving away from mixed cities to white, middle-class suburbs or tightening the discipline in high school. The social stakes were high, as far as these critics could see, since rock 'n' rollers, whatever their race, could easily spread lower-class values to middle-class kids. With their cocky attitudes, their unconventional dress, and their frank acknowledgment of their own sexuality, teenage rock 'n' rollers mocked the cardinal rules of respectable high school life and social mobility. More interested in the present than the future, and eager to enjoy their high school years, they were already determined to strike out on their own.

chapter ten

Rock 'n' roll goes worldwide. *Library of Congress, Prints and Photographs Division, Subject file [LCUSZ 6254400]*

The Perils of Prosperity
Teenage Rebels, Teenage Sex, and the Communist Menace

As far as record promoters and mass marketers were concerned, the rise of rock 'n' roll signified a healthy expansion of teenage culture. When young consumers were spending $50 million a year on records alone, as they did in the late 1950s, even magazines like *Good Housekeeping* were willing to admit "It isn't all junk." *Seventeen*, which never noticed the rise of teenage rhythm and blues and barely mentioned Elvis, now happily endorsed rock 'n' roll as an exciting and totally appropriate expression of popular teenage culture. "Teenagers all have the same basic problems and interests," explained a young columnist in 1958, "it's only natural we create our own special brand of music."[1]

Depending on how and where the music was played—and who was doing the listening—rock 'n' roll could still be considered a threat, though. It was one thing for teenagers to dance along with "American Bandstand" while their mothers and kid sisters looked on. It was quite another when they danced on the seats at a live rock 'n' roll show in a mixed crowd of frantic teenagers. According to Jeff Greenfield, rock 'n' roll was everything that middle-class parents feared: elemental, savage, and dripping with sexuality,

155

qualities that respectable society usually associated with "depraved" lower classes. Before the rise of rock 'n' roll, middle-class high school students like Greenfield might never have encountered such people on their own, but thanks to Alan Freed and his rock 'n' roll shows, they were discovering an exotic new world of independent teenagers who felt no compunction to follow adolescent rules.

"These people are different. They do not look the way I do," Greenfield remembered thinking as he took in the scene at his first rock 'n' roll show. There were tough-looking boys dressed in black muscle shirts who looked as if they read "auto specs at night, not college catalogues." There were big-busted girls in revealing sweaters and tight black pants (or pastel pink toreadors) who thought nothing of appearing in public with their hair rolled up in curlers (camouflaged by tiny black kerchiefs they wore tied under the chin). These teenagers were loud. They chain-smoked cigarettes. They seemed to know each other very well, if not in the Biblical sense then close to it. If that was not different enough, there were black teenagers swaying to the music, an eye-opening experience for sheltered, suburban teens whose parents had fled the city just to avoid meetings like this.[2]

As far as hostile critics were concerned, this cultural exchange was a recipe for disaster. The younger generation was going to the dogs! It was bad enough that roll 'n' roll singers could not sing, critics charged, but that fact that their teenage audience did not seem to care was even worse. According to Mitch Miller, a record producer who likened rock 'n' roll to musical baby food, teenagers could not tell the difference. "They don't want recognized stars doing *their* music. They don't want real professionals. They want faceless young people doing it in order to retain the feeling that it is their own." This startling lack of good taste, he and others feared, reflected a dangerous decline in popular standards. Teenagers seemed almost compelled to join fan clubs, purchase records, and watch teenage movies for hours on end, despite the low quality of the products and the obvious waste of time—tendencies that did not bode well for the future.[3]

Adults were now making the same charges against rock 'n' roll that their parents had made against swing, and for the same reasons. The teenage world was changing dramatically, and they feared they were losing control, but the cultural context of that teenage world was remarkably different, too. In the first place, the teenage market had grown into a $9 billion enterprise, a magnitude that early promoters could not have imagined. Secondly, teenagers were now in charge, and this fact guaranteed a major shift in the style and content of teenage life. Back in the days of the swing music craze, adults still set the social pace and the direction of the teenage market. Up until around 1954, teenagers still appeared to be adolescent bobby soxers, ready, willing, and even eager to take their social cues from adults.

In fact, from the time that a majority of teenage youth found their way into high school in the mid-1930s to the moment rock 'n' roll found a national audience twenty years later, adult-directed adolescent culture had dominated the commercial teenage world. Represented first by *Scholastic* in the 1930s and then perfected by *Seventeen* in the 1940s, it was a culture of careful transition to adulthood. Adolescent "teenage" culture emphasized healthy growth, discriminating tastes, and mature acceptance of social conventions. *Seventeen*, for instance, set high standards for young readers at the same time that it hawked teenage wares; articles concerning fashions, fads, parties, and dates were always carefully balanced with solid advice about college, jobs, and planning for the future. In *Seventeen*'s adolescent world, teenage independence was a privilege to be earned, not a prerogative of age or a mark of high school status.

The advent of rock 'n' roll changed the nature of the teenage culture business, expanding the market well beyond its traditional middle-class base. Thanks to rock 'n' roll and the rebel culture associated with the music, teenagers now had a choice of social identities, whatever their family background. They could see themselves as adults-in-training and use their high school years to hone their skills and discover their talents, as adults had been preaching for years. Or they could join the fast-paced teenage-only world of (loud) music, (fast) cars, and styles that mocked the very notion of adult guidance. Like the jitterbugs, zoot suiters, and teenage cats who preceded them, teenage rebels wanted to walk on the wild side while they were still young enough and free enough to enjoy it. In the process, they turned the concept of adolescent culture on its adult-approved head: In the rock 'n' roll world of teenage rebels, the future was now and the culture was age-exclusive, defiant, and reckless to boot.

With neither a depression nor a world war to hold them back, teenage rebels had their own ideas about who they were and what they wanted to be. They were virile men, not adolescent school-boys, and they did not care who knew it. They wore their hair long in arrogant ducktails. They flaunted tough-looking, black leather jackets. They dated girls who were as daring as they were, girls who wore tight skirts, big hair, and heavy makeup. Some boys were known to play "chicken"—branding their hands to show they could "take it." Others proved their manhood with their cars. "The really big thing . . . is 'digging out' from a dead stop at an intersection," a teenage boy explained. "You jam the gas pedal down in low gear and make the tires squeal."[4]

To no one's great surprise, teenage rebels resurrected the specter of juvenile delinquency, largely because they looked the part. "We keep a watchful eye on these boys with black shirts, ducktail haircuts, and zoot suits," a police captain explained, "because they're usually up to no good."[5] Rock 'n' roll and rebel culture were blamed for everything that seemed wrong in the postwar world, from alleged teenage sex clubs that scandalized sleepy Midwestern towns and gang fights that seemed to grow more frequent and violent to vandalism, car theft, and an obvious decline in respect for parental authority.[6] Determined to keep young rebels in line with a show of force, if necessary, police offi-cers in some towns had standing orders to arrest teenagers who "lounged" on the sidewalks—a popular pastime that infuriated adults who were forced to cross the street or walk around them. "Bring some of these adolescent apes into the station and don't treat them gently," one captain told his troops. "These punks have more respect for a cop's night stick," he explained, "than for the entire Code of Criminal Procedure."[7]

During the war, the experts had argued that juvenile delin-quency was a temporary predicament. With fathers overseas and mothers busy in factories, neglected teenagers had been forced to fend for themselves in a hostile environment. However, the end of the war had not solved the problem. If anything, teenagers had grown more insolent, critics charged. An editorial cartoon in a 1956 newspaper captured public fears. It featured a showdown between an oversized teenager (who represented a gang of "hood-lums and rioters") and two adults (labeled "civic authorities" and "police") quivering in their boots. Dressed in cuffed blue jeans complete with a pack of cigarettes in the pocket, the teenage hoodlum brandished a switchblade knife as he cried, "Well! What'cha goin' to do about it?" The message was clear: Because adults had failed to hold the line against teenage rebels, they had permitted a new breed of mindless criminal to evolve.[8]

The idea that teenagers were potential delinquents at heart was a potent one in the mid-1950s. Even middle-class parents were "fed up with teenagers," as one mother told *McCall's* magazine. They were being spoiled and muddled and encouraged to think that it was "perfectly normal for them to be 'problems.'" They seemed to take it for granted that adults were old fossils, and incompetent old fossils at that. Old folks had nothing of value to pass on to the younger generation—in a modern world, it seemed as if adults were obsolete.[9] In 1953, congressional committees opened hearings on the subject that continued into the 1960s. Witnesses agreed that delinquent behavior was now part of the fabric of teenage life, not just a lower-class aberration. Even in the best of homes, they claimed, it was almost impossible to raise healthy children when movie directors, record producers, and comic book writers shamelessly ridiculed parental authority and encouraged teenagers to see themselves as a troubled class apart. Commercial vendors had seduced young innocents out of their adolescent cocoons, they insisted, and into a delinquent world of leather jackets, rock 'n' roll, and flippant attitudes toward school.[10]

Hollywood bore much of the blame. The public was willing to concede that "sympathetic" parents, teachers, and professional experts had raised a crop of impudent, irresponsible teenagers, but it was Hollywood that made them stars. For instance, no one knew what teenage rebels looked like until Marlon Brando played the sullen leader of a motorcycle gang in the 1953 hit, *The Wild One*. Since then dozens of movies had exploited the trend, including *Running Wild*, *Teenage Crime Wave*, *The Delinquents*, and *Rebel Without a Cause*. By far the most popular movie of its kind, the last starred James Dean as a handsome, tormented, middle-class teenager, the victim of bumbling, incompetent parents. The fact that Dean fatally crashed his Porsche just days before the movie opened guaranteed his status as an authentic rebel star: He lived fast, died young, and left an exceedingly good-looking corpse.

Hollywood refused to plead guilty, however. After all, movies did not create teenage tastes, they reflected them. They did not exploit delinquent behavior, they provided a forum for serious debate. Or at least that was the industry's line. For instance, the opening scene of *The Blackboard Jungle*, the movie that first associated rock 'n' roll and delinquency in the public mind, featured a sober prologue designed to establish its serious intent. "Today we are concerned with juvenile delinquency," it said, "its causes, its effects. We are especially concerned when the delinquency boils over into our schools." By making moviegoers more aware of the problem, producers argued, they were taking an important first step to finding a solution.

On one level, they were right. The public was gravely concerned with questions of delinquency and school. In fact, a shocking exposé in the New York *Daily News* had characterized public high schools as training grounds for drug addiction, vandalism, gang warfare, and sexual promiscuity.[11] According to critics, though, movies like *The Blackboard Jungle* only promoted the behavior they were purportedly trying to check. What was the point of entertaining teenage audiences with smart-mouthed boys who drove recklessly, smoked in high school bathrooms, and harassed and almost raped an inexperienced teacher? The fact that teenagers apparently cheered the delinquents on when they beat up their teachers or destroyed their property on screen did not help the producers' case. *The Blackboard Jungle* was banned in several cities, denounced by teachers, lawyers, and critics, and voted the picture that hurt America most in foreign countries by the American Legion.[12]

Critics also blamed the picture's graphic violence for teenage "riots" that erupted in movie houses, but they were missing the larger point. Teenagers "rioted" when management tried to make them stop dancing to the movie's rock 'n' roll theme, or told them to quiet down and take their feet off the seats. Adults had been trying to control teenage conduct as long as movie houses had existed, but now that teenagers dominated the audience, they intended to set the tone. Apparently, even teenagers from good neighborhoods were acting up in movie theaters, according to *Variety*. Their delinquency ranged from old-fashioned vandalism (ripping up seats and rifling candy machines) to moral turpitude (indulging in necking sessions that went far beyond "anything that is permitted on the screen"). Teenagers regularly disturbed adult patrons by laughing, throwing "missiles" from their balcony seats, and competing for the attention of unescorted girls, a situation that sometimes led to out and out brawls.[13]

Obviously, the interpretation of delinquent behavior was in the eye of the beholder: One man's riot was another's revelry. At the time, though, it was hard to tell the difference. Sensational stories of senseless teenage violence were regular newspaper fare—even the comic strip *Little Orphan Annie* offered readers a daily dose of muggings, switchblade knives, and tough-talking teenagers in 1956.[14] At the same time, official government statistics drew no real distinction between violent crimes (like rape, assault, and armed robbery) and status crimes (underage drinking, curfew violation, and driving without a license). As far as the adult public was concerned, "the numbers were going up," and that was all that mattered. According to the FBI, juvenile delinquency rose 45 percent between 1945 and 1953, and 55 percent between 1952 and 1957, but a closer look revealed that truancy and incorrigible behavior led the list in Jacksonville, Florida, for instance. In Chicago, it was curfew violation and disorderly conduct.[15] In fact, according to police estimates, only one teenage gang in ten ever committed violent crimes, and only 1 percent of the teenage population ended up in court, despite an exceedingly broad definition of criminal teenage behavior.[16]

This aggressive minority was never the real issue, however. Images of violent teenage thugs were used to sell newspapers and movie tickets, not to drum up taxpayer support for misguided, neglected, delinquent youth. There was no demand in the postwar world for government-funded training programs or teen canteens. Nor was there any concerted effort on the part of private citizens to give poor teenagers something better to do. As one social reformer put it in 1957, Americans preferred to hire more policemen to keep delinquents in line than to address underlying problems like inadequate schools, "pig-pen" housing, and racial discrimination.[17]

He had a point. Respectable parents were determined to contain delinquency, not rehabilitate delinquents. Their attention was focused on their own offspring, whose delinquency ranged from talking back and refusing to share in household tasks to going steady, staying out late, and taking the family car across state lines in order to buy beer. An article in *Cosmopolitan* put the issue in perspective when it asked the popular question "Are You Afraid of Your Teenager?" "In your neighborhood there are probably no gangs armed with switchblades, garrison belts, or zip guns," the author pointed out, but there were gangs of another kind. Teenage gangs "who get together to sandbag their parents with the cry: 'Aw, gee, Mom. Why can't I? All the others are going.'" Before a parent knew it, the teenager was off with his friends to experiment with "liquor, sex, and fast, fast cars," the motto of a defiant generation whose only question seemed to be "What are you going to do about it?"[18]

The fact was, when middle-class parents condemned juvenile delinquency, they were usually referring to working-class teenage style. High school students who refused to conform to the traditional adolescent mold could seem just as threatening as knife-wielding thieves to parents with big plans for their children's future. Working-class rebels (like Elvis Presley) mocked middle-class notions of social respect and upward mobility, reason enough to brand them as delinquents in some adult eyes. There was nothing much parents could do to shield their offspring, either, especially if they lived in the city and attended public schools. In large, centralized, comprehensive high schools, which served academic and vocational students, the best and the brightest college-bound teenagers now walked the halls with a tough-looking crowd. Even the U.S. Children's Bureau blamed the mixed population of comprehensive high schools for the alarming spread of lower-class values and "delinquent" teenage behavior.[19]

School authorities solved the immediate problem with dress and behavior codes. Tight blue jeans, ducktail haircuts, and excessive makeup were prohibited in school. "Dress Right" campaigns set appropriate high school styles that drew national attention in the late 1950s. Boys were required to wear shirts and ties, standard trousers (or neatly pressed khakis), and polished shoes (or clean white bucks). Girls were required to wear dresses or skirts and forgo pincurls, dungarees, and slacks. As an article in *Newsweek* explained the theory, "Bejeaned girls behave better when they're in ladylike dress."[20] There was a direct connection "between undisciplined dress and undisciplined behavior," high school administrators believed. In fact, one went so far as to make the link explicit. The gangster of tomorrow, he explained frankly "was the Elvis Presley type of today."[21]

Whether middle-class critics realized it or not, the classic, clean-cut adolescent styles they tried to force on high school stu-

dents had no influence on teenage behavior outside of the classroom. Strict dress and behavior codes helped weed out troublemakers who refused to toe the adult line, but they did not raise
teenage standards or change teenage minds. In fact, they usually
had the opposite effect. Students were more likely to resent adult-
imposed dress codes than they were to adopt them, especially
when the styles in question had nothing to do with their lives.

All high school students may have shared the same basic problems of growing up and establishing adult identities, but they were
not heading for the same place no matter what they wore to
school. An article in *Seventeen* on the uses of rock 'n' roll hinted at
the differences. According to the teenage author, the music provided a perfect background for day-to-day high school life, but it
was far better suited to some activities than others. Take doing
homework, a task that thousands of teenagers accomplished each
night with the help of their transistor radios. Rock 'n' roll might
be the perfect accompaniment to repetitive courses like stenography, but it just was not conducive to more complicated subjects
that required concentration, like advanced algebra or chemistry.
The fact was, rock 'n' roll could easily "make you throw down
your pencil and dance," and this, the author sagely advised, could
get in the way of serious study.[22]

The point was, some teenagers studied advanced algebra and
worked hard to get into "good" colleges; they followed a rigorous
academic program of languages, laboratory sciences, and mathematics. If they were aiming for a high status career (or a high status husband), they had no choice but to put their free time to
good use, racking up impressive experience on school newspapers, student government, and community service projects. These
were the students who honored adolescent rules of respectable
behavior and dress, the teenagers who were more likely to listen
to Pat Boone than Elvis Presley. Since their plans depended on
cooperative parents to foot the bill for college, foreign travel, or
perhaps a car and teachers to award high grades and write glow-
ing letters of recommendation, they had good reason to adopt the
wholesome, casual style adults endorsed. And since they had a
long educational road ahead of them, they had no choice but to
be as disciplined in their private lives as they were in school—or
at least to keep up appearances, which often achieved the same
result.

Others, however, the vast majority, had no special plans beyond getting a job and marrying as soon as they were out of school. These were the students who took stenography or other vocational courses. During the war, these teenagers might well have dropped out of high school in order to get a head start on "real" life, but now they were expected to stay in school long enough to graduate. Educators argued in favor of filling their days with undemanding classes and social activities that would keep them off the streets and safely occupied, but rarely challenged, in high school. Girls took home economics, typing, and life-adjustment classes (like Human Relations or Social and Personal Living) and organized sock hops, dances, and proms.[23] Their boyfriends took shop classes, played sports, and harassed their teachers, or smoked in the bathroom whenever they were feeling defiant. Once school was out, though, these students were gloriously on their own. Unconcerned with exams or grades, they could spend their free time cruising the streets with their friends, hanging around drive-in restaurants, or maybe playing pool or taunting their rivals, if that's what an evening's entertainment happened to bring.

These teenagers were not doing homework when they listened to rock 'n' roll. They were drinking beer, dancing at taverns, or cuddling with their steady dates in the back seat of a car. Content with life as they found it, for the most part, they relished the freedom and camaraderie teenage life offered. They did not expect to be teenagers for long, a fact of life that spurred them to test their limits and enjoy their youth while they had it. They may have been rebels, as their critics charged, but they were not rebelling against the adult world. They were chafing at the bit to move into it—to get out of school, get a job, get married (which was, in the 1950s, the only legitimate way to have sex). What they rebelled against was an artificial adolescent culture designed to keep them "innocent" and dependent on adults too long, goals that had nothing to do with their lives. With no plans for college or a career, they were actively seeking love and commitment during their high school years, and if they discovered passion along the way, so much the better. From their point of view, there was nothing delinquent or even precocious about going steady and falling in love. In an age that equated adulthood with marriage, these teenagers were merely getting on with their "real" lives.

By almost any measure, teenage rebels were luckier than previous generations. The consequences of taking life easy or making poor choices were not nearly as dire in the 1950s and early 1960s as they had been in the past (or would become again in the future). That was probably the most unique and potentially liberating feature of postwar teenage life. Factory jobs were plentiful, and that took the edge off academic failure for those with no talent for book learning. "You didn't have to go to college to earn a good living," explained a boy who grew up in Gary, Indiana, a steelmaking center. "Steel workers earned more money than teachers," he said. Even unskilled jobs in unionized industries paid good wages and benefits, and this made a big difference to teenage boys who wanted to test their limits before settling down. "I knew when I graduated that the steel mill was there waiting for me," another boy explained, "so I was pretty carefree during my teenage years."[24]

Before the war, working-class boys might well have taken jobs to help out their families as soon as they reached age sixteen. Now their earnings went to their clothes, their dates, but most often, their cars. There were teenagers who worked as many as forty hours a week to purchase new wheels, a serious investment in time and money that produced a wealth of social benefits. "The guy with his own car got the girls," everyone agreed, and if it happened to be a dragster or a convertible, so much the better. "If you had power packed dual exhausts, you gained instant recognition," a teenager explained. "Chicks would flock to you for a ride."[25]

Whatever type car a teenager could afford—and the choices ranged from a souped up 1930s Ford to the ultimate symbol of coolness and speed, a brand-new Chevy—teenage rebels expressed their personalities and their pride through their cars. They used everything from bright paint colors like Candy Apple Red to flame painting and dice hanging from the rearview mirrors to distinguish themselves on the road or at the drive-in. One teenager was especially proud of his 1953 Plymouth: a four-door sedan with a modified engine, a new paint job, scroll work around the door handles, and the name "Summer Nights" written in script on the fender.[26] He and his friends were so devoted to their customized cars that their girlfriends were known to get jealous, particularly when the boys spent their free time simonizing fenders or checking carburetors late into the night.

To some adults, of course, "hot rods" were just another sign of juvenile delinquency. It was bad enough that teenage "motorheads" spent time and money on their cars instead of their schoolwork, but the teenage love affair with the automobile also opened up a world of aimless amusement that was completely beyond a parent's reach. This was not a postwar phenomenon. Even in the early 1940s, high school students had a reputation for driving as far and fast as their cars could go.[27] At the time, however, it was only the high school elite who could afford to waste whole afternoons in their cars, and nobody seemed particularly alarmed by the prospect. These teenagers were not the type to pose a public threat!

After the war, however, the mainstream majority could get into the game. In hundreds of towns and cities teenagers took over the roads on weekends, "cruising" for hours on end. If kids couldn't drive, they walked—the girls waving as car horns tooted, the boys jumping in with their friends when a car slowed down. "Guys could be cruel though," recalled a girl who spent many an evening cruising on foot. "Once I was walking with a friend who was a little chunky, and somebody yelled 'Hey Streamline.' My girlfriend turned around, and a boy yelled, 'Not you, boxcar!' "[28]

Cruising routes also doubled as drag strips, a popular but dangerous way for boys to show off. "We'd have the top down and the radio on, being cool," a weekend racer recalled. "At stop lights guys would pull alongside you. You'd look at each other and smile, each thinking, 'I'll show this punk.' " When the light changed, they'd take off with their souped-up motors roaring. That is, unless, the police interfered and stopped them for reckless driving. Then there would be fines to pay and forced attendance at a driving school, where there would be horrifying pictures of accident victims to remind young rebels of their own mortality.[29]

Cars offered teenagers much more than status and speed; they also offered privacy, still a prized commodity in the working-class world. A boy with a car had a place that he could call his own, where parents, grandparents, and kid brothers could not barge in, unlike what he could expect at home. A boy with a car had a place to entertain dates and a perfect opportunity to get to know them better. After an evening of dancing or movie watching, teenage boys could easily suggest a drive to the beach to "watch the submarine races"—typical code words for parking or "making out."

"When we first got there," a girl remembered her parking days, "we would cruise around and talk to other couples. Then when the guys got a few beers into their systems, they'd try to get something." Apparently, everyone knew that if a car window was really steamed up, the couple was making love, or coming quite close to it. Friends were known to knock on the glass to slow the action down![30]

This was not something people talked about, however, except in the abstract. It was not something that teenage girls entered into lightly. A girl's good name still carried a great deal of weight in high school, and even teenage rebels took their reputations seriously. They had to; if they were looking forward to marriage and a family, they had to command respect. Boys rarely felt any social obligation to girls they considered sluts. "Most of the girls I went out with nobody would have wanted for a steady girl friend, if you know what I mean," a promiscuous boy remembered. But nobody held it against him. It was still a girl's place to set the sexual standard, and she bore all the blame when passion went too far. As one father put it bluntly after his teenage daughter revealed her accidental pregnancy, boys would always be boys, but girls who let them get away with it were "damn stupid."[31]

Sylvia Plath, the future poet and a Smith College student in the early 1950s, deeply resented the duplicitous roles "good" high school girls were still required to play. The ambitious daughter of a widowed mother, she knew she had no choice but to follow the straight and narrow path that led to a college scholarship, but that did not mean she enjoyed the game. Practical enough to live by adolescent conventions, she privately seethed at a code of sexual ethics that rewarded boys and punished girls for the very same behavior. "I have too much conscience injected in me to break customs without disastrous effects," she wrote in her high school journal. "I can only lean enviously against the boundary and hate, hate, hate, the boys who dispel sexual hunger freely . . . while I drag out from date to date in soggy desire, always unfulfilled." Summing up the credo that guided high school students, she added, "We go on dates, we play around, and if we're nice girls, we demur at a certain point."[32]

Plath was describing a sexual double standard that would never completely disappear, but her frustration had as much to do with her plans for the future as her sex. Had she been willing to marry young, as teenage rebels tended to do, she would have had other options. In fact, in the mainstream world of less ambitious teenagers, heavy petting was a fact of high school life. As one reporter put it in 1951, "Students insist it is not a thing that 'some girls do, but nice girls don't'—almost everybody does it." And the experts were on their side. They believed that girls like Plath were headed for a lifetime of frigidity. Teenagers needed to learn that "good body feelings were permissible," *Parents* magazine pointed out and that there existed "safe and harmless ways of finding temporary, partial gratification."[33] That is, they needed to learn that "sexual experience, short of intercourse" could solve their frustrations and prepare them for a happy family life.[34]

If the Kinsey Report and others could be believed, however, teenage rebels did not need expert advice or permission to indulge—and apparently neither had their parents. As one woman who came of age in the mid-1950s put it, the real difference between good teenagers and bad was a matter of appearance: Good teenagers kept their private lives private, which meant, in effect, they remained "technical virgins." "You pretended that the old proprieties still held," she explained "but went to the edge of breaking them."[35] However, she and her friends took it for granted that they would marry soon after high school, sometimes even sooner than they expected. Whatever the experts thought about appropriate teenage boundaries, there was a direct connection between "good body feelings" and sexual intercourse. After all, what the experts called petting in the teenage world of beach blankets and back seats was usually called foreplay in adult bedrooms.

Teenage rebels understood the rules of the game. Going steady marked the beginning of the end of teenage life, since it started a couple's sexual clock. From that point forward a girl could measure a boy's sincerity and set a level of physical affection that matched the strength of his commitment. One girl recalled how she decided to let her boyfriend go "above the waist" after attending a formal high school dance. "We had been going steady for about six months, and I knew that he really cared about me, so I let him go a little farther than ever before." By the time they were seniors, they were already engaged to be married, so on prom night she let him go farther still, almost "all the way." Her gradual acceptance of an adult relationship was typical for steady couples. "Most of my friends lost their virginity to high school sweethearts about a year or so into an intense relationship," a woman remembered, a step that almost inevitably resulted in marriage.[36]

No one was particularly worried when working-class rebels married young. On the contrary, their decision to settle down often came as a relief to their elders. Premarital sex could not be hidden for long when condoms, withdrawal, and vinegar douches were the most accessible forms of birth control. In fact, eighteen was becoming the most popular age for brides. By 1960, 24 percent of eighteen-year-old females had already walked down the aisle. When middle-class teenagers began to follow their lead, going steady while they were still in high school and favoring sex and romance over higher education, though, the situation seemed more ominous.[37] Even *Seventeen* was forced to acknowledge that teenage couples were more experienced than they looked. "What seems to have happened," sociologist David Riesman explained, "is that the middle class has been losing its traditional orientation to the future ... and that the permissiveness ... [of] the lower strata has now become a matter of principle" among educated youth— a scholarly way of saying that the virus of rebel culture had infected the better classes, as critics had feared from the start.[38]

It was one thing for teenagers with no talent for school to waste their youth on rock 'n' roll, hot rods, and romance, but it was a political catastrophe, in some adult eyes, when the best and the brightest middle-class teenagers also adopted rebel ways. Or at least that was what politicians concerned with the cold war and the spread of communism seemed to think. The nation was in dire need of doctors, scientists, engineers, and highly trained technicians, these cold warriors insisted. How could the United States hope to beat the Soviet Union in future contests, they wanted to know, if the cream of the teenage crop favored risk and romance over serious schoolwork?[39] Indeed, after the Soviet Union successfully launched its Sputnik satellite in 1957—the same year that "American Bandstand" began broadcasting to a national audience—the link between teenage rebel culture and the communist threat seemed clear.

An article in *Life* magazine, "Crisis in Education," illustrated the connection. Contrasting the experience of two high school students, a teenager with a steady girlfriend in the United States and an adolescent just beginning to notice the opposite sex in the Soviet Union, the article pointed up the political consequences of a teenage leisure world. The American joked his way through math class and relied on comic book condensations to write book reports, and despite his obvious intelligence he seemed totally unconcerned with his mediocre grades. His English-speaking Soviet counterpart, on the other hand, took five years of physics, four of chemistry, and math, astronomy, and technical drawing classes, along with very demanding courses in literature and history. After school the young communist continued his education, visiting science museums, practicing the piano, and playing chess for amusement. The American teenager, however, followed a far more leisurely pace, dating, dancing, and swimming his young life away instead of earnestly preparing for his future. Could anyone be surprised that the Soviet Union beat the United States into space after comparing these high school experiences?[40] Considering the technological demands of cold war competition, could any American now deny that the rock 'n' roll generation would have to set its sights a good deal higher than dating, mating, and living happily ever after?

James B. Conant, former president of Harvard University, and a chemist who had helped develop the atomic bomb during the Second World War, did not think so. With a grant from the Carnegie Corporation, he visited fifty-five high schools in eighteen states in 1958. His goal was to measure the rigor of American schools and to study the programs of high-ranked students to see if they were being adequately challenged and trained to assume leadership in a technological world. High school students needed four years of English, mathematics, and foreign languages to be competitive, he concluded, and three years of science and social studies. They also had to spend at least fifteen hours a week on homework, an assignment that would almost certainly limit their free time for rock 'n' roll and romance. When a colleague complained that this "get tough" policy ignored the fact that high school students were at "the most social and fun-loving period of their lives," Conant dismissed the criticism as irrelevant. Instead, he saluted another colleague who agreed that too many high school teachers favored "leisure" over "learning," a side effect of progressive educational reforms that he believed had been gutting high school programs since the 1930s.[41]

While Conant was preparing his report, which was published in 1959, the federal government was also priming the educational pump, an accomplishment it took the communist threat to achieve. The National Science Foundation increased its educational budget from $1.5 million in 1952 to $84.5 million in 1962, and federal funds to beef up academic high school programs were also made available through the 1958 National Defense Education Act. Thanks to the cold war, and especially to Sputnik, the number of foreign language labs increased from sixty-four to over a thousand between 1958 and 1960, while the number of specialists in science, math, and foreign languages increased by a factor of five. "Schools forced math and science down our throats with little regard for our aptitude," a former student remembered. "And some schools changed their hours, adding extra periods and cutting into free time. If political propaganda didn't make us hate the Communists," she added, "the education race did."[42]

This cold war push for more rigorous high schools and more competitive students was designed to separate the middle-class wheat from the rebel chaff, but it was couched in the language of democracy: An educated teenage population was the best defense against the communist menace, reformers insisted. In this context, democracy was just an ideological foil, not a practical way of life. New and improved high school programs were never intended to boost the learning power of the teenage population overall, or open doors to teenagers who did not grow up in educated homes or were not usually welcome in professional circles. At best, Conant intended to rescue the "right kids" (about 15 percent of the high school population, in his estimation) from a teenage rebel culture of mediocrity. In the process, he would groom them to play strategic roles in the competitive adult world.

Although nobody said it out loud at the time, Conant made his plans with boys in mind, white middle-class boys. After all, these were the students that had always counted. To be sure, the educator had no intention of barring girls from demanding classes if they could keep up with the work, but as far as Conant was concerned, girls would not be playing professional roles in the future; they were destined for motherhood, in his estimation. He had even lower expectations for the mass of high school students. Since they had no talent for science or technology, they simply were not worth investing in, Conant privately believed. In fact, he thought they should be encouraged to drop out of high school at the first opportunity.[43]

Conant was hailed as a great educational reformer and modern patriot, but his ideas seemed strangely rooted in the past. The schools he envisioned were state-of-the-art, but his ideal student body harked back to the days before the Great Depression, when only a tiny minority earned a diploma. His conception of high school students was equally dated. Conant seemed to believe that adults could produce the kind of teenagers they wanted by tightening high school requirements and channeling students into adult-approved roles. He was overlooking the fact that high school students, even the best and the brightest high school students, drew their own conclusions from the world around them, no matter what lessons adults intended to teach in school. Even if they "dressed right" and grudgingly played by the rules, as middle-class teenagers were wont to do in the 1950s, that was no guarantee that they internalized the rigid social codes their elders valued. Even if experts like Conant persuaded teenagers that their patriotic duty was to take school seriously, they could not determine how teenagers would use their education or even which teenagers would actually benefit from this advice.

For instance, Conant may have aimed his cold war message of ambition and excellence at an all-male audience. Like it or not, though, girls heard the message, too. Many took it seriously, an unintended consequence of cold war rhetoric that ironically pushed girls into college and nourished professional dreams. "No one said, 'Just boys—just you boys study hard.' This was on everyone's head," a girl who grew up to be a college professor pointed out. "We had to get A's as well," she added, "to fend off the red peril and save our country and ourselves." In the process, many girls discovered they could do anything boys did in school, and they could do it just as well.[44]

No one said "just whites," either, although that was not something that needed to be said in the late 1950s. As the debate over rock 'n' roll and the spread of rebel culture indicated, the forces of social segregation still ran strong in the postwar world. Cold warriors might preach an inspiring gospel of democracy when it came to iron curtain countries, but as far as life in these United States were concerned, they inevitably preferred to keep to their own kind in their neighborhoods, their churches, but especially their schools.[45] In fact, by the end of the decade, it was painfully clear that many upstanding American citizens were willing to violate the law of the land if that was what it took to keep their high schools "lily white." And they were willing to demonstrate, in courts, on the street, and on national television, that the "American way" they promoted overseas did not apply to black citizens in the South.

Ultimately this duplicity proved to be far more damaging to the fabric of American life than teenage rebel culture ever was. Wholesome high school students or rock 'n' roll fans, teenagers tended to lose respect for adult authority whenever they caught their elders in a lie. As Holden Caufield, the privileged prep school character in J. D. Salinger's *The Catcher in the Rye* had pointed out in 1951, teenagers had a low tolerance for adult phonies.[46] Whether this was a sign of adolescent idealism or naiveté was not the point. Teenagers expected adults to practice what they preached, especially when it came to ethical issues like justice, fairness, and equality. They were learning every day, though, that adults played by different rules. "We as a generation received the earliest lessons in hypocrisy in history," Jeff Greenfield put it bluntly.[47]

At the time, he was talking about the impact of television on middle-class rebels. Weekly favorites like "I Love Lucy," "My Little Margie," and "Beulah" gave the younger generation a crash course in adult reality. They learned that "dishonesty, fear and pretense were the dominant values of domestic life"; that "Negroes could be maids . . . or fools . . . or bug-eyed elevator operators," but they could not live on the same blocks or even in the same neighborhoods as whites; that "grown-ups did not do what they told us to, and did not live by the precepts they taught us."[48]

Disillusion was nothing new, of course; it was part of the process of growing up. But the pace of that process was accelerating in the late 1950s and 1960s, transforming the teenager's traditional desire for autonomy into mocking contempt of the adult world. In a sense, the superior education the younger generation now enjoyed (or endured) only strengthened this aspect of teenage culture. The best and the brightest teenagers, both black and white, had higher expectations of what the world could be, and what individuals should be, than their elders could ever remember imagining. By the late 1950s they were determined to do something about it.

chapter eleven

Central High School, Little Rock, Arkansas, 1958. *Library of Congress, Prints and Photographs Division, U.S. News and World Report Magazine Collection [LCU9 1538]*

The Content of
Their Character

Black Teenagers and
Civil Rights in the South

BY 1957, TEENAGERS HAD ALREADY TAKEN THEIR PLACE AS THE
nation's most exciting new consumer market. Magazines like *Cosmopolitan* were publishing special teenage issues with articles entitled "The Nine Billion Dollars in Hot Little Hands." Eugene
Gilbert had done enough marketing studies to prove that Americans were not living in the Atomic Age or even the Feverish
Fifties: They were living in the Time of the Teenager. High school
rebels set the pace in the world of popular music, movies, fashion,
and car design. Even old-line companies like Elgin Watch and
United Fruit were paying attention to teenagers. "When kids
speak, we listen and act accordingly," an advertising executive
explained. "You're out of business," an article in *Variety* reported,
"unless you get the teens."[1]

But the "kids" and "teens" they were talking about and the
teenagers featured in national publications were by no means a
cross-section of the high school population. They were invariably
white. As far as the national market was concerned, there was no

other kind of teenager. Rock 'n' roll may have brought black music and black teenage stars into the public spotlight. It may have catapulted the teenage market out of high school and into the street. But the rise of rock 'n' roll and the vast expansion of the teenage market did not create the racially integrated culture that adult critics feared. Black teenagers were still invisible as far as mainstream society was concerned.

That was par for the course. Black adults were invisible for the most part, too, except in their traditional roles as entertainers, domestic workers, and porters. In fact, in the mid-1950s, *Variety* reported that negro actors were being eliminated from television shows. Apparently their presence made white viewers feel guilty![2] Before the decade was over, however, white Americans would get to know a whole new cast of negro characters who would dominate the evening news—lawyers, ministers, and freedom fighters who tapped the energy of black teenage rebels to build a national civil rights movement. When the U.S. Supreme Court ruled against racially segregated public schools in *Brown* v. *Board of Education* in 1954, the decision eventually thrust black teenagers into the public eye in a way that rock 'n' roll only hinted at.

Initially, there was no indication that the *Brown* decision would have any real impact on American life except to speed up white flight to the suburbs.[3] Legal decisions were one thing; legal enforcement another, especially in the lily-white South, where racial segregation was a way of life. There were those who firmly believed that the *Brown* decision was the first step toward "mixed marriages, miscegenation, and the mongrelization of the human race," a notion that was key to their rabid opposition to rock 'n' roll. Unfortunately for the rest of the nation, these white supremacists held the balance of political and social power in the South.[4]

In Mississippi, for instance, state officials vowed to ignore the *Brown* decision. In fact, a local judge launched the White Citizens' Council to protect "blue-eyed, golden-haired" Southern girls from mixing with brutish black classmates. A newspaper editor backed him up, issuing a stark warning to those who supported integrated schools. "Human blood may stain southern soil in many places because of this decision," he said, and "the dark red stains of that blood will be on the marble steps of the United States Supreme Court Building." His words took on an eerie ring when Emmett Till, an "uppity" black teenager from Chicago, was brutally murdered in Mississippi for the crime of whistling at a white woman—just the kind of insolent behavior fostered by integrated schools, opponents thought. "Did you hear about that fourteen-year-old boy who was killed in Greenwood?" a white woman asked her fifteen-year-old black housekeeper. "He was killed because he got out of his place," she pointed out.[5]

According to this woman, and those who thought like her, Southern black teenagers would never make the same mistake. After all, they were reminded every day that they neither inhabited the same social world as their white counterparts nor deserved the same opportunities to develop and prosper. Their schools were underfunded and dilapidated, their textbooks used and out of date. Their teachers were forced by practical circumstances to uphold the rules of racial etiquette that governed life in the South. A white Southerner who spent his teenage years in the rural South remembered those rules well. "When a black person approached a doorway at the same time as a white adult, the black stepped back and sometimes even held the door open for the white to enter," he explained. "The message I received from hundreds of such signals was always the same: I was white; I was different; I was superior. It was not a message with which an adolescent boy was apt to quarrel."[6]

Black teenagers, on the other hand, had no good reason to internalize these rules. Like teenagers everywhere, they did not always learn the same lessons from life that adults intended to teach them. When a thirteen-year-old contemplated the differences between white and black water fountains, for instance, he did not assume that he somehow deserved a broken-down, dirty fixture. On the contrary, such obvious inequality awakened him to the hypocrisy that shaped American life and shook his faith in some of the things he learned about in school, like the Constitution of the United States. "I couldn't believe that on the one hand they're saying this is the greatest country in the world with all this freedom, and I can't even go to the movies here if I wanted to," he said.[7]

Although their parents often warned them that black people had no choice but to go along to get along, teenagers were not easily persuaded. Fifteen-year-old Claudette Colvin, for instance, understood that white people held all the economic cards that mattered in the South. Yet she still resented the fact that adults accepted life as given: They were always respectful to white people and never said much about it. She and her young friends were more rebellious and looked for ways to subvert the system, especially if they could have a good laugh at white expense. When a local department store refused to let them try on hats, for instance, the black teenagers quietly broke the rule anyway. They got a friend who was light enough to "pass" to try on hats and shoes.[8]

Because she lived in Montgomery, Alabama, where the National Association for the Advancement of Colored People, or NAACP, was active, Colvin got a better high school education than she would have gotten elsewhere. Booker T. Washington High attracted good teachers educated in the North who were determined to "prick" their students' minds, as Colvin put it, to get them to start thinking. For instance, a very dark teacher announced to the class that she was African and proud of it, a radical statement at a time when light complexions (and white blood) were still a mark of status in the black community. The same teacher made it clear that there was no such thing as "good" or "bad" hair, heresy to black high school students obsessed with the subject. These discussions forced Colvin to rethink her values, and she decided to stop straightening her hair. Her friends thought she was crazy, since Claudette would surely lose her boyfriend. On that score they were right. When the fifteen-year-old came to school with tiny braids all over her head, her boyfriend wanted nothing to do with her.

At this point in Colvin's young life, however, popularity had lost its luster. She was more concerned with the question of negro rights. A fellow student had been falsely accused of raping a white woman, and authorities had kept him in jail until he was old enough to be executed. Although they no doubt intended to intimidate young blacks with this cruel and unjust treatment, their ruthlessness enraged her.[9] She did not set out to challenge the racial system, but in March 1955, she took a stand that paved the way for the Montgomery bus boycott, which put the civil rights movement on the national map. Seated directly across from a white woman when she rode the bus, she refused to give up her seat, although she was clearly in violation of local law.

Her impromptu sit-in ended with handcuffs and a visit to the police station, but it also drew the attention of Montgomery residents already involved in the movement. Rosa Parks, who would gain national fame that December when she refused to give up her seat on the bus, introduced Claudette to high school students who were just as angry as she was. That there were others, many others, in fact, who shared her outrage surprised Colvin, who was always odd girl out in her working-class neighborhood. Most of the kids she knew were more concerned with their social lives than the world around them. Had she lived on the other side of town, however, the middle-class side that housed activists like Rosa Parks, E. D. Nixon, and Dr. Martin Luther King, she might have had an easier time in school, she thought.

She was probably right. In Montgomery and other Southern cities, middle-class teenagers were providing the shock troops for the civil rights movement that took off in 1956. They did not have the experience, the fears, or the comfort of community status that sometimes paralyzed their elders. In fact, they were not only willing but eager to put segregation to the test. A group of teenage boys in Birmingham, Alabama, who called themselves the Eagles, for instance, moved the "colored" sign whenever they rode the bus. Or sometimes they defied it, choosing to sit right behind the driver. When he got off to call the police, as the driver inevitably did, the Eagles would disappear, ready to take up the lethal game again another day, on another bus.[10]

Much like the military during the Second World War, the civil rights movement depended on aggressive, adventuresome teenagers to make legal victories a practical reality in the South. In a sense, it depended on teenage naiveté, too. The teenagers who led the fight to integrate high schools, for instance, did not expect the violent resistance they met. Leslie McLemore, a teenager in Wall, Mississippi, just took it for granted that he would attend a white high school when the term began in the fall.[11] He and other optimistic teenagers had not counted on the rise of White Citizens' Councils or the fact that congressmen from eleven states would sign a "Southern Manifesto" against school integration.[12] Hard experience would teach them that they had to take their rights since no one in authority was going to pave the way. White people were not giving anything away, teenage activists told their friends. If they wanted change they would have to change, too. They could not just sit back and wait.[13]

They could not expect to be protected, either, once they accepted the challenge to integrate schools. Even the most sympathetic white teachers would not take up their fight. Instead, adults encouraged black teenagers to fade into the background. If they wanted access to the same facilities and programs that white students took for granted, black teenagers had to give up all rights to participate in high school life and mask their personalities in unfailing politeness. They had to accept the fact that there would be no playing on the football team, no joining the band, no going to the senior prom. They also had to realize that if they lost their temper or responded to cruel or petty remarks they would be on their own. "They were brave kids," a woman who remembered the struggle said, much braver than she had been at the time. "I knew the kind of personality I had," she readily admitted. "I would not [have been] able to withstand that kind of abuse."[14]

She was wise to recognize her limits, since abuse was a core ingredient of the fight. At Clinton High, in Tennessee, one of the first white schools to act on integration, it took the National Guard to prevent townspeople from attacking twelve black teenagers assigned to the school. Apparently a rabid segregationist was passing around pictures of white women embracing black men, to remind white parents of their children's integrated fate. The unruly mobs initially won the battle by frightening the students away, but their terrifying tactics eventually lost the war. As one student put it, the experience of being beaten on the street by grown women shouting "nigger" unleashed something in his soul that was much more powerful than fear. "I won't say I wasn't afraid after that," he told a reporter who covered the story for *Collier's* magazine. "But it came to me for the first time that I had a right to go to school. I realized that it was those other people who were breaking the law, not me."[15]

Unfortunately, those other people, hateful though they were, set the ground rules in the South. More often than not they got their unconstitutional way when it came to school integration. Ricky Shuttlesworth and her sister Pat, for instance, tried to integrate Phillips High School in Birmingham in 1957, but they did not come close to a classroom that year. As the daughters of a Baptist preacher active in the civil rights movement (whose home had been firebombed on Christmas 1956), they had no expectations of a warm welcome. However, they did not expect the angry mob that surrounded the school, either. Before the girls could even get out of their parents' car, they saw the crowd beat their father with chains, an experience so personally devastating that Pat and Ricky never discussed it. When they learned that their mother had been stabbed as well, they felt even worse.[16]

The sad fact that no one interceded or tried to stop the crowd both amazed and infuriated local teenagers. "We actually saw hundreds and hundreds of white people standing around watching others beat a black man," Myrna Carter said. "And no one was going to his defense." James Roberson was enraged when he realized that nothing would come of the episode, either. How could it be that people could stab a woman for no reason at all and get away with it? He had a strong feeling at the time that people like that did not deserve to live. "I wished I could just go out and get a gun and kill them all," he recalled, reliving the rage he felt that day.[17]

Hoping to avoid such violent outbursts, school administrators in Little Rock, Arkansas, had been trying to devise a workable desegregation plan since the summer of 1955. By the time it was put into practice in 1957, however, its primary purpose was to pacify racist opponents, not to protect black teenagers. Originally a school committee at Central High had planned discussions with parents and students to prepare them for the coming change. The committee even invited a prominent black physician to address a school assembly in order to demonstrate to students that blacks could be capable and productive citizens. That plan was dropped before it even got started, however. Instead, the district superintendent assumed full responsibility and warned teachers not to get involved. "So we did nothing," admitted the vice-principal for girls, Elizabeth Huckaby, a decision she came to regret in 1957, when white racists took the upper hand in Little Rock.

The superintendent's plan was designed to contain the problem. Only one senior high school would accept black transfers, limiting the number of students affected. At the same time, high school officials had whittled down the number of black applicants from eighty to seventeen and then hand-picked the final nine. As far as the superintendent was concerned, no one had any reason to worry—no one that mattered, that is. Before the school term opened, though, there were unmistakable signs that even this conservative plan was too much for white racists. Late in August a newly organized Mothers' League applied for a court injunction against integrated schools. With Governor Orval Faubus's help, they won their case. He testified that teenagers in Little Rock were armed and ready to do battle, although no one else could confirm this plan. A federal court overturned this decision, but Faubus upped the ante in this state's rights tug of war: He called out the National Guard and explicitly ordered them to keep the Little Rock Nine, as the black teenagers came to be called, out of Central High.

Even after a federal court responded with an order to integrate the school, the governor and his racist band stood firm. With state troops to back them up, an angry mob of parents and students effectively kept the nine out of school. On September 23, a federal court order replaced state troops with local police who were pledged to protect the students, not the angry crowd. They were not enough to turn the tide in Little Rock, however. Although black students took their places in class without incident that day, local radio stations reported a violent response that panicked parents, who now barged into school to take their children home. Unable to control the adult crowd, the chief of police dismissed the black students instead, and they in turn chose not to return until their safety could be guaranteed. Ernest Green, the only senior in the group, remembered that afternoon well. After watching the rioters on television, he realized how life-threatening the situation had really been. When neighbors warned him that the federal government would never support the Little Rock Nine, he began to fear that he wouldn't graduate high school that year.

Within two days, however, the U.S. 101st Airborne Division took over Central High, and the atmosphere immediately changed. Segregationists were outraged by this federal occupation, which President Dwight D. Eisenhower only reluctantly permitted. At the same time, they were a little less willing to harass black students in public. "These were no lounging, half-trained civilians in uniform," Elizabeth Huckaby reported. "These were armed professionals, moving with astonishing efficiency." With playing fields overrun with trucks, jeeps, field kitchens, and pup tents, and armed guards in and around the school, there was no question that the military intended to keep order. There was no question either that the Little Rock Nine would now attend classes, since they could count on a military escort to protect them. "For the first time in my life," explained Minniejean Brown, one of the most outspoken members of the young group, "I felt like an American citizen."[18]

As long as the Airborne Division patrolled the corridors, it looked as if life would proceed normally at Central. Huckaby was relieved and noted the change in her diary: "Atmosphere more relaxed; pencil thrown at Melba in Miss Dewberry's class. Lipstick writing, 'Nigger go home,' on rest room walls . . . some positive items, too. Colored and white at one table in cafeteria . . . home room president [shook] hands with Ernest Green when they were introduced." This was just the lull before the storm, however, induced by the military presence. When the Airborne Division was ordered out on September 30, and the now federalized Arkansas National Guard replaced them, the black students were on their own again in enemy territory. School administrators, still underestimating the power of the racist crowd, had requested federalized troops to stay in the background. Even after the Airborne Division returned temporarily, the situation continued to deteriorate for the nine.

During the first few months of the conflict, students like Ernest Green had felt almost confident. The combination of federal troops and national news coverage encouraged the most rabidly segregationist students to boycott classes. Once they realized that black students were at Central to stay, however, the racist crowd returned. From that moment on, Central High became a combat zone.[19] Without troops in the hallways, teenage segregationists thought nothing of tripping black students, pouring ink on their clothes, or threatening the few white students who were brave enough to speak to the nine. Convinced that they had a constitutional right to harass black students, the most hostile teenagers routinely called them "nigger" to their faces, or tried to force them out of school.[20] There were some teachers, including Huckaby, who allowed black students to hide out in their offices or classrooms, but there were others who flaunted their racist beliefs. Ernest Green remembered gym class as one of the most dangerous and disappointing, since his instructors made it clear that he was not welcome there. "You got the feeling they deliberately put you with the most hostile kids," he said.[21]

Minniejean Brown soon emerged as the favorite target. She was the most volatile of the group and thus the most vulnerable black student, too. When antagonists tripped her she always tried to fight back. When they called her "nigger," she called them "white trash." Since she refused to follow the code of "good" black behavior, which required her to defer to whites of any age, she had few allies at Central. Although her teachers witnessed the organized hate campaign she was forced to endure every day, they believed she was asking for trouble when she stood up for herself.

If her teachers had been willing to do their professional duty and support her constitutional rights, Minniejean might not have had to fight so hard. As it was, however, even sympathetic teachers thought the "crisis" would work itself out when black teenagers learned how to fade into the crowd and avoided "offending" white sensibilities. No teacher, for instance, would back a black student's request to play on the football team, attend a dance, or appear on stage with white students. In fact, when Minniejean asked Mrs. Huckaby if she could audition for the junior show, since she had a very fine voice, the vice-principal calmly turned her down. "You know as well as I do that it wouldn't do, Minniejean," she explained, as if local custom were the law of the land. The principal took the same cautious approach when he barred the black teenager from performing with the Glee Club at a Christmas show, although she was an active member of the group.[22] Like Huckaby, he seemed more concerned with the outraged feelings of racist taxpayers (who paid his salary) than he was with the students he was hired to serve.

So when white racist students harassed poor Minniejean in the lunchroom, just days before Christmas in 1957, she did what any other angry sixteen-year-old might have done: She dropped her bowl of chili over the heads of two boys who shoved chairs in her way and called her names.[23] In so doing, however, she played right into segregationists' hands: She was suspended, and eventually expelled. But it wasn't the chili that sealed her fate. As Mrs. Huckaby explained, the real truth was "that we could no longer run the school if Minniejean was there. There were plenty of marginal youngsters who would be glad to . . . gain the approval of their group by souping Minniejean week after week—or even day after day." Since Minniejean was, in Huckaby's estimation, "too impulsive, too ready to come back at people, too unprepared to accept the heavy responsibilities of her difficult situation"—in other words, too "uppity" to avoid attacks—the school had no other choice. No wonder the racist teenagers viewed her expulsion as a victory and confidently passed out cards boasting, "One down, eight to go."[24]

Without the support of the local NAACP, black fraternities and sororities, and their families, the eight students left at Central High might have followed Minniejean out the door. There was precious little support for their efforts in the school itself. White students who started out being friendly were ostracized for their efforts. Students seen talking to blacks in the halls received threatening phone calls at home. In fact, when a few white students joined the blacks on a radio program, their efforts to bridge the racial divide only resulted in hate mail. Unbeknownst to white or black students at Central, however, there was one teenager working undercover to sabotage the racist crowd. Sixteen-year-old Ira Lipman, a senior who belonged to the country club where Ernest Green worked, was feeding information to John Chancellor, the television reporter who made the struggle at Central High a national issue. Lipman always whispered when he made his calls from a pay phone outside the school, since he knew the risk he was taking, but he wanted to help dismantle a system that would not allow him to associate with Green, a teenager who struck him as a pleasant, intelligent, and gentle individual, the kind of person Lipman valued as a friend.[25]

The fight to integrate high schools in the South met with mixed results in Little Rock. Ernest Green graduated with his class, but no senior sat on either side of him, and no one cheered when his name was called. Only his family clapped. "It was eerie, quiet," Green remembered, but he was not particularly concerned. At the time his mind was not on the cosmic issues his graduation raised. He just wanted to get across the stage without tripping and then go home to celebrate with his friends.

Years later he took pride in the job that he and his friends began in 1957. Although Central High closed its doors in 1958, it opened the following year as an integrated high school. "We were all ordinary kids," Green explained, kids who learned that "you really do have the ability to do a lot more than . . . you've been led to believe by your surroundings. If given the opportunity," he added, "you'd be surprised at how much you can do, how much you can achieve."[26]

The fight was reenacted in school district after school district for the next ten years. The results were not particularly encouraging. Only 11 percent of almost seven thousand school districts in the South and border states had integrated by 1961.[27] Three years later, less than 2 percent of black students in eleven Southern states attended racially mixed schools. When thirteen black students integrated Lanier High School in Montgomery, Alabama, in 1965, white students still harassed them in the hallways and refused to sit next to them in class. By this time, however, black students were getting used to struggling to claim their rights, and they kept their eyes on the prize of opportunity. "We weren't going there to be liked. That's why I didn't get all uptight about it," Delores Boyd explained. "I went there to do as well as I could and go on to the next stage. I wanted to be a lawyer." Her plan worked out and she reached her goal, but in the process she learned a more important lesson. "I realized I shouldn't make white people my standard. It's not that we're looking for association because we think association makes us as good as they are. It's that there are opportunities here that we are not being given."[28]

Black teenagers and college students took the struggle for civil rights beyond the classroom and into the community in the 1960s, organizing sit-ins at segregated lunch counters, bus stations, movie theaters, and restaurants—public accommodations, which by law had to serve blacks as well as whites. This phase of the campaign began in Greensboro, North Carolina, when four black college students wearing jackets and ties sat down to eat at a whites-only lunch counter at Woolworth's. Refusing to leave without being served, they stayed at the counter until closing time. The following day they came back with twenty-five others, and the day after that twenty-five more. Within five days some three hundred students made it clear to television cameras that they knew their place, and it was at the lunch counter. Their daring determination touched off similar demonstrations at Woolworth stores North and South. By March there were sit-ins in fifty-four cities in nine states, and by April these young black demonstrators had organized the Student Nonviolent Coordinating Committee, or SNCC, to end segregation through direct action.[29]

"In order to change the law, we had to break the law," explained Ricky Shuttlesworth, who was just sixteen years old when she joined the campaign. "The only way you could change things was to demonstrate."[30] That required enormous self-discipline, however. The point was to occupy all the seats at a counter (to keep money from coming in), not get beaten up in an angry brawl. There were teenagers who thought the fight would be over that much sooner if they could just get angry and burn something down, a woman who went to high school in Selma, Alabama, recalled, but she came to appreciate nonviolence as a strategy once she realized how dangerous a sit-in could be. It could lead to jail, it could lead to violence, it could lead to getting seriously hurt, but that was just part of the process for teenagers determined to win their rights. "We had our minds set on freedom," as one woman put it, "and that was it."[31]

High school and college students who manned the lunch counter sit-ins in 1960 and the Freedom Rides in 1961 awakened the nation to the stark reality of race hatred. The undeclared war in the South between black and white citizens tested the nation's commitment to its core values. Teenagers steeped in the rhetoric of postwar democracy and universal brotherhood took concepts like equal rights and equal opportunity seriously. When they saw (or read about) angry mobs that beat Freedom Riders while local police looked the other way, they lost what little faith they still had in the wisdom of adult authority. "When I saw black people . . . fighting back, something about what they were doing . . . struck a chord in me," a white student reported. "I wanted to fight back, too, and I wasn't black, but I already knew something was wrong."[32]

He was not alone. By 1962, some of the best and the brightest white college students were joining black freedom fighters on the lines, getting arrested at sit-ins, and risking life and limb as Free-dom Riders.[33] In 1964, over a thousand students paid their way to travel to Mississippi to take part in Freedom Summer. Working in some of the poorest, most deprived rural regions, they launched voter registration drives and organized Freedom Schools to teach black history and other subjects. "The freedom school was the first time I had a social relationship with whites," recalled a participant who was fifteen at the time. It was also the first time he learned anything about his heritage or realized that there were other kinds of people in the world, people who were nothing like the ones he knew.[34]

The education worked both ways. White students were discovering the real face of rural poverty, and it was not what they expected. As an SNCC organizer put it, these privileged college students were beginning to identify "with these people who come off the land—they're unsophisticated, and they simply voice . . . the simple truths that you can't ignore because they speak from their own lives." Watching the nation's most dispossessed people find the courage to register and vote, despite beatings, bombings, and lynch mobs, college students learned a lesson in human dignity and courage that no classroom lecture could communicate.[35] When they went back to school in the fall, their world was not quite the same. Their vision of the future, and their country, had changed.

"All over America, little knots of students were looking for ways to forsake the predictable paths of career, propriety, family," reported Todd Gitlin, an early member of Students for a Democratic Society, or SDS. Some returned to the South to work with SNCC, others took off for the Peace Corps. Still others began organizing their college friends to take a more active interest in politics. That upwardly mobile college students were willing to explore unconventional paths to adulthood or devote themselves to social movements was a measure of their sheer dissatisfaction with the "respectable" adult world, a world that valued appearances over truth and social conformity over social justice.

Their determination to change that world was also a measure of their own self-confidence—a characteristic of the baby-boom generation. Motivated by a sense of personal security that reflected the prosperous years of their youth, these teenagers fully expected to build a better world than their parents had, a world free of atom bombs, unsatisfying work, and social hypocrisy. "Without thinking about it," Gitlin remarked, "we all took the fat of the land for granted," an attitude that allowed middle-class teenagers in the 1960s to reject the conventional world they had been raised to inherit.[36]

Part IV

Adversaries

chapter twelve

Beatlemaniacs, Washington, D.C., 1964. *Library of Congress, Prints and Photographs Division, U.S. News and World Report Magazine Collection [LCU9 11375]*

A Hard Day's Night
Beatles, Boomers, and the Bomb

ON A HOT SUMMER'S EVENING IN AUGUST 1964, THE PAST AND the future were about to collide. Benny Goodman, the king of swing, whose band gave birth to bobby soxers in the 1930s and 1940s, was scheduled to meet the Beatles, the phenomenal British rock 'n' roll group that was currently thrilling teenage audiences. "I'll tell you one thing," the fifty-five-year-old musician informed his daughters, "I'm not exactly looking forward to the shindig." Although he had never heard a single Beatles record—despite the fact that the "Fab Four" had racked up seven number one hits since February—Goodman had already decided that the Beatles were not worth his time. "Can I say what I really think of them?" he asked after agreeing to review their Forest Hills concert for a local radio station. "How about . . . 'Anybody who listens to that crap is out of his mind?' "[1]

For a man who owed his own celebrity to the enthusiasm of teenage fans, Goodman's assessment seemed rather harsh. As far as he could see, though, the Beatles had no talent to speak of. Who even knew whether they were playing their instruments once their fans started to scream? The tidal wave of Beatlemania that

was sweeping the nation had more to do with hysteria and publicity agents than hard work and determination, the older musician concluded—a dangerous shift from the good old days when
celebrities *earned* their fame. "We were always busy playing the
music," Goodman insisted, "now they're busy growing their hair. We
didn't have the time to mess around with their kind of publicity."[2]

If he expected the Beatles to bow to his judgment on the basis
of his superior skill and experience, however, Goodman was sorely
disappointed. His young successors knew plenty about hard work
and more about popular music than he did. John Lennon had
formed his first band in 1956, when he was only sixteen, and Paul
McCartney and George Harrison had been younger still when
they signed on. By the time Ringo Starr joined the Beatles in
1962, the group had learned the music business from the bottom
up, playing for free at school functions and local Liverpool clubs,
ferrying their equipment around on public buses, and finally getting steady work in the gritty, seaport city of Hamburg, where
they hit their professional stride. Looking back on those early
days, a longtime fan remembered the dark crowded clubs where
the Beatles played and the sense of excitement the young band
generated. "I was drawn to the music, because it was something I
always imagined could exist but which I had never seen," she
explained. "It was just like boom—an explosion. These boys on
that stage there had everything I'd ever dreamed of," she said voic-
ing a sentiment that amazed members of Goodman's generation
but united teenage fans the world over.[3]

Like Goodman in the heyday of swing, these working-class boys
had created a musical style that exhilarated their audience. That
style was rooted in rock 'n' roll and teenage rhythm and blues,
musical traditions that grew out of the postwar experience and
spoke directly to a younger crowd. Goodman had fired up teenage
jitterbugs with his incredibly cool and liquid style; the Beatles
tapped into a much more direct vein of teenage energy. They had
cut their musical teeth on Chuck Berry, Little Richard, and Elvis
Presley, a generation of rebel stars who meant nothing (but trouble) to adults of the swing music era. Goodman's bobby soxers and
the Beatles' fans may have been part of the same cultural trend—
the rise of independent, teenage consumers—yet by the mid-1960s

the distance between these groups was greater than even the thirty-year gap implied. Neither knew enough or cared enough about the other's history to recognize any common ground—musical or otherwise. They inhabited two different worlds as far as tastes, experience, and expectations were concerned, worlds that were becoming increasingly distant, if not downright hostile.

In fact, when the past and the future finally met, a few hours before the Beatles' concert, there was silence across the generations, according to Goodman's daughter, Rachel. No more impressed than Goodman by the prospect of such a meeting, the Beatles barely recognized the veteran musician's name when they were introduced. "I had a seventy-eight of yours once," Ringo offered, perhaps reflecting the fact that he was the oldest Beatle. Unfortunately, he couldn't remembered which one, so the conversation lagged. Communications were no easier with Paul, who casually remarked, after Goodman praised a Boston Pops recording of a Beatles song, that big band music was "fruity." Even cocktails could not bridge this cultural divide, a generational fact of life that Goodman reiterated in his concert review later that night. "There was a very strong beat," he reported truthfully, "but otherwise. . . . I'm afraid there's not much I feel qualified to say about it."[4]

That was exactly the point. Even if Goodman had shared his opinion that the Beatles were not worth listening to, he was in no position to pontificate. Just as he matter-of-factly dismissed the Beatles as if they had no talent and no genuine appeal, their teenage fans were not about to take anything Goodman said seriously. Who was he, anyhow? As far as they could tell, Goodman was just a cranky blast from the past, another crotchety complainer who didn't like their music, didn't like their style, didn't think they were old enough or bright enough to know their own mind anyway. Frankly they could not have cared less. By 1964 teenagers were used to shocking Goodman's generation with their "low" taste for popular culture and their eagerness to waste good money on "sucker stuff." No doubt they would have rolled their eyes at Goodman's reaction to the prices of Beatles tickets—some teenagers paid as much as $7 to see the group live. "What kind of allowances are being given out," he wanted to know, "for kids to be able to spend like that?"[5]

The question pointed up how much the world had changed since bobby soxers first plunked down 25 cents to hear Goodman play. Back in those days, even records were well beyond the reach of most teenage fans: It took almost two hours of work to earn enough to buy a 78 rpm disk in the mid-1930s, and high school students lucky enough to find a job were not likely to invest their earnings in dance music or record players.[6] The generation who entered their teens during the Great Depression (and who were middle-aged by the 1960s) came of age at a time when thrift and self-denial were the watchwords of a secure life, a painful lesson in practical economics that often stuck with them long after their personal circumstances had changed. These adolescents had very little teenage space to call their own when they were growing up—the concept of teenagers as a group apart was only just beginning to take off. In the 1930s, the majority of teenagers was still fighting for the right to enjoy a private social life, and many were still fighting for the right to go to high school: Only 40 percent of the age-group managed to earn high school diplomas, and only a fraction of these went on to college.[7]

The generation that included Beatles fans, on the other hand, knew no such boundaries. As far as they were concerned, prosperity was a fact of life and material comfort a birthright. The first wave of the postwar baby boom, these teenagers were better educated and better dressed and had higher expectations, for the most part, than their parents did. Just about everyone their age attended high school (only 5 percent did not), and about half of these went on to college, a shift that produced an "education gap" that intensified the otherwise typical "generation gap" in the 1960s. Brought up in an affluent world of television, rock 'n' roll, automobiles, and travel, this teenage generation was the first to take the concepts of individual choice and personal identity for granted. Thanks to the cold war focus on rigorous education and democratic ideals, they had an unprecedented belief in their own importance as a group and their place in the postwar world. "I always had a sense that our generation was bigger and better than any that had come before," explained a member of the high school class of '65. "We were the chosen, we were gonna make the world right. . . . We had the luxury of free time and economic security. . . . You could just go in any direction you wanted," he said.[8]

The size of the teenage generation in the 1960s had a lot to do with this confidence. For the first time since teenagers took their place as a recognizable consumer group, their tastes and their interests were determining national styles—for adults, as well as the high school crowd. There were 22 million teenagers in 1964, and their numbers were increasing three times as fast as the overall population, reaching what one demographer called "a critical mass . . . as fissionable as any nuclear pile."[9] It was no secret that teenagers comprised a $12 billion consumer market and spent $13 billion of their parents' money, too. The group spent about $100 million a year on records and $3.5 billion on clothes (and that was just the girls) and purchased more than half of all the soft drinks and movie tickets sold nationwide.[10]

Ever since the days of Elvis Presley, the youth market had loomed as the most dynamic component of the domestic economy. Eugene Gilbert's classic book, *Advertising and Marketing to Young People*, had been published in 1957, and by the 1960s his network of teenage interviewers was working overtime to compile information for his syndicated column "What Young People Think." Major magazines like *Life, Look, Esquire, Time,* and *Newsweek* were stepping up their coverage of teenage tastes and opinions, extending teenage culture well beyond the cities and towns where it first appeared. If anyone doubted the importance of teenagers to the national market, Pepsi Cola advertised itself in 1961 as the drink "for those who think young"—a major shift from the 1940s, when the idea of teenage consumers was still a hard sell. Even car manufacturers were taking teenagers seriously in the 1960s, and not just because they influenced their parents. Models like Ford's Mustang and Chrysler's Barracuda were directly marketed to teenage buyers and "youthful" adults.[11]

The first generation of teenagers large enough and affluent enough to deliver the kind of market that advertisers dreamed of, the baby boomers transformed "delinquent" teenage culture into a prosperous big business. In the 1950s it was a mark of social rebellion when middle-class teenagers ventured into the lower-class world of rock 'n' roll. By the 1960s, middle-class teenagers dominated the market, recasting rock 'n' roll as a respectable category of teenage pop music. Television stars like Ricky Nelson ("The Adventures of Ozzie and Harriet") and Shelley Fabares

("The Donna Reed Show") showcased their hit songs as music
the whole family could enjoy. Lesley Gore, who grew up in affluent Tenafly, New Jersey, interrupted her rock 'n' roll career to go
on to college. When Chubby Checker started doing "The Twist"
(a record that had gone nowhere when Hank Ballard released it
in 1958), adults started dancing along with him.[12]

But it took the Beatles to prove the power of baby-boom
teenagers to turn "youth culture" into a national phenomenon.
Whether it was their British accents or their charm, they made
rock 'n' roll as acceptable as high school yearbooks in 1964. They
recaptured the bobby-soxer spirit of irrepressible youth that had
been lost to teenage rebels since Elvis Presley's day. As one professional promoter put it, the Beatles "were new, they were clean-cut,
they were fun. We'd had a bad winter," she explained, referring to
the assassination of President John F. Kennedy late in 1963. "We
needed a change. We needed to laugh."[13]

The Beatles seemed to fit the bill precisely, as they roused the
nation out of mourning with their upbeat tunes, their quick and
clever wit, their nonthreatening appearance. In their early days
they may have been rebels who grew up playing rhythm and
blues, but that meant nothing to their fans, who thought "Roll
Over Beethoven" originated with the Beatles. By 1964, the "moptops," as they were known in the press, had perfected the marketing process that Dick Clark pioneered on "American Bandstand."
They could easily "pass" in the middle-class world. They may have
stirred up the same kind of hysteria that Elvis did in the 1950s,
but their message was crafted for sheltered, suburban teens. The
first group to ignite middle-class teenage passions, the Beatles
drew their fans from affluent teenagers, kids who wanted to be
rebels but not "greasers."[14]

Their winning combination of good looks and innocent songs
like "I Want to Hold Your Hand" and "This Boy" made the Beatles
the perfect fantasy boyfriends for kids who were not ready for the
real thing. Fifth graders could collect Beatles bubble gum cards (at
5 and 10 cents a pack) and moon over their handsome photographs for hours. Junior high students, still the most avid record
buyers, were known to spend whole days in school scribbling
"Paul, Paul, Paul" all over their notebooks, or practicing Ringo's

distinctive signature—he dotted his "i" with a star! "The Beatles became my life," recalled a fan who grew up in the suburbs. "We weren't going to scream, oh no," another remembered, but when she saw the Beatles live at the Hollywood Bowl, "then we screamed like everyone else. . . . We thought they were cute," this affluent teenager added, an explanation that made more than enough sense to thousands of young Beatles fans but began to worry their parents, who thought teenagers could find something better to do.[15]

Although this turn in teenage culture was evolutionary—from bobby soxers, to rock 'n' rollers, to middle-class rebels—the impact of the baby boom made it seem like a revolution. The economic power of Beatles fans boosted the teenage market to new heights, making it much more visible and influential. The group grossed $12 million in less than a year's time (which may have had something to do with Benny Goodman's hostility), and that did not count the revenue from "official" Beatles products, including fan magazines, clothing, calendars, even wallpaper. Capitol Records, the Beatles' American label, operated plants around the clock to keep up with teenage demand and hired the facilities of eighty other companies, including RCA and MGM. Hordes of teenage fans were helping the Beatles break box office records, altering the economic structure of show business in the process: The Beatles were able to demand a higher percentage of the gross than promoters were used to paying, causing established performers like Bob Hope to demand a larger share, too. Few could match the Beatles' draw, though. In Kansas City, the group set an industry record, earning $150,000 for a one-night stand. In Indiana, they took in more money in two performances at the state fair than Tennessee Ernie Ford and Andy Williams did in ten shows each. When the Beatles appeared on the "Ed Sullivan Show," they drew the largest audience in the history of the Nielsen ratings, registering a 72.7 audience share.[16]

Beatlemania boosted the fashion industry, too. Even the youngest teenagers could adopt the British look, since it was a much softer style than the leather jackets and high teased hair popular in the days of Elvis Presley. Boys grew their hair a little longer and stomped around in the same high-heeled boots the

Beatles wore on stage. Girls wore their skirts a good deal shorter and sported patterned stockings in eye-catching prints. Yardley lip gloss was a perfect match for fresh-faced, British-minded teenage girls, and waiflike models like Twiggy, with her short blond hair, underdeveloped body, poorboy sweaters, and British accent, captured national attention and a larger market share for British designers like Mary Quant. Even adults were jumping on the "youth culture" bandwagon, a definite shift from the 1950s, when rebel style attracted congressional attention. "Now fashion starts in the street," designer Rudi Gernreich explained. "That's why I watch the kids."[17]

The idea that teenagers could set national trends seemed ridiculous and even dangerous to critics, who had been railing against the popular power of teenage tyrants ever since the middle class gave its allegiance to rock 'n' roll. They had been chastising amoral marketers and unconcerned parents as partners in this social crime. "The mission of the adult world is to help teenagers become adults by raising their standards and values," these critics insisted, and "to make adolescence a step toward growing up, not a privilege to be exploited." Instead, the demographic power of youth was lowering the standards of civilized society, since adults were now apparently willing to follow their children's lead. Unwilling to take on the hard job of disciplining and educating the next generation, irresponsible adults were adopting the teenage preference for "self-indulgence over self-discipline." If the adult world abdicated its duty and permitted teenagers to set the national pace, these critics warned, the fun ethic would soon replace the work ethic, and the very concept of responsible adulthood would be lost in the process.[18]

Beatlemania seemed to prove their point. No matter how innocent promoters tried to make the popular quartet appear, the Beatles were apparently leading well-brought-up teenagers down some unsavory paths, and adults seemed powerless to stop them. When an organized charity booked the Beatles for a benefit performance in New York City, for instance, they had no trouble at all moving $50 tickets—a price that must have chilled Benny Goodman's blood! But Beatles fans happily dipped into savings accounts, or badgered their elders for the money, pitifully declaring that they could never lead a "happy life" unless they saw the Beatles. "Kids 'Won't Speak to Me,' So Grandmas Get up $50," *Variety* gleefully reported, an amazing display of teenage leverage at home and in the marketplace that must have made promoters proud.[19]

If that wasn't bad enough, a couple of teenage girls in Cleveland shocked city fathers (and no doubt their own) when they cashed out their college savings accounts and tried to buy airline tickets to England, in hopes of following the Beatles back home. That college-bound teenagers were willing to trade their education for a chance to see the Beatles live seemed unbelievable to the juvenile court judge who handled the case. Enraged by such poor judgment, he tried to outlaw future concerts, arguing that presenting groups like the Beatles to teenage fans was similar to "feeding narcotics to children."[20]

He was not the first to offer that analysis. Critics of the swing music craze had railed against "addictive" popular culture, too. As he and others were forced to concede, though, an industry as profitable as the teenage-culture business was not about to take the advice of critical judges, journalists, educators, or worried parents. Even presidential candidates, in the 1964 campaign, had to face the fact that they could not defeat the teenage market. When a national political party tried to preempt "Shindig," a rock 'n' roll variety show, in favor of a candidate's speech, television executives just laughed at this request, since the Beatles were scheduled to perform during the half-hour in question.[21]

Law enforcement officers likewise had to take a back seat to the Beatles where rabid fans were concerned. Middle-class or not, Beatles fans had no intentions of settling down and behaving just because a policeman ordered them to, which made them no better than juvenile delinquents in some adult eyes. Even at the $50 benefit performance in New York City, well-heeled Beatles fans gave no consideration to older ticket holders and then defied police who tried to quiet them down. In fact, when a teenage girl ventured too close to the stage and police attempted to hold her back, she stunned adults around her by "boldly and blandly" running down a long line of seats to escape her uniformed captors, stepping right on the laps of outraged $50 ticket holders—with her shoes on, no less![22]

This volatile mix of youth's high spirits and contempt for authority shocked adult critics, but it was a crucial component of teenage
culture in the suburbs or the city, one that the Beatles heartily
endorsed. Once considered juvenile delinquents themselves, the
lads from Liverpool were no fans of authority, either. When police
at a Milwaukee airport whisked the Beatles away without even
driving by a screaming crowd of faithful fans, for instance, Paul
McCartney objected when he learned that the Beatles had been
blamed for the plan. "It's a dirty, lying policeman who says the idea
was ours," he allegedly responded, supporting the teenage belief
that police just wanted to spoil their fun for no good reason at all.
In Cleveland, the birthplace of rock 'n' roll, police added fuel to
this teenage fire. They tried to end a Beatles show after teenagers
charged the stage. According to *Variety*, however, they were forced
to reconsider when both the band and the fans defied them.
Apparently, the officer in charge had marched to the center of the
stage to proclaim, "This show is stopped." However, the Beatles
refused to move off stage and the audience booed loudly. In the
meantime, John was allegedly making faces at police officers, and
Ringo was quoted as saying, "The police are stupid."[23]

This was hardly the wholesome image that professional han-
dlers used to promote the Beatles, but it was the image that caught
teenage attention and inspired Beatlemania—something the professionals never quite understood. They seemed to believe that the
mass media "ran" American teenagers. As *Esquire* magazine put it
in 1965, adult promoters determined what the younger crowd
would "say, think, wear, sing, do and look like." This was wishful
thinking, something promoters said to boost their business and
prove to their critics that the market was under adult control. Real
Beatlemania, like real teenage culture, flowed from the bottom up.
Conformists or not, teenagers still set their own standards when it
came to music, fashions, and fads, and what caught their eye (and
opened their pocketbooks) was not always discernible to adults.
For instance, when promoters tried to push a look-alike group on
Beatles fans, the plan failed dismally. Although the manufactured
group wore the same type of haircut and dress as the Beatles did—
which promoters thought would guarantee success—teenagers
passed them by.[24]

John, Paul, George, and Ringo may have seemed wholesome enough to parents, who were known to bring Beatles records home for the kids, something they would never have done for Little Richard or Elvis Presley. Nonetheless, they were also clever, irreverent, and decidedly snide—a delicious duality that middle-class teenagers immediately recognized. The Beatles had an edge and a mocking sense of humor that appealed to teenagers who had grown up with *Mad* magazine and had already learned from television—and their own experience—that the adult world was not all it was cracked up to be. When John Lennon instructed a very posh audience at a royal command performance to "rattle their jewelry" if they liked the show, he may have startled them with his brashness, but his fans who were part of the television audience had a good laugh at their expense.

A year or so later John shocked the adult world by announcing that the Beatles were more popular than Jesus, a remark that seemed true enough on its face to Beatles fans but outraged just about everyone else. By that time, however, teenagers already knew that the Beatles thought social pretensions were a "giggle" and social conventions a lark, as anyone who followed their movies or read their interviews could easily see. Rumor had it that the Beatles had lounged on silk bedspreads at New York City's elite Plaza Hotel still wearing their muddy, high-heeled boots—a symbol of contempt for the respectable world that groups like the Rolling Stones (another British import) would later hone into a profitable art form. Whether parents recognized it or not, the Beatles represented a form of personal liberation to suburban, middle-class teenagers who were already questioning the social conformity that governed their lives.

Frightened yet fascinated by this troubling aspect of teenage culture, adults began to analyze the phenomenon. To *Variety*, Beatlemania was a cross between show business and psychopathology that was not completely genuine; hysterical "screamagers" were merely trying to live up to their newspaper image, the trade paper decided.[25] A Presbyterian minister took a more sympathetic approach, pointing out that the Beatles' "hair and music" were an obvious cry for help. The *New Republic* reported that "the girls who shriek when they see the Beatles" could not explain "why they feel the way they do," and neither could the nation's psychologists, according to a report in the *Science News Letter*.[26] On the other hand, a college professor offered a straightforward explanation: Beatlemania was a crystal clear expression of teenage rebellion against adult authority. "Anyone who dismisses the Beatles by saying they need a haircut does not know what is going on in the world," he said.[27]

He had a point, for the rise of Beatlemania coincided with a real shift in middle-class teenage behavior. By the mid-1960s, even college-bound, suburban teenagers were defying their parents' authority, not only behind their backs (as countless teenagers had done for decades) but right in front of their faces. Boys were growing their hair too long, girls were wearing their jeans too tight, and teenagers were talking back to parents and teachers as if they had every right in the world to contradict their elders.

Others went even further, adopting a personal style that advertised their contempt for conventional life. By 1964, some of the best and the brightest teenagers were fascinated with the notion of living life at the margins. They had already traded their plaid skirts and matching sweaters (or chino pants and button-down shirts) for the sun-bleached look of West Coast surfers in search of the perfect wave. Or they had adopted the worn blue jeans and freewheeling intensity of "folkies" like Joan Baez and Bob Dylan. They worried about nuclear war, despised their parents' racism, and rejected the notion of taking their place in the adult rat race. They were looking for stimulation, not security. They demanded social justice, not the privileges of class. And they looked forward to college as a place to try out new ways of living and learning, not as a passport to conventional success.[28]

Whatever their intentions, their appearance was a constant reminder that some teenagers were beyond an adult's reach, an uncomfortable fact of life that flew in the face of conventional adolescent theory. Adult experts still believed that they could shape teenage culture (and teenage behavior) by presenting appropriate models of teenage life, a theory that guided television executives in the 1960s when they ventured into the teenage world. When Patty Duke debuted in her own television show in 1963, for instance, she was the picture of a "wacky" but harmless adult-approved teenager. She was crazy about dancing, talked a wild streak of slang, and kept on good terms with family and teachers alike, a modern-day Andy Hardy in curls. "Patty has become a heroine—and an example—to her own generation," *Variety* boasted. High school girls from Maine to California were not only sporting her hairdo (a bouncy flip); more important, they were copying "her gentle manners," too.[29]

Not according to Ellen Levy, though, a middle-class teenager from suburban Long Island who punctured this cherished myth. A stand-in for Duke (who was now touted as the "princess of teendom"), she got to know the actress, serving as her liaison to the real teenage world. "Is this what it's like, Ellen? . . . Is this what high school's like for you guys?" the actress wanted to know after they filmed a scene of two girls happily chatting after class. "Well . . . no, not at all," she answered, "It's really not like this at all." Ellen was a member of a high school clique known as the Pinkos, a group of outspoken teenagers who were more concerned with democracy than they were with rock 'n' roll—too concerned, in fact, according to their elders. Disillusioned by the casual racism they witnessed at home, which did not square with the lofty ideals they were taught in school, the Pinkos refused to say the Pledge of Allegiance. Angered by cold war hysterics that they believed threatened their future, the Pinkos also refused to participate in air raid drills. They boycotted gym class as an act of civil disobedience against an authoritarian teacher, an activity that was not likely to make its way into a television script in the early 1960s.

Ellen and her friends were on the cutting edge of a new wave of teenage culture: Their self-awareness and obvious disdain for middle-class conventions marked them as high school radicals in the early 1960s, but their left-wing politics and their taste for confrontation also marked them as arrogant troublemakers or middle-class delinquents, something promoters of the teenage market had not counted on.

Determined to set these teenagers straight and remind them of their own insignificance, *Esquire* magazine offered some "friendly" adult advice. The "sick" minority of teenagers who rejected the adult world as "boring, phony, and full of dangerous things like bombs," the magazine pointed out, had the mistaken idea that they were equal to adults. They were confusing demographic power with social influence. Even if the commercial world valued teenagers as consumers, that did not mean they were interesting in their own right. Far from it. Adults were paying attention to teenagers because there were so many of them, not because teenagers had anything valuable to say. "Remember that no matter how many millions of dollars are spent catering to your taste in music, your taste remains very bad: Even more millions are devoted to the study and treatment of your pimples, but that doesn't make pimples a good thing."[30]

Esquire's hostility held no more weight with teenage radicals than Benny Goodman's did with Beatles fans. Over the next few years, adults would learn the hard way that they could not retain their traditional upper hand without a fight. Nor could they expect the current crop of teenagers to cover their tracks and hide their identities the way that "nice" teenagers had thoughtfully done in the past. Adults who welcomed teenagers as adult consumers in the marketplace could not expect them to remain children at home or at school. Adults who encouraged teenagers to be part of the crowd could not expect to define that crowd, especially when teenagers had the numbers and the money to call their own tune. By the late 1960s, even the Beatles would drop their wholesome disguise, and teenagers like Ellen Levy would prove far more popular, and influential, with the high school crowd than adult-approved models like Patty Duke. "Kids are very discontented with life today in the U.S.," an eighteen-year-old would tell *Look* magazine in 1966. That same year *Newsweek* would feature a seventeen-year-old who denounced what she called "mainstream" society.[31]

That these privileged children of middle-class America would lead the charge against their parents' world seemed a strange and sometimes incomprehensible inversion of the American dream. Critics would blame the usual suspects for the revolutionary change in attitude they perceived: popular culture, permissive parents, and short-sighted, hedonistic teenagers. But that only reflected the fact that they rarely paid attention to what was going on in their children's world until trouble actually erupted. They were rarely as critical of their own behavior, or its consequences, as they were of teenage culture. Had adults been as concerned with the rumblings on college campuses in the early 1960s as they were with the Beatles' hair, they might have realized that dissatisfied, disillusioned students were setting the stage for a decade of social conflict. By 1964, it was already evident that they had the determination to shake things up, at home, at school, and in the larger world. And now that teenagers had the numbers, adults had no choice but to pay attention.

chapter thirteen

Campus demonstration, University of Maryland, College Park, 1971. *Pete Daniel*

Lies My Father Told Me

Berkeley, Vietnam, and the Generation Gap

WHEN THE MONTHLY MAGAZINE *CHANGING TIMES* SUGGESTED that troubles were brewing on college campuses, no one seemed particularly interested in the 1962 report. Enrollments were at an all-time high, and colleges were enjoying their greatest boom since the GI bill sent veterans to campus. The number of college students had jumped 56 percent between 1950 and 1960, despite a slight decline in the college-age population, and by 1962, six out of ten high school graduates enrolled in college, the highest proportion to date. The vast majority were white, middle-class males, of course, since they were the target population, yet female students doubled their numbers between 1955 and 1965, and so did black students between 1960 and 1970, proof that the national investment in high school education was beginning to pay off.[1]

By all indications, this growth would continue. Population trends certainly favored college expansion, and so did middle-class opinion. Anyone who kept up with national affairs already recognized the link between higher education and an affluent life, and by the 1960s ambitious parents expected to send their children to school—the best schools they could afford. Regardless of their children's plans (to train for a profession, or to marry young, as 50 percent of female high school grads did), college was well worth the expense. Once enrolled in a "good" college, their sons would make lifelong friends and business connections through eating clubs and fraternities and their daughters would meet the right sort of dates, men with good prospects for the future. After all, that was what parents wanted most from college, a chance for their children to lead happy, prosperous lives.

As *Changing Times* had discovered in 1962, however, some of their children had other plans. There was a new breed on campus more critical than their classmates. They had no interest in the rah-rah culture of campus life, and they expected college to offer more than middle-class credentials and engagement rings. They wanted to be engaged, but intellectually and politically as full-fledged members of the college community. They were usually disappointed, however. Football teams and marching bands seemed more important than the outdated curriculum on most college campuses. Undergraduate education was not a priority; it was a chore for talented faculty to escape. According to Todd Gitlin, an honors graduate of the Bronx High School of Science, even Harvard University let good undergraduates down. At age seventeen, he arrived on campus intending to immerse himself in higher mathematics, but Gitlin soon concluded that off-campus politics were far more rewarding than course work. Political activism "made me feel useful, gave me good company, books to read, intellectual energy," all the things he had come to college to find but failed to experience in the classroom.[2]

Like other bright, critical teenagers, Gitlin had discovered the lively world of student activism with the help of some red-diaper-baby friends, children of radical parents who were used to taking ideas seriously. They had grown up "breathing a left-wing air" that Gitlin found intoxicating, and they recognized him as a kindred spirit who shared a healthy fear of social conformity and cold war politics. By his sophomore year, Gitlin was a member of Tocsin, a student organization opposed to nuclear war. Fascinated by the prospect of building a left-wing flank of college students to work with the national "ban the bomb" movement (much in the same way that black college students were pushing the civil rights movement), Gitlin and his friends picketed the United Nations to support test-ban talks in 1961. They also used their Harvard connections to meet with members of the Kennedy administration in hopes of changing national policy. "It was heady stuff for world-savers still in their teens," he recalled, "getting taken seriously in middling-high places."[3]

By the time he was graduated in 1963, Gitlin had amassed an impressive political resumé. He had organized a protest against civil defense policy in Washington, D.C., marched in support of civil rights workers, worked in numerous political campaigns, and joined the fledgling Students for a Democratic Society, or SDS. If his undergraduate experiences were not typical, by any means, they were not so unusual either. Student activism was already a tradition in large college towns like Ann Arbor, Michigan, Madison, Wisconsin, and Berkeley, California, where issues of civil rights, political radicalism, and student repression were everyday fare. Although SDS was only a skeletal organization in 1963, its concept of "participatory democracy"—that is, that individuals should have a say in decisions that affected the quality and direc-tion of their lives—was gaining a national constituency. Even Vassar, a prestigious women's college at the time, had a chapter in 1963, although it counted just five members at the start.[4]

SDS never claimed to represent the majority of college stu-dents, who still "wanted to make families," as Gitlin put it; it attracted the new breed, the active minority "who wanted to make history." But it was getting a boost from an increasing num-ber of dissatisfied students fed up with the "absurd" quality of col-legiate life. They had discovered the "hollowness of the American dream" for racial minorities (who were segregated even on cam-pus), and they recognized the political "bankruptcy of America's Cold War policies." They deeply resented the fact that colleges still emphasized social life over the more serious business of learning and rewarded conformity, not creativity, in the classroom. Frustrated by their inability to effect change on campus, they refused to participate any longer in "fake student governments in which they have no real voice."[5]

The fact that colleges operated *in loco parentis*, or in place of a parent, also rankled the new breed, since it meant, in effect, that college students were considered dependents on campus, subject to adult rules. The same students who risked physical abuse when they sat in at segregated lunch counters needed their parents' per-mission to do so (at least officially) and had to register plans well

ahead of time to take an "overnight" away from school. "It was a
system of arbitrary authority," according to Tom Hayden, who
attended the University of Michigan between 1957 and 1961, and
authored SDS's political manifesto. "You couldn't have girls in the
room, or even in the library," and boys were expected to dress for
dinner in coats and ties, an unpopular requirement that led to a
food fight during his freshman year—and the expulsion of the
participants without benefit of a hearing. The rules could be even
more intrusive for women. Students at Vassar could be expelled for
failing to live up to the college's highest standards, which included
temperance and chastity in 1962.[6]

Ironically, undergraduates were still ignored in university classrooms, a chronic problem that reached crisis proportions when
baby boomers began to swamp college campuses in 1964. The gap
between image and reality in higher education was shocking to
students who had taken adult advice seriously. After years of being
told that entrance to a "good" college was the chief goal of their
adolescent life, they discovered that the coveted prize had not
been worth the investment. These students had taken the hardest
high school programs and invested long hours in homework and
extracurricular activities, while their less ambitious friends
enjoyed high school and did just enough to get by. Now they
were rewarded with overcrowded classrooms, unavailable professors, and irrelevant courses—not at all what they had bargained
for. "I went through the realization that the dream . . . was not too
much of a reality," a disappointed student explained. The experience shattered his faith in adult promises and led him and his
friends to reject adult advice with the words, "We don't believe
what you are saying any more."[7]

Students at the University of California at Berkeley were
among the first to make the statement out loud. The campus was
already a mecca of sorts for student radicals, and the administration had grudgingly come to tolerate political activity that ranged
from demonstrating against capital punishment to disrupting local
hearings of the House Un-American Activities Committee. After
Berkeley students took part in a campaign to force local business-
men to hire black employees during the 1963–64 academic year,
though, university administrators took a harder line. When students returned to campus in the fall, they discovered that political
recruiters were prohibited from raising funds on campus or orga-

nizing illegal protests, and many suspected that conservative politicians were behind the ban.[8]

The fact that student leaders had spent the summer battling conservative forces in Mississippi intensified the conflict. According to Mario Savio, they recognized a disturbing parallel between the racist paternalism they had witnessed in the South and the denial of their own free speech rights on campus. Using their training in civil disobedience, they mobilized the student body against the university's unpopular stance. Five activists set up unauthorized recruiting tables and collected unauthorized funds, and they were summoned to the dean's office to explain. When they arrived for the meeting on September 29, they brought some three hundred students with them. All insisted that they had broken university rules, and all demanded similar treatment. Ordered to disperse, since the dean was obviously not equipped to handle such a crowd, they ignored authorities and remained in the building overnight.[9]

The situation escalated on October 1, when a protester again violated university policy and police promptly arrested him. This time, though, some seven thousand Berkeley students responded, blocking the police car for thirty-two hours and demonstrating to the university at large that they would claim their rights as citizens, by any means possible. "There is a time when the operation of the machine becomes so odious, makes you so sick at heart, that you can't take part," Savio declared, speaking from the roof of the car. "And you've got to indicate to the people who run it . . . that unless you're free, the machine will be prevented from working at all."[10]

To prove his point, the Berkeley Free Speech movement proceeded to disrupt a major university, publicly undermining its proud claim to combine high standards with mass education.[11] Protesters ridiculed the massive bureaucracy that dominated campus life with slogans like "UC Student: Do Not Fold, Spindle, or Mutilate." Student activists manned the bullhorns each day, loudly denouncing the administration, the faculty, the regents, and the system in general. They protested the federal grants that directly linked universities to cold war policies they despised. They took enormous pleasure in stripping the administration of its vaunted authority. Student activists had persuaded the university not to discipline them for their actions and also demanded the right to advocate and organize illegal protests off–campus without fear of retribution. Their victory was more apparent than real, at this point, however, since neither the faculty, the administration, nor the Board of Regents would grant this last demand, and by December the original agreement had collapsed, too.

So the fight resumed in earnest when leaders of the Free Speech movement were called before a faculty disciplinary committee. This time when students occupied the administration building to protest, folk singer Joan Baez led the crowd in song. And this time, Governor Pat Brown called out the state police, thereby drawing national attention to the crippled California campus and putting the Free Speech movement on the map. Like the shot heard 'round the world, the picture of police arresting eight hundred college protesters alerted the public that the fight for student rights was a serious one. The December uprising demonstrated that students would no longer defer to authority once they judged that authority to be arbitrary, corrupt, or just plain incompetent. It also taught students beyond Berkeley's gates a practical lesson in politics. The university could ignore student rallies and petitions, as it had been doing for years, but it could not ignore the damage of national publicity, a point that was driven home when the chancellor of the university resigned his position.[12]

Student activists were only a small percentage of the national student body, but their numbers were impressive nonetheless, considering the size of the population overall, and they had more influence than percentages might suggest. Studies showed that 3–5 percent of the student body at universities like Berkeley, Chicago, and Columbia were willing to court arrest over pertinent issues, but 10–20 percent were willing to support the cause, and a third to a half of the student body agreed that activists were on the right track.[13] Their no–holds–barred strategy of civil disobedience also galvanized public attention. As the dramatic uprising at Berkeley demonstrated, student dissent generated the kind of "man–bites–dog" excitement that the news media thrived on. When Mario Savio complained that "students are permitted to talk all they want so long as their speech has no consequences," a journalist felt obliged to set the record straight. The Free Speech leader "not only spoke freely on campus," he pointed out, "but expressed his views in hundreds of newspapers, national magazines, and on TV. No undergraduate in history has enjoyed so large an audience," he said.[14] A study of student dissent and mass circulation magazines confirmed his point. In 1963, only 18 articles dealt with the issue, but thanks to Berkeley the number jumped to 110 in 1965.[15]

In the process, this publicity changed the dominant image of college students from self-centered panty-raiders to student radicals determined to shake things up. In the *New York Times*, James Reston remarked that "instead of chasing girls, the boys are chasing college presidents." Even Art Buchwald felt moved to comment on why "college students are doing so much demonstrating."[16] The shift was particularly apparent in educational circles. Prior to Berkeley, concerned professors had worried about apathetic students, who seemed all too willing to take their place in the corporate world; after Berkeley, they zeroed in on how to placate student radicals, suggesting that faculty be retrained to become more "solicitous of student feelings" and more "receptive to student concerns."[17] Sociologist Paul Goodman, an intellectual hero of the Free Speech movement, put the new, confrontational image of college students in context. "At present, in the United States today," he said, "students—middle class youth—are the major exploited class."[18]

The idea seemed ludicrous to Nathan Glazer, a sociologist who taught at Berkeley. At first sympathetic to the Free Speech movement, Glazer changed his mind after he helped to negotiate the original truce with student leaders. These students failed to understand that a university was an educational institution, he said, not an incubator for political radicalism. He steadfastly maintained that teachers had the right to set the rules, and students the duty to follow them. The hierarchy was implicit in the nature of the institution, he argued, although he did admit that the system was out of balance. But the cure was worse than the disease, he warned. Berkeley was one of the most tolerant campuses in the country, and students there had an opportunity to make their voices heard.

No wonder student radicals preferred Goodman to Glazer; the Berkeley sociologist had missed the point entirely. His basic assumption—that students were children entrusted to the faculty's care—was just the kind of "natural" hierarchy that had kept black citizens disenfranchised in the South. If Berkeley students had the option of working through the system, no one in authority paid attention until conditions on campus deteriorated to near-riot levels. Likewise, the relative freedom they enjoyed did not change the fact that undergraduates were the "forgotten men" on campus; only four out of ten entering freshman stayed in college long enough to graduate. That students now threatened the university at its roots was hardly surprising under the circumstances. That they were intoxicated by the power of civil disobedience made logical sense, too. The Free Speech movement spread the tantalizing message that sit-ins and strikes could succeed on campus where petitions had failed, thus opening up new possibilities for student activists nationwide.[19]

Just in time, too. In August 1964, about a month before the Berkeley movement took shape, the U.S. Congress had authorized President Lyndon B. Johnson to escalate the undeclared war in Vietnam. As campus radicals had predicted, cold war politics now directly threatened teenage futures. Monthly draft calls jumped from an average of 17,000 to 27,000 in September 1965, and 40,000 soon after.[20] This "Americanization" of the war in Vietnam had a profound effect on the radical student movement. In October 1964, 7,000 Berkeley students challenged authority on campus; in October 1965, over 100,000 college students participated in antiwar activities and organized protest marches in thirty American cities.[21] Free Speech leaders had rallied students to protest a university system that ignored their rights and interests. Now a national network of student activists geared up to protest a military system that compelled young soldiers to kill and be killed, whether the fight was justifiable or not.

In fact, as soon as the president stepped up the bombing in February 1965, organized students immediately challenged his decision. "The bombing raids . . . serve to highlight the sordid war the U.S. government is engaged in," wrote angry students at Cornell University in an open letter to the campus. "The Government's explanation of the events are . . . transparent lies (upholding, to be sure), a hallowed principle of U.S. foreign policy. The only solution to the dirty war in Vietnam," these students insisted, "is American withdrawal."[22] They were not alone. In San Francisco, students picketed federal buildings, echoing the call for withdrawal. In St. Louis they staged a sit-in at a federal courthouse. The University of Minnesota's student government passed a resolution against the war, and at George Washington University in Washington, D.C., a small but committed band of students began to fast for peace.

"Sane men in capitals throughout the world today are hoping and praying that you will not escalate this mad war further," an SDS spokesman telegraphed President Johnson, but to no avail, of course. In April an SDS march in Washington drew more than 20,000 students who believed they had a duty as well as a right to protest this controversial turn of foreign affairs. Determined to present themselves as respectable young citizens who wanted to make their voices heard, they dressed in jackets and ties (or skirts and sweaters) for the momentous occasion.[23]

The president ignored this earnest group, though, since they posed no threat to the great war machine. Yet in doing so he invited a much more strident response. There was a strong corps of baby boomers who had no intention of disguising their contempt for the war or conforming to adult standards of respectability to get their message out. As far as they were concerned, President Johnson was a "colossal, intransigent liar" who was sacrificing American youth to protect his enormous ego, and they did not care who knew it.[24] Determined never to repeat the mistakes of so-called good Germans who failed to stop the rise of fascism before the Second World War, these students were amazed when less militant friends tried to keep them in line.

"If we're going to make them listen, we have to look like them. We have to stop looking like Beatniks," an Ivy League protester reportedly told a friend from New York's City College. But she was having none of it. "So in other words, you want to cloak our disapproval of a fascist president and an illegal military action in a respectable outfit. Is that it?" she wanted to know.[25] She and others would not camouflage the moral outrage they felt in skirts and sweaters; on the contrary, when they marched to protest the war, they brandished provocative posters of Vietnamese women and children, the innocent victims of American bombs. Or they burned their draft cards in disgust, horrifying angry onlookers, who sometimes retaliated with violence.

If the Free Speech movement first brought the image of student radicals into public view, it was the war in Vietnam—and the emergence of a national, campus-based antiwar movement—that gave that image force. The war was fought at home as well as in faraway jungles, and if the two conflicts could not be compared in terms of sacrifice or horror, they were nevertheless inextricably intertwined. As Dr. Martin Luther King, Jr., put it, the bombs in

Vietnam exploded at home, and student activists were the first to lead the raucous chorus of opposition.[26] For good reason, too; American youth was expected to pay the highest price for this military adventure, although no one could give them a good reason why. In the course of the brutal debate that ensued over the question of military service, student activists made it clear that they would not sacrifice innocent life—including their own— merely because adults told them to. The immediate issues of life and death could not be disguised by empty notions of duty, honor, or respect for authority. Adults, including Lyndon Johnson, who tried to do so soon lost whatever moral authority they had once enjoyed.

Perhaps because the pool of draftable eighteen-year-olds was so vast in 1965 (1.9 million, a 35 percent increase over the 1964 total), President Johnson assumed he could field an army and wage a foreign war without destroying domestic tranquillity. After all, neither fathers nor college students would be called to serve, and monthly draft calls were far below totals for the Second World War (450,000 a month in 1943) or Korea (80,000 a month).[27] Although the draft had never appealed to Americans in any war, the tradition of compulsory military service was well established by 1965. The Selective Service had been in business for twenty-five years, and teenage boys were regularly counseled in high school to factor military service into their future plans. Even Elvis Presley had been drafted, at the height of his popularity in 1958, and he had served the required two years on active duty, no questions asked. In fact, "the service" was such an established fact of young male life in the early 1960s that 40 percent of the nation's conscripts had volunteered to be drafted in 1962.[28]

As the president steadily raised the number of U.S. troops in Vietnam, though, from 184,000 in 1965 to 542,000 in 1969, he also changed the meaning of military service for hundreds of thousands of potential draftees. A survey of high school students demonstrated the shift. In 1960, six out of ten teenage boys who expected to be drafted "liked" the idea; by 1969, the figure had dropped to 14 percent, and 7 percent admitted that they would only serve under duress or would refuse to serve altogether.[29]

Once an accepted rite of passage into adulthood (and a vocational training school for working-class youth), military service now looked like a brutal sacrifice of young American life. A veteran of the war who was just nineteen when he was drafted in 1966 put this shift in perspective: "I didn't look forward to the army, but I didn't dread it either," he said. "I wanted to be a man." A year of guerrilla warfare changed his opinion of the value of service, though. "All the men we sent over there . . . all the money we put in was wasted," he mourned, "because we didn't have a chance to win. We shouldn't have been there at all."[30]

Student protesters agreed. "If I don't want to join the Army, I shouldn't have to," a nineteen-year-old college student told *Look* magazine in 1966. "I think the draft boards should be made up of artists and writers asking people *why* they want to get into the army, because war is so horribly absurd. I'll serve my country [but] I'll do it my way," he added. No president could force him to kill or be killed in an immoral war. "Daddy is *not* always right," he insisted, a point that SDS also championed.[31] "We are not afraid to risk our lives—we have been risking our lives in Mississippi and Alabama," SDS argued in its official statement on the draft. "But we will not bomb the people, the women and children of another country." Instead, the group challenged government officials to make "service to democracy" grounds for military exemption. As SDS saw it, alternative service would demonstrate the fact that draft-age baby boomers would "build not burn" once they were given a choice.[32]

The idea that youth could pick their wars or choose their methods of service seemed preposterous to men like Lieutenant General Lewis B. Hershey. Director of Selective Service since 1947, he was fed up with "youngsters who say that two years in the service is two years down the drain." A society that "didn't have the guts to make people do what they ought to do"—in this case, defend their country—did not deserve to survive, he believed.[33] He was willing to use the force of government to prove his point. When thirty-five students from the University of Michigan sat in at the local draft board, Hershey suggested drafting them as a lesson to other students, and within a few weeks several of the group lost their deferments. "Reclassification is quicker at stopping sit-ins than some indictment that takes effect six months later," he explained.[34]

Many Americans agreed with him, especially during the early years of the war. "It was impossible for those of us who were alive and conscious during World War II and Korea to take the same easy path as radical youth," a sociologist explained. "We had known the country and its army in different times and different wars. We valued the country, its international role . . . its capacity for change and correction."[35] Rank–and–file war veterans often shared this view, although they were no more likely to talk about it than they were to talk about their combat experiences. They had done their duty, whether they wanted to or not, and now it was another generation's turn. Military service in time of war was never a matter of choice; nobody wanted to die. It was a matter of personal honor, and in the eyes of many, the unquestioned duty of loyal men.

It was here that generational communications most often broke down. "The issue isn't a moral one," a college student explained.[36] Honor, personal or otherwise, had nothing to do with the fight, as anyone who watched the nightly news could plainly see. What was honorable about antipersonnel bombs designed to inflict as much pain as possible? Where was the honor in defoliating jungles and destroying whole villages? Why was it the duty of loyal men to take sides in a civil war that even the generals knew we could not win? The best and the brightest American youth did not believe that Tonkin Gulf was Pearl Harbor or that the fall of South Vietnam could somehow threaten American shores. National security was not at stake in Vietnam, they insisted, and no amount of political rhetoric could change that basic fact. Yet the government continued to escalate the fighting, as if sustaining national myths of honor, duty, and American invincibility were somehow justifiable and worth the sacrifice of human life on either side.

The consequences were costly. In 1966, one hundred student leaders sent President Johnson an open letter warning that potential draftees would refuse induction if his policies did not change. The *New York Times* followed up the story, estimating that 25 percent of all college students could be counted on to refuse, and a Harris poll confirmed the figure. As the editor of the Cornell *Daily Sun* put it, after students passed a series of resolutions against the war, opposition was no longer "the affair of the radical student fringe."[37]

As students moved from protest to revolt, the tenor of campus demonstrations changed, too. At Cornell, students joined a national boycott against the Selective Service Qualifying Test (which ranked college students in case the government decided to draft them), and protesters occupied the president's office for half a day. At Harvard, an SDS crowd forced Robert McNamara, the secretary of defense, out of his car and into a shouting match that ended with police escorting him off campus. At the University of Wisconsin, in 1967, angry students kept a recruiter from Dow Chemical (the manufacturer of napalm) from keeping his appointments. Riot police in full gear freely bashed demonstrators with their clubs and then used tear gas and Mace to disperse thousands of student supporters who came to their aid. Fighting back with rocks and bricks, the students surrounded the police, let the air out of paddy-wagon tires, and sent seven policemen (along with sixty-five students) to the hospital. A month or so later, when Secretary of State Dean Rusk visited the campus, five thousand students joined a peaceful demonstration, but militants threw bottles and paint and then took over city streets in protest.[38]

By 1968, violent eruptions on campus had become a new ritual of spring. Students at over two hundred colleges and universities were demonstrating against the war, and bomb threats, arson, and vandalism were replacing folk singers and peace signs as the dominant symbols of collegiate life. A violent outburst at Columbia University in New York City offered compelling evidence that conflict over the war in Vietnam, was destroying an already fragile campus community. In April, black and white draft opponents and community activists occupied university buildings and the president's office for ten explosive days. In an open letter to the president, they quoted the unambiguous words of Leroi Jones, a militant black activist: "Up against the wall, motherfucker. This is a stick up." The cycle of mass demonstrations, strikes, and sit-ins that had begun in Berkeley in 1964 had come full circle: Militant students who started out with the hope of reforming an unbalanced university system now rejected the corrupt adult "establishment" entirely. The process had forged a new public identity for American youth, one that said in effect, as Todd Gitlin put it, "To be young and American is to have been betrayed; to be alive is to be enraged."[39]

As in Berkeley in 1964, antiwar student radicals were prominent in the news. They had come a long way since the suits and ties of the 1965 march. Activists were known for long hair, indifferent dress, and a matter-of-fact disdain for authority of any stripe. A high school cheerleader offered her impressions in *Look* magazine: "We saw this movie, 'While Brave Men Die,' in school, and it had all these dirty, beatniky types out demonstrating against the war. Yes, they have a right," she conceded carefully. "But I don't know if I would like to call that type of person an American."[40] Nicholas Katzenbach, the U.S. attorney general, was not sure either. Back in 1965 he had suggested that "Reds" were leading the student movement, and conservative journals like *U.S. News and World Report* and the *National Review* had publicized the claim.[41] It could not be easily sustained, however, especially as the movement embraced high school students, by 1968, as well as a host of liberal adults. In fact, Katzenbach was forced to modify his opinion, although he kept that fact from President Johnson, who was having trouble stomaching the familiar chant, "Hey, Hey, LBJ. How many kids did you kill today?" Unbeknownst to the president, even Katzenbach's daughter and all of her friends were marching against the war. In fact, he knew very few parents of teenage children who could not make a similar claim.[42]

But if antiwar students were not communists or traitors, the majority were not militant resisters, either. The bulk of high school and college-age war opponents tended to avoid the draft, not fight it. Going to college was still the easiest way to steer clear of Vietnam, as the booming number of male students attested. Boys who might have otherwise taken a job right out of high school, on the line at General Electric or Westinghouse, for instance, now took their place in college and stayed as long as they could. Many students ignored the war until graduation (and the end of their student deferments) drew near. "My position on the war was shaped by self-interest," admitted an antiwar activist who saw the light in 1968, just a year before he was scheduled to graduate. He was opposed to the war because he did not want to fight and he could not see any reason why he should.[43] After graduation he enrolled in law school but also took a part-time job as a schoolteacher to avoid the draft. As long as a student had a talent for schoolwork (and was willing to become a teacher, an engineer, or a doctor), he could escape dangerous service in Vietnam.[44]

If he lacked that talent, the task was harder, but it could be achieved with money, ingenuity, and a strong survival instinct. The question was, as a UCLA dropout put it, how do you avoid being classified 1A? In his case, the answer was controlled starvation. He slimmed down to a mere 107 pounds, the minimum requirement for his height. He was disappointed to discover, however, that his weight-loss program was only worth a three-month deferment. Desperate for a new strategy, he began to move frequently, confusing his draft board in the process. He regularly switched his papers to a new office, creating a bureaucratic nightmare that bought him a measure of freedom. Since he came from a wealthy family, he was able to keep moving until the draft lottery was established in 1970. At that point, his troubles were over: He pulled the very last number, 366, finally freeing himself from the war.[45]

A traitor in some eyes, a survivor in others, he was just one out of hundreds of thousands of potential draftees who managed to outwit the system. Some took off on treks around the globe, a legal strategy for teenagers who left before their eighteenth birthday.[46] Others purchased whatever medical consultations they needed to disqualify themselves from service. College students made a game of staying up for days on end before their Army physicals in order to raise their blood pressure high enough to protect their freedom.[47] Others gave up bathing entirely, established unstable (and unpleasant) identities, or pricked their arms with pins to simulate a heroin addiction. Still others used family connections to reserve a safe place in the National Guard, probably the most respectable way to evade service in Vietnam. The truly desperate cut off parts of their thumbs, shot themselves in the foot, or got punched in the nose hard enough to cause a deviated septum. If all else failed, those determined not to serve took off for Canada or parts unknown.[48]

Overall, by the time the draft was phased out in 1972, half a million young American males failed to register or committed draft violations, 110,000 burned their draft cards, 172,000 registered as conscientious objectors, and 50,000 fled or assumed false identities and disappeared underground. Less than 10 percent of the 27 million males who came of age between 1964 and 1973 actually served in Vietnam—about 2,150,000. Of these, 50,000 were killed, 250,000 were injured, and 21,000 were permanently disabled. By and large, these were not the sons of the middle class or a cross-section of American youth. Only 12 percent of college students were estimated to have served in Vietnam, as opposed to 21 percent of high school graduates and 18 percent of high school dropouts. Only 9 percent of these saw combat, as opposed to 17 percent of the high school group and 14 percent of the dropouts. "As a rule, middle-class kids did not have to go and fight the war," a draft counselor explained. "They knew about lawyers, psychologists and college deferments."[49]

A Harvard student concurred. He had just convinced his military examining board that he was suicidal and therefore not fit for service. As he watched the next batch of inductees arrive, though, he realized they probably did not know, as Harvard students did, that they could avoid service by deliberately failing the test. Working-class youth, or "Boston proles," as he put it, they had only recently graduated from high school. They looked as if they had "no idea that there might be a way around the draft. They walked through the examination lines like so many cattle off to slaughter," he remembered, a characterization they would have certainly resented.[50]

In a sad twist of social fate, these young inductees were seen as losers, not heroes or even duty-bound Americans who had answered their country's call. Indeed, by 1971 a national survey suggested that it was common knowledge that only "suckers" went to Vietnam, those who lacked the education or the social connections to avoid military service. Returning veterans could vouch for the survey's accuracy, since their own time in Vietnam had earned them little but contempt at home. "People just look down on you," a veteran explained. "I went up to the campus to see my girl, and I got called pig and murderer and all kinds of things just because I was in uniform."[51]

Pawns in an old man's game of war, these young veterans were denied the respect, the national gratitude, and even the skills that veterans of the Second World War—a "good" war—had enjoyed. Instead, they were blamed for carrying out President Johnson's bankrupt policy, as if they had as much choice in the matter as their middle-class counterparts did. A veteran who chanced upon an antiwar demonstration soon after he returned home had very mixed feelings toward student protesters: "At first I smiled; kids at it again, just a fad," he remembered. "Then I started getting sore. About how I had to go and they could just stay out. My Negro buddy didn't like the war, but he went in, too. I just stood there and got sore at those spoiled rich kids telling people to 'resist the draft.' What about us poor people? For every guy who resists the draft, one of us gotta go. . . . One of their signs read 'We've Already Given Enough.' And I thought 'What *have* they given?' "[52]

Kingman Brewster, the president of Yale University, offered an indirect response that addressed the question of national losses, losses that were profound. For if the government had played fast and loose with the lives of poor teenagers and young adults, it had also lost the confidence—and the respect—of its most privileged students. In the process, it had undermined both the values and the institutions of middle-class culture. Patriotism had no meaning when a president lied about the conduct of a war; duty had no value in a corrupt military system; and respectability counted for very little in world that rewarded those best able to take care of themselves and condemned the rest as "losers." As Brewster put it, the result was "a cynical avoidance of service, a corruption of the aims of education, a tarnishing of the national spirit . . . and a cops and robbers view of national obligation."[53]

Americans would later blame these losses on a popular teenage culture of sex, drugs, and rock 'n' roll that mocked authority throughout the turbulent 1960s, but they were confusing cause with effect. It was the war in Vietnam and the hypocritical values it exposed that pushed mainstream teenagers to finally reject old notions of middle-class respectability. "Our values were all wrong," a mother remembered the endless battles she had with her teenagers and their friends. "We had brought the world to the brink of disaster. Vietnam was our fault. . . . The bottom was falling out of everything. . . . It was a terrible time. . . . The only thing worse than being a child," she said, "was being a parent in those days."[54]

chapter fourteen

Antiwar demonstrators, Washington, D.C., 1971. *Pete Daniel*

Up the Down Staircase
Sex, Drugs, and Rock 'n' Roll

THE WAR IN VIETNAM AND THE DOMESTIC CONFLICT THAT RESULTED did not create the generational tensions that came to symbolize "the sixties," the turbulent decade that actually began around 1965. Although journalists spotlighted the "generation gap" as if it were a new phenomenon, the distance between parents and children, or experience and exuberance, was built into the relationship. What was new was the frank expression of that distance—through popular culture, personal style, and political protest. Up until the 1960s, discretion had been a key component of middle-class teenage culture. After the 1960s, teenagers were much more willing "to let it all hang out."

After all, it was one thing to follow adult rules, hypocritical or not, when they promised a prosperous future, but in the life-or-death context of war and the draft, rules lost their potency. Who would follow an adult chain of command that apparently led to oblivion? What kind of crazy adult world valued respect for authority above all else? The Selective Service system proved every day that there was no reward for following the rules, a disillusioning realization for idealistic teenagers who had trusted the system.

Now they had to decide for themselves what constituted an honorable life, an exercise in growing up that took on a distinctly political spin in the 1960s and 1970s. As the image of teenage protesters—at college, in the streets, and in high school classrooms—dominated the public scene, a new teenage identity took shape. Alienated youth, the middle-class version of teenage rebeldom, moved out of the margins and into the mainstream.

By all appearances, the ties between middle-class youth and the world of their parents still remained remarkably strong, but the times were definitely a-changin', as folk singer Bob Dylan pointed out in 1964. Unlikely as it seemed at the time, his scruffy, freewheeling style would soon set teenage standards, even in the best of homes. The Beatles had started the process rolling with their long hair and cheeky wit. The uproar at Berkeley had raised hostility to new political heights. Fusing the trends into a musical style called folk-rock, Dylan launched a popular culture of discontent that rocked the foundations of middle-class propriety. An uncompromising original in a plastic world of mass marketing, Dylan sang in a nasal twang that defied conventional tastes. Unpolished and abrasive, he expertly tapped a bulging vein of teenage alienation, giving voice to the defiance that middle-class teenagers had been brought up to repress. His 1965 release, "Like a Rolling Stone," was a sneering, hostile, mean-spirited ballad and one of the top-selling records of the year.

Dylan's explosive entry into the pop music scene marked the official rise of an alternative youth culture. "Respectable" teenage pop like Herman's Hermits' "Can't You Hear My Heartbeat?" and Petula Clark's "Downtown" still topped the charts in 1965, but Dylan's commercial success opened mainstream doors to other renegade artists. In what had to be one of the most unexpected turns of popular teenage culture, singer Barry Maguire had a number one hit with "The Eve of Destruction," a brutally frank, uncompromising protest song. Making a clear connection between racial injustice, escalating violence, and the failure of hypocritical, middle-class values, the song alerted a whole new segment of the teenage audience to changes going on in the world. It broadcast the message to the community at large that mainstream teenagers were on the warpath.[1]

By that time hostility, or at least irreverence, was already a marketable commodity in the teenage world. The Rolling Stones, a hard-driving, authentic-sounding rock 'n' roll band from England, had developed a bad-boy image to make their name. Their hair was longer and wilder than the Beatles' bangs, and they looked as if they regularly slept in their clothes. They strutted and snarled their way into the pop charts, making no effort to disguise the sexual energy that drove their music. As one critic put it, "The Beatles' songs had been rinsed and hung up to dry. The Stones had never seen soap and water."[2]

In fact, their rebellious style nearly banished them from Ed Sullivan's Sunday night stage after the Stones turned in a particularly sexy, surly performance. "I was shocked when I saw them," the veteran starmaker reported, and he promised never to book the group again. But just as he had promised not to book Elvis Presley way back in 1956—for many of the same reasons—he was forced to change his mind. Whether the respectable world approved or not, there was a growing teenage audience for the Rolling Stones' erotic defiance. The innocent young "chickadees" who had screamed so loud when the Beatles shook their heads on Sullivan's stage were now demanding "Satisfaction," and they would not be denied.[3]

And why not? As anyone who kept up with popular culture could attest, the concept of teenage sex had come out of the closet. Movies like *Where the Boys Are, Blue Denim*, and *A Summer Place* all featured nice teenage girls willing to go all the way, and teenage love songs like "Will You Still Love Me Tomorrow?" only sounded ambiguous to the youngest teens. In 1964, Mary Stolz, a well-known writer of young adult fiction, acknowledged the change when she published *A Love or a Season*, a novel that featured a well brought up sixteen-year-old in love for the first time and eager to lose her virginity.[4] That same year, television producers confirmed that public standards had changed when they launched "Peyton Place," a prime-time soap opera that boldly linked teenage characters to premarital sex, a decision that did not hurt the show's ratings. "There's no question but that a large segment of the viewing public—particularly teenage girls (and their boyfriends) . . . dig 'Peyton Place,' " *Variety* reported.[5]

If teenagers were considered adults on their own time and in the marketplace, though, they were still required to be children in school. If they wanted to earn a high school diploma and go on to college, as the majority did in the 1960s, they had to forgo their rebel ways and toe the respectable line in the classroom. Principals still used dress codes and conduct rules to set appropriate behavior standards, and they rarely tolerated individuals "who cannot adjust," as one educator put it.[6] Troublesome teenagers were not welcome in high school, a group that ranged anywhere from long-haired boys caught smoking in the bathroom to girls unfortunate enough to find themselves pregnant. According to adults in charge, the high school ideal "was chastity and strict morality, obedience and respect for authority," and they had every intention of enforcing those rules in school, even if parents could not enforce them at home. Apparently, they had the legal right to do so. Back in 1930, a judge had decreed that high school students were entitled to as much protection as bootleggers were, and that decision had not changed significantly in thirty-five years.[7]

That being the case, students were still required to dress "right," at least for the duration of the school day. That usually meant no dungarees or sneakers, no leather jackets, no long hair, no short skirts, and no tight pants. Principals held fast to their conviction that there was a direct correlation between dress and behavior, and 97 percent of high school teachers surveyed in 1960 apparently agreed.[8] As long as they were in school, teenagers could assume only one appropriate identity, that of dutiful teenage students subject to adult rule.

Up until the mid-1960s, they rarely argued the point out loud. High school students were more likely to mock adult authority than challenge it. An entire class of boys might "forget" to wear their required belts after an official reminder. Or they might wage a quiet campaign of petty vandalism—bending all the forks in the cafeteria, for instance—to protest silly rules or pompous orders from above.[9] For the most part, though, they accepted the generational bargain that had regulated middle-class life for decades. "Nice" teenagers could see for themselves that adults controlled access to the good things in life, so it was worth their while to follow the letter, if not the spirit, of society's laws. "Act well-adjusted and well-behaved," an eighteen-year-old advised younger teenagers. "Be a hypocrite," he said, since that paved the way to freedom.[10] Brought up in a world that valued the perception of propriety even more than propriety itself, teenagers had learned to keep their private lives private and undetectable at home or at school.

That bargain was getting harder to negotiate, however. Whatever adults thought, their authority always depended on a teenager's decision to cooperate. By the mid-1960s, it was easy to see that adults had lost their influence. Boys were wearing their hair too long to suit conventional tastes, a notorious symbol of disrespect (and delinquency) that stretched back to the pachucos in the 1940s. "Not even members of *crews* have crew cuts anymore," *Life* magazine lamented. Worse yet, even boys from solid middle-class homes were refusing to comply with school rules. Instead, they held fast to the motto, "It's my hair and I can do what I want with it," a defiant attitude that seemed like a declaration of war at the time.[11]

It was hard to say whether adults were more upset by teenagers' rebellion, their questionable taste, or their apparent rejection of conventional masculinity. Did long hair mean teenage boys were "queer"? The highly publicized uproar that ensued suggested that all three were serious concerns. It was probably just as well that the Beatles never publicized the fact that a German woman had inspired their haircuts because hostile critics would have had a field day.[12] As it was, sarcastic gym teachers were already handing out pink hairnets to boys with long hair, while magazines wondered what it meant when boys spent as much time and money on their long curly locks as girls did. In Richmond, Virginia, a long-haired seventeen-year-old was forced to contend with a father who called him "she." He probably had an easier time of it, though, than the Los Angeles teen who refused to cut his hair and was convicted of disturbing the peace![13]

Teenagers wondered what the problem was. "I . . . couldn't see how something like my hair could be considered disruptive," a fourteen-year-old remarked. "It wasn't that I was so proud of my hair," explained another. "But when they told me to cut it, I felt it wasn't a reasonable thing for them to ask." This student was a surfer from a wealthy community in California who was as well known for listening to the radio in class (and turning up the volume for Jan and Dean or the Beach Boys) as he was for his collar-length, sun-bleached hair. It was true that his hair was a mess. It looked like straw, he conceded. But that did not give his school the right to determine its length. "What business of theirs was it how long I had my hair?" he wanted to know, as long as he kept up his grades. Unwilling to conform to standards he did not accept as his own, an attitude that was becoming more common every day, this student added simply, "I felt I should fight it." As far as he could see, he was merely claiming his constitutional rights as any American might do. Years later, though, when he returned to his high school as a teacher, he realized how deeply some adults had resented his fight. A gym teacher who remembered him from his student days still refused to acknowledge him.[14]

It was not long hair in and of itself that enraged adult critics. It was the arrogance they perceived in teenage style, the public nature of the challenge, and the disrespect it implied that raised adult tempers. Long hair was a direct assault on adult prerogatives, critics argued. It challenged traditional standards and values and weakened the ties between age and authority, experience and wisdom. "Long hair and mod clothes are . . . not only signs that adults are losing, or have already lost, control of the young," an analyst reported, "but signs that they may be losing control generally." To a high school principal, he pointed out, "a Beatle-type hair style can be as frightening a symbol as a switchblade."[15] He was not alone. "These days," another critic complained, "teenagers tell their parents how things are going to be at home. Students tell administration how school is to be conducted. . . . Kids dictate to our Federal government what our policy is to be on domestic and foreign affairs." Enough was enough, he said. It was time to hold the line in high school and "stop giving in to the kids."[16]

Others were not so sure. They questioned the wisdom of forcing teenagers to conform to standards just to prove who was boss, especially when adults all around them no longer abided by the rules. As a teacher in Des Moines put it, "A principal who sends a girl home for wearing slacks runs a considerable risk of having the mother appear in slacks for a parental conference. Should the mother then be sent home for more suitable apparel?" the teacher wanted to know.[17] As college administrators had learned the hard way, an ironclad strategy could easily backfire. "We believe there is nothing gained and much to be lost in taking a quick, hard and fast stand in cases of student defiance," a group of pragmatic educators reported. It only resulted in publicity, they said, and that, after all, was what the students wanted in the first place.[18]

They had a point. Rebellious teenagers had no trouble at all gaining a public forum. There were 12.9 million high school students in 1965, which represented an 80 percent increase in ten years' time, a sizable population by any measure. All over the country they were coming to school with their hair too long, their skirts too short, and their pants too tight to comply with existing dress codes. And people were paying attention. Newspapers and magazines chronicled the conflict in articles like "School Slacks Issue Skirted" (when girls lost a fight to wear pants to class in Washington, D.C.) and "Splitting Hairs over Moptops, or How Lunatic Is the Fringe?" A teenager writing in *Seventeen* declared dress codes to be "irrelevant, immaterial and insulting," while another told *Senior Scholastic*, "It's not the clothes, but the person inside those clothes, that matter." Convinced that personal appearance was a personal matter of no concern to parents or teachers, teenagers wanted to know, "Do you have to be bald for an education?"[19]

Mass circulation magazines picked up the story as part of their ongoing coverage of teenage culture. For years they had run light-hearted features on teenage slang, high school fads, the younger generation's amazing capacity to shop. Now these happy-go-lucky stories were balanced, and sometimes outweighed, by more frank appraisals of teenage life. The combination of an irreverent popular culture, tensions unleashed by the Vietnam War, and the baby boomers' astonishing demographic power had generated a class of teenagers who were bolder and more aggressive than adults had come to expect. "They have become the enemy," Stephen Birmingham concluded in *Holiday* magazine, destroying property at lavish parties, rioting on city streets, sniffing glue, smoking marijuana, and taking a dangerously casual attitude toward sex—comments that usually described lower-class delinquents, not the affluent offspring of the better sort.[20]

If magazine editors still tipped their hat to the teenage majority's "essential goodness," there was no denying that the dominant image had changed. The innocent energy that had defined teenagers since the word was coined in the 1940s had given way to hostility. Indeed, the most outspoken teenagers wanted nothing to do with hypocritical adults. "They're so stupid. They're so untrustful. . . . They think they've just got to clamp down," complained a sixteen-year-old from Los Angeles.[21] "Today's teens feel they cannot talk to most old people," another added. That included parents, according to a seventeen-year-old from Berkeley High. "They just say, 'Oh, no, you've got long hair and you hang around with the wrong people, and I'm going to ground you for three months," she said. A self-identified student activist who expected to spend ten years in college, at least, organizing and earning a degree, this teenager saw no reason to rush into the kind of life her parents led. "I could never join the mainstream of society now," she said. "Society is just going to have to accept us. Either that, or this darned society is just going to collapse."[22]

The superficial advice adults had been offering the younger generation for decades—how to shop, how to dress, how to achieve popularity—now seemed ludicrously out of touch. Adults didn't have a clue about real teenage life. "Adults live without a personal identity," complained a teenage boy from Buffalo. Thus they had no insight into why their children might fight so hard to express their individual style at school. Even if they tried to understand, they usually missed the point. When *Newsweek* interpreted new "unisex" styles (high-heeled boots, hip-hugger pants, and ruffled shirts) as evidence of female dominance in the teenage world, young readers complained about the coverage. "We protest against the pitiful, closed-minded people (all looking the same to us) who stare at us as we walk down the street. We try to be direct opposites of them," this teenager wrote, "so that there will be no chance for us to turn out anything like them."[23]

Even religious leaders could not escape such harsh criticism. They had to earn their respect like everyone else. When a Catholic editor commented on "Today's Rebellious Generation" in 1966, for instance, he noted that modern teenagers had "never grasped the reality of Christianity." How on earth could they, teenagers wanted to know, with the poor example adults set? "The older generation does not believe in many of the things that it holds as true, and it is this hypocrisy which is handed down to the new generation—nothing else." Others were even more frank: "We 'young people' are not impatient," a teenager insisted. "We have realized that this monolithic corporation run by old men in

Rome is not alive to the needs and desires of its stockholders." Adopting a tone that certainly would have earned him a slap in Catholic school, another added that "many of the parish priests give the impression that they are nothing more than old, senile fuddy-duddies. All teens ever hear them say is 'We need money for this,' or 'Don't hold hands with your girl friend, it will lead to other things,'" complaints that made it clear that even the most harshly disciplined teenagers could not be forced to hold their tongue in public.[24]

Although the press continually made the point that teenagers, by and large, were contented kids "who wanted what adults wanted them to want," the articles they published gave a different impression. When Newsweek offered its special teenage issue in 1966, for instance, it highlighted the generation gap that was growing wider by the minute. "Sometimes I feel like dropping out," a sixteen-year-old told interviewers, and she was talking about society, not high school.[25] A few months later Look surveyed teenagers who were just as dissatisfied. A third of the respondents agreed with the statement that the United States was no longer a democracy, and the great majority believed that the war in Vietnam was immoral and unjust. Forty-two percent distrusted their hometown police force, and more than half agreed that the nation's economic system did not work for everyone.[26] High school fared no better. Nearly 60 percent of the survey group thought the curriculum was uninspired and the teachers mediocre and unprepared.[27]

Respectable behavior standards had also fallen, if these teenagers could be believed. As Beat poet Gregory Corso put it after interviewing an outspoken group of teenagers, "Yesterday's taboos are today's jokes." The survey in Look, which was not scientific by any means, backed him up. Two-thirds of the middle-class respondents thought premarital sex was acceptable behavior, and 45 percent agreed that couples could live together without benefit of marriage. A shockingly high 83 percent were opposed to shotgun weddings, and more than a third of these were female. This did not mean that the younger generation had lost all sense of right and wrong, as some adults seemed to fear. It meant that they saw no reason to hide their opinions behind moral platitudes. In fact, 82 percent of the survey group thought both generations were on the same moral plane but adults were reluctant to admit it. "It's easier for adults to conceal what they do," a boy from Arizona explained, and a girl from New York agreed. "Adults are just phonies about morals," she said.[28]

Given the fact that most high schools still ducked the question of sex education, it was clear that adults were not comfortable discussing the subject, despite the fact that advertisers used sex to sell everything from cars to records. Teenagers, on the other hand, seemed surprisingly at ease. "Sex is the biggest topic in any high school, and you can't tell me it isn't," a teenager told *Newsweek* in 1966. But if sociologist Edgar Friedenberg applauded what he called "a growing sense of 'erotic authenticity' " among American teenagers, *Newsweek*, for one, was not about to probe the subject too deeply. Although the magazine surveyed a cross-section of thirteen- to seventeen-year-olds on any number of topics, it carefully avoided the question of sexual experience. "Partly because the legality of such inquiries among minors is in doubt," the editors explained, "and also because such questions evoke an often meaningless jumble of wishes, facts, and boasts." Undoubtedly, they also avoided the question because nobody wanted to hear the answer. If it turned out to be true, as a New York City teenager insisted, that "the majority of teenage girls sleep with the boy they're going with," what would be gained by the knowledge? Wasn't it better to assume, as most authorities did, that premarital sex was an issue confined to television characters and college students, who were leading the so-called sexual revolution on campus, and not high schoolers at all?[29]

Reliable numbers were hard to come by, but that did seem to be the case. Between 1925 and 1965, various studies estimated that about 10 percent of white teenage females (and 35 percent of black) had lost their virginity by age nineteen, and the numbers did not change significantly until around 1973. "There hasn't been any real increase in premarital coitus" among younger teenagers, experts Ira Reiss and Paul Gebhard maintained.[30] Anecdotal evidence tended to back them up. "When it came to sex . . . you said no all the time and you said no fairly forcibly," a woman who was raised in an upper-middle-class family explained. "But even then you didn't have to be that forceful about it," she admitted. In her experience, nice boys rarely forced the issue (before 1969, at least), since they took it for granted that virginity mattered, at least to respectable girls.[31]

If they did not, however, girls joined forces to protect themselves. "We used to get together . . . to talk about virginity," recalled a cheerleader who graduated in 1965. She and her friends kept each other apprised of their dates, and if a boy came on too fast the others always knew about it. The word would go out to keep away from him. Even the most adventurous girls held on to their virginity, whether it was strictly technical or not. "It was your bargain for marriage," said a girl who played in a rock 'n' roll band. Although she might have admitted to fooling around in her high school days, "nobody actually admitted to losing their virginity," she said.[32]

College was a different story. More teenage girls were postponing marriage to earn college degrees—tripling their numbers between 1965 and 1969.[33] This profoundly altered their perceptions of the future. The vast majority still intended to marry, but this was no longer the key to their happiness, self-worth, or economic security. Now that reliable birth control had become available (the pill had come on the market in 1960 and had passed a constitutional challenge in 1965), the rules that regulated teenage virginity no longer seemed persuasive. "I mean we all get sort of the same 'nice girls don't' routine at home," a Radcliffe student reported in 1964. "But then I came up here and there they were— all those nice girls, much nicer than I if you talk about family and background—and they were doing it. I felt betrayed," she admitted, and lost her virginity four months into her freshman year. Like so many others of her age and status, she assumed that her personal life was a personal choice, not an issue of morality at all. "I used to think it was terrible if people had intercourse before marriage," another confessed. "Now I think each person should find his own values."[34]

The sexual revolution on college campuses was neither as swift nor as widespread as the mass media implied. Before 1967, sexually active college females still tended to be pinned or engaged to their partners, a pattern that dated back to around 1925. But if attitudes shifted more quickly than behavior did, there was no denying the fact that the climate on campus had changed radically since the early 1960s. "The big difference was being in charge of myself," a woman who entered college in 1965 remembered. "I mean, wow . . . there was nobody standing behind me." The Berkeley Free Speech movement may have involved only a minority on campus in 1964, but it had ignited a national campaign for student rights that was changing college life from the bottom up. Fraternities and sororities lost their prestige (and half their population between 1964 and 1972). College officials dropped or relaxed their parental roles. The rigid rules that once separated males and females in the dorms, the cafeteria, and the library were gone by 1965 in some schools and on their way out in most. Now it was up to the students themselves—or duly elected governing boards—to devise their own social standards.[35]

As college students were learning, that was more difficult than it looked. Social freedom was harder to handle than social hypocrisy any day. "That was when boys started saying on the first date, 'Well, obviously you have a psychological problem. You're uptight if you're not going to go to bed with me,'" a girl who started college in 1969 recalled. "You could suddenly have anybody in [your room] at any time, and in a way it was good because it allowed us the freedom to develop relationships," she said. "But in a way it was bad, because it put girls under a real pressure to have sex. The opportunity was there now. . . .You could no longer say to a guy, 'No, you can't come up. Those are the rules.' "[36]

This sudden burst of freedom changed the nature of the college experience. The hallowed halls of academe now became a sanctuary for students who wanted to experiment with new ways of living, some of them legal, some of them not. "That's when I had my first sexual experience," a Berkeley student recalled, "and that's when I smoked dope for the first time."[37] Her experience was hardly unique. By the mid-1960s, marijuana had become the collegiate drug of choice. Although adults feared the prospect of bright futures going up in smoke, students seemed remarkably unconcerned. In fact, the casual acceptance of the illegal substance was probably more significant than the cumulative effect of the drug itself. "It was a social thing," an occasional smoker pointed out, "to show that you weren't stuffy, that you were contemporary," she said.[38]

Another pointed out that all his friends at Berkeley smoked marijuana, and a third reported that he didn't know anyone at

UCLA who wasn't smoking dope—not even his professors! The fact was, marijuana was part of a social ritual, a passport to the counterculture that was evolving nationwide. As one student described it, "the curtains would go down, the Indian music would come on, the incense would start. Someone would roll a joint. Then everybody would . . . space out."[39]

Although nobody knew for sure how many students actually inhaled—or dropped LSD, for that matter—there was no denying that popular culture had picked up on the trend. It was common knowledge on college campuses that in order to "get" Dylan's "Mr. Tambourine Man" you had to smoke dope, Todd Gitlin remembered. "To get access to youth culture, you had to get high," the SDS leader pointed out. Otherwise "you were an outsider looking in."[40] When LSD entered the public picture, around 1966, the connection between drugs and the counterculture seemed unmistakable. There was nothing ambiguous in Tim Leary's well-publicized message to "Turn on, tune in, drop out." The psychologist-turned-psychedelic guru was promoting the use of LSD, marijuana, peyote, and other nonaddictive drugs and grabbing headlines with his "anti-establishment, anti-church, anti-parents, anti-rat-race, anti-cop" message.[41]

San Francisco's Summer of Love in 1967 put a softer face on alienated youth, turning national attention to teenage hippies, flower children, and their "groovy" kind of love. "It was really idealistic and the drugs were great," a participant who was sixteen at the time recalled.[42] LSD (which was not yet illegal) shaped everything from psychedelic posters (by Peter Max) to the Beatles' album "Sgt. Pepper's Lonely Hearts Club Band." In fact, rumor had it that the song "Lucy in the Sky with Diamonds" was an ode to LSD (although John Lennon always denied it). Even prime-time television shows were caught up in the psychedelic scene—without ever actually mentioning drugs, of course. For instance, an episode of "Get Smart" featured a Leary-like guru who hypnotized college students with messages like "Yeah, yeah, yeah, bump off a square," or "Make trouble, rebellion is hip." "Can you imagine what ten million kids could do to the country?" the Chief asked Max, who was investigating the guru's Temple of Meditation and Inner Peace. "I thought they'd already done it," he said.

The remark was meant to be funny, but it was actually on target. By 1967, the drug-laced counterculture had filtered down to the high school crowd, usually in the form of marijuana, although LSD was not unknown. Educators estimated that on a typical school day one out of ten students was high in class.[43] "It was incredibly easy to get," a girl explained. "Everybody knew somebody—an older brother or sister at the university . . . who could get hold of dope." These were not the troubled, pathological youth adults usually associated with drugs. "We were part of a rich, middle-class community. We saw ourselves as college-bound for good careers," she said.[44]

A student at Northwood High School, in suburban Maryland, confirmed her point. "The question is: Who exactly does all the pot smoking at school?" she asked. Obviously, long-haired radicals headed the list, along with "greasy looking potential drop-outs." But high school athletes were also known to toke up (even during training). So were "quite a few of those innocent-looking, school spirited, collegiate, social-climbing 'young ladies.' "[45] Even teenagers in out-of-the way New Hampshire were getting high by the late 1960s, although Budweiser was still the more popular vice. "If a person's liberated and hip and creative-thinking . . . then he smokes," a teenager from Durham pointed out, "and if he's dull and crew-cutted and Republican . . . then he doesn't," she said.[46] Across the country in sunny California, the same distinctions held. "If people smoked pot, then they were probably into music, too, and chances were good we could communicate," explained a boy from a wealthy family who started smoking early in his teens. It did not take long for him to discover that "long hair, dope, and music were attractive to girls. It was a near-delirious discovery," he added, since he lacked "the other things that attracted girls . . . like a surfboard, or blond hair and blue eyes, or . . . the nerve to approach them."[47] Dope did not interfere with his schoolwork, either, he was careful to point out. On the contrary, he kept up his grades since he had no intention of giving his parents "the slightest provocation to get involved" with his private life. As far as he could see, smoking dope was an enjoyable, sometimes enlightening experience. "Getting high gave me the freedom to be what I wanted, to escape who I was and where I was. . . . I appreciated music more when I was high. . . . I even discovered that with a little buzz I actually liked reading." Aware that adults blamed "peer pressure" for the rise of dope-smoking teens, he thought they were missing the point. "I kept waiting for my friends to put the screws to me but they never did," he recalled. "Peer pressure. It's a myth. . . . The pressure comes from within. It's *me* pressure," he said.[48]

The controversial counterculture of sex, drugs, and rock 'n' roll suggested that the generation gap was now unbridgeable—and not just because the mass media said so. In the past, teenagers had amused adults in movies (*The Bachelor and the Bobby-Soxer*), television shows ("Dobie Gillis" and "Patty Duke"), on the dance floor, and on the athletic field. Or they had aggravated them with their laziness around the house, their bad taste, and their infuriating addiction to the telephone (if they were girls) or their cars (if they were boys).[49] Now they reviled adults by taking up the psychedelic colors of an enemy army of youth. In a war-torn world, age and experience did not count for much, and teenagers made the most of their golden opportunity to tell their elders off.

"When I look at adults, I see greed and ambition," a teenager explained. "I feel sorry for my parents," another added. "They have wasted their lives dreaming of money." As far as he could see, his father did not live life, he calculated it. Yet for all his material success—two houses, two cars, and a country club membership—his family was bitter and disillusioned. Did these narrow-minded, status-seeking conformists see the error of their ways? Did they try to escape the middle-class rat race that had trapped them? Of course not, bitter teenagers complained. Worse yet, they wanted their children to take the bait, too. "The message is clear," a suburban teenager wrote in an underground student newspaper. "Sure you'll be dealt with as cogs, you can expect to be abused and trampled upon; but that's the way things are, so if you can learn . . . to work hard and excel . . . then there is money to be made and authority to be had and 'respectability' and it all clicks into being 'successful.' " And the outcome? "Politeness, ambition, and discipline—which in many respects means dishonesty, game-playing and self-suppression as a way of life—become desirable qualities."[50]

A vibrant, underground high school press had emerged by 1968, demonstrating how determined some teenagers were to challenge the "system." Adults still held the balance of power in high school: Teachers were not only free to censor student expression but considered doing so part of their job. Students who risked becoming involved with unauthorized publications (often some of the brightest students around) were amazed to discover that they had no right to free speech in school. "You will definitely encounter resistance and hassling from the administration of your school, or even from the local board of education," experienced editors agreed. Suspensions, expulsions, parental involvement, and the dreaded notation on a permanent record card were all routine responses. "The suppression we encountered was frightening," an editor reported. In a New Hampshire town, police shut down an unauthorized student paper in a Catholic school, and in Milwaukee they began investigating "subversive influences," which, authorities presumed, were responsible for the underground paper there.[51]

But if school officials believed that harassment, legal fights, and even arrests would silence dissatisfied students, they had not been paying attention. Suppression only egged defiant students on, pushing them to expose an educational system that denied students their right to an uncensored opinion. "The existence of anti-distribution laws for student literature . . . is a violation of our constitutional rights," an editor from Ann Arbor High School reminded students. Just to insure that teenagers understood the principles at stake, the American Civil Liberties Union (ACLU) offered legal support. Students denied the right "to have access to varied points of view, to confront and study controversial issues, to be treated without prejudice or penalty for what [they] read and write" could count on an ACLU lawyer to defend them in court. That did not mean the fight would be easy or hassle-free, however. "Remember," an independent-press organizer wrote, "if you are going to offer an alternative to the system's way of doing things, it will get a lot of people annoyed and hung-up. Expect it!" he said.[52]

That was good advice given the tone of these alternative publications. "This paper belongs to the people of our generation. And it will talk about issues which really affect our lives—authoritarian and oppressive high schools, police harassment, racism, drugs, the draft, entertainment, sex," one began. "This school system needs drastic changes—interesting classes, an end to compulsory attendance and hall passes, an end to the racist crap they try to force feed us from their still-biased textbooks. . . . What is this anyway," students wanted to know, "a school or a prison? Or have the two come to mean the same thing?"[53]

From some points of view, it certainly seemed so. "We will no longer tolerate a high school system that condemns all behavior that it itself has not conditioned," students in Framingham, Massachusetts, announced, and those in Milwaukee backed them up. "Until more freedom is granted in dress and school rules," they wrote, "all Milwaukee city schools are going to have trouble."[54]

This was not an empty threat. In New York City, girls won the right to wear pants to school after students staged a strike. In Wellesley, Massachusetts, students had organized and overturned a draconian dress code: no long hair, no dungarees, no boots for boys or girls, no makeup, no mustaches, no untucked shirts, and more. They had done so by forcing the principal to practice what he preached and to give the majority a voice in their own affairs. Students circulated petitions, formed joint committees with faculty to devise proposals, and then gave the student body a chance to vote on the issue. With four plans to choose from, students overwhelming supported the "no dress code" option. "We'd put [the principal] up against the wall," student activists boasted. He had to go along with them.[55]

High school students were also testing their legal rights in court. With the ACLU's help, they challenged the constitutionality of dress codes and adult censorship, and they claimed the right to protest the Vietnam War by wearing black armbands to school. This time, however, the courts were on their side. In a 1969 decision, *Tinker v. Des Moines*, the Supreme Court recognized a high school student's constitutional right to free speech and expression, a revolutionary change that put students at the center of school policy. The justices also decreed that the process of education mattered as much as the content. Thus, high schools had to practice democracy as well as teach it. Principals could no longer suppress unruly words and nonviolent deeds. Nor could they impose values and standards in the name of efficiency or order. Since the larger world was notoriously "disputatious," the court argued, a degree of disorder in school was not only acceptable but educational. As a related decision argued, it was far more important for teachers to encourage diversity and adaptation to it than to enforce a rigid code of homogeneity in school.[56]

High school administrators did not fight these court decisions; in fact, many welcomed them as a way of ending the disruptive battles that now passed for high school life. Dress and grooming conflicts were only the tip of the iceberg. Black power had also come into its own, bringing a new degree of separateness and hostility into the classroom. In Cambridge, Massachusetts, black students raised clenched fists for their yearbook pictures, and when the principal objected, they held a sit-down strike outside his office that went on for weeks. In Denver, the Black Student Association protested faculty racism and demanded the reinstatement of suspended black students. In San Diego, angry black students shouted "Kill the whites" at a pep rally and then ordered teachers to leave. All over the country, dissatisfied students demanded black faculty, black student centers, and courses in black history and literature. And the protests were angry enough to bring results.[57]

What was true in the world of high school was not necessarily true in the wider world, however, as continued protests against the war in Vietnam demonstrated. By the late 1960s and early 1970s, high school activists had joined college students in the streets, but the experience proved as frustrating as it was dangerous. Supporters of law and order were not as willing to placate teenage protesters as high school administrators were. Students who challenged the power of the state soon discovered what power really meant. "My throat is red and raspy from the riot-gas of the Illinois National Guard," a seventeen-year-old wrote. "My head is swollen from the 'Sons of Liberty' who beat me up because I'm a 'hippy-Jew.' My voice is hoarse from trying to explain the way I feel," he added. "I no longer give a shit if anyone understands."[58]

The point was made more graphically by President Richard Nixon in 1970, when he decided that it was time to show the country who was boss. It was on his watch that the National Guard shot down unarmed student protestors at Kent State University on May 4, killing four students and wounding eleven others. To Nixon, these deaths were justified because young protesters were "bums, you know, blowing up the campus."[59] To students, however, this was a horrifying show of generational power and stunning proof that youth and their elders inhabited two different worlds. If the president was willing to gun them down, if that was what it took to silence critics, then this could not be the free country they had been brought up to believe in.

The Kent State killings did not achieve Nixon's ends. Students continued to protest the war in greater numbers than ever before. In fact, the level of student dissatisfaction was high enough to persuade the U.S. Congress to give eighteen-year-olds the vote in 1971, end the draft, and withdraw all troops from Vietnam by 1973.[60] But this was the students movement's grand finale, not a sign of things to come. As early as the fall of 1970, the number of students identifying themselves as "radical or far left" had dropped for the first time since 1965, and the number of "conservatives" increased for the first time since 1968.[61]

Having won most of their immediate objectives, students were not as interested in transforming society as the original leaders of SDS had been in the early 1960s. They were less convinced than their predecessors had been that they could live off the fat of the land. By the early 1970s, students who majored in liberal arts were already having trouble finding jobs.[62] They were also less inclined to romanticize revolution (after facing reality at Kent State), or the counterculture (after rock stars Janis Joplin, Jimi Hendrix, and Jim Morrison all died ugly drug-related deaths). The end of a turbulent era, however, did not mean the end of social change for teenagers. Those who came of age in the 1970s never experienced the social repression and regimentation that generations of teenagers had taken for granted. High school dress codes were gone by the early 1970s, for the most part, and rigid discipline was giving way to a more open, less hostile (and some would say, less demanding) high school system. Students had more opportunities to choose electives in "relevant" subjects such as black history and culture, psychology, and film studies, and teachers made more of an effort to integrate popular culture into the curriculum. Special programs, or even alternative schools, were launched to keep radical students satisfied (and marginal students in school). As one educator put it, rights and feelings now took precedence over academics in public high schools, an attitude that would have shocked James Conant and his cold war critics in the 1950s. After a decade of conflict and confrontation, though, the time seemed right to try a new approach.[63]

In a sense, teenagers in the 1970s had won the battle for freedom that high school students had been waging since the 1930s. They not only gained a voice and vote in their own affairs, at home and at school, but they had the right to live life as they pleased. Whether adults approved or not, they had to accept the fact that teenagers—girls included—were likely to drink in high school. They had to face up to the unpleasant fact that high school students needed access to reliable birth control, whether parents were willing to discuss the subject or not. Finally, adults had to concede that teenagers lived by their own social rules, rules that had nothing to do with old-fashioned notions of middle-class propriety or respect for their elders.

"There's nothing they won't write on a piece of paper," an English teacher reported. "Why, I got one this morning, a poem on sex." Ten years earlier, he said, students would not have offered such a piece.[64] They would not have come to school in such casual, revealing clothes, either. One teacher reported in 1975 that a student came to class in a low-cut sweater, one that made it obvious that she wore no bra. Ten years earlier, as a student at this very school, he had fought for his right to wear long hair, but now, watching his students do whatever they pleased, he was not persuaded that teenage freedom, without the fight, taught students anything valuable. Moreover, he was glad that he had grown up when he did, at a time when achieving freedom in high school was still a challenge for teenagers.[65]

A former classmate had to agree. She understood the teenage hunger for freedom and self-expression; she had fought for those rights in school. But she wondered whether the pendulum had swung too far. When teachers did not set boundaries, how would students—especially indifferent students—stay on track? "The students today don't seem to have any sense of responsibility," she said. "They come and go as they please, they dress the way they want, and school's just more or less something to keep them busy." She knew only too well how dangerous that kind of freedom could be for teenagers who were not the type to take their education seriously. Back in her own high school days, she had been more concerned with turning heads with her high teased hair and her well-developed figure than with classes or homework. "I don't think I could take it today," she readily admitted. The opportunity to get into drugs, or whatever it was teenagers were doing, would be much too much of a temptation.[66] She needed a more structured environment in and out of school.

So the cycle had come around. The free spirits of the turbulent 1960s, who had done so much to liberate the teenage world, now wanted to shelter their children from it.

conclusion

Jennifer Beasley and Christopher Grose, Dahlgren, Virginia, 1995. *Brad Piepmeier*

Back to the Future

IN THE SPRING OF 1991, THE *NEW YORK TIMES* FEATURED A BED-
time story that surely disturbed the sleep of a good many readers.
Alarmed by reports of increasing street violence and the spread of
AIDS among teenagers, a new breed of "sympathetic" parents was
now permitting their sons (but not usually their daughters) to
entertain guests of the opposite sex in their rooms—overnight. "I
feel better knowing where my child is," a suburban mother
explained, "so I decided that his room is his territory, his privacy."
Like other parents who had reached the same startling conclusion,
she believed that permitting sex at home was a practical way of
protecting her offspring. "Parents feel caught between two very
profound worries," a clinical psychologist explained. "On the one
hand they feel that if they don't accept that their kids are having
sex and provide a safe place, the children will have it with people
the parents don't know and in places that could be dangerous. On
the other hand parents fear that by doing this they are encouraging their kids to act out sexually," an analysis that almost invites
the teenage response, "Well, duh."[1]

Hardly a trend outside of affluent suburbs, adult-approved
sleepover dates represent the cutting edge of adolescent culture in

the 1990s. Sixty years ago, when high schools first began to enroll a mixed population, concerned parents engineered a social life for their children to steer them away from unacceptable dates. Now their modern descendants are trying to screen their children's sexual partners in order to eliminate risky mates. This time, however, the experts are not on their side, and not only because the strategy is faulty. Sex in a good neighborhood is by no means safer than sex in the back seat of a car, as far as the AIDS virus is concerned. Whatever parents have in mind when they welcome their teenager's overnight guests, they are fostering a false sense of security, the experts warn. Moreover, they are neglecting their family duty. "Parents need to set limits," a psychologist points out, "and it's the children's job to push them." A mother of an independent seventeen-year-old daughter agrees. "We have raised her to be careful, to know about birth control and AIDS, but if she wants to have sex she has to be responsible for finding the place. She should not expect to have it in my face," she said.[2]

Although the debate raised some intriguing questions about modern parenthood, the appearance of the article in the *New York Times* was probably more significant than the thorny issue itself. That a major newspaper might so casually document the fact of premarital sex among middle-class teenagers demonstrates how far the high school crowd has come since the days of sheltered adolescence. In the 1930s, the editors of *Scholastic* could barely raise the question of teenage necking, and it was not until the late 1950s that *Seventeen* did in any serious fashion. Even at the height of the so-called sexual revolution in the 1960s, teenagers were not part of the public discussion. Although adults used the idea of sexually active teenagers to sell movies, television shows, and popular music, high school students were still presumed to be innocent. Up until the 1970s, they were not supposed to think about sex at all, except in the context of a sacred relation between (married) men and women.

Female chastity and adherence to social rules were the keys to keeping this system in balance. Girls still had a social duty to keep boys in line by refusing to go too far, and boys had an obligation to respect their wishes. Ignorance and obedience were also part of the plan. Although parents might agree that boys needed to know something about practical "protection," girls were supposed to be better off not knowing anything at all, except how to avoid trouble. As late as the 1970s, *Seventeen* still limited practical advice to questions of etiquette, fashion, and diet, as if the subject of passion and its consequences had no bearing at all on teenage life. Long after the number of teenage brides (and premature babies) shot up in the 1950s and early 1960s, adults still believed they could control teenage behavior by setting rules and withholding information. For instance, the subject of birth control was almost never raised in public. To even consider the possibility of controlling pregnancy outside the bonds of marriage (and thereby admit that some teenagers enjoyed illicit sexual lives) was to confront a long-standing contradiction between teenage image and reality that most Americans preferred to ignore.

Consider the case of the 1954 book *Two by Two*, by Mary Stolz, an intensely romantic novel that featured a teenage love affair that was almost consummated—the girl's unsuspecting father came home at just the wrong moment. Originally the book was marketed to adults, but by 1964 it was deemed appropriate for teenage readers and reissued as *A Love or a Season*. Since the original version had included what the author called "certain areas of sophistication" that fell outside the realm of teenage interests, however, some cutting had been done.[3] Although readers might assume that the high school couple's decision to go ahead and "do it" might have been deleted, that was not the case. What was cut was the sixteen-year-old girl's vague question about birth control and her seventeen-year-old boyfriend's promise to take care of it.[4] Apparently it was permissible to introduce teenage readers to a high school couple intent on losing their virginity as long as no mention of birth control marred their romance!

This illogical approach to sex and contraception went unquestioned, for the most part, as long as sexually active teenagers were willing to do the right thing and marry young. But when 50 percent of these marriages ended in divorce, as they did in the mid-1960s, it was obvious that something had to change. Dr. Mary Calderone urged high school educators to adopt what she called "comprehensive" sex education. Once teenagers had reliable information about abortion, illegitimacy, and venereal disease, she believed, they would forgo sexual experience until they were ready for it.[5] Dr. Eli Ginzburg, on the other hand, favored a more realistic approach. According to the sociologist, American society had "one simple choice" if it hoped to cut down on teenage marriages and divorces: It could adopt a "different attitude" toward teenage sex and birth control. An alarming rise in illegitimate births to teenagers between 1963 and 1970 settled the question, at least temporarily. Although adults were still reluctant to discuss the subject, by the mid-1970s teenage girls had access to the Pill through private doctors, agencies like Planned Parenthood, and in some cases high school clinics that steered students to the services they needed.[6]

This shift in attitude and accessibility was revolutionary as far as the connection between sex and marriage was concerned. Once individuals had the chance to control their own fertility, teenage girls had the same opportunities that boys did to explore their sexuality without committing themselves to family life. Once pregnancy was no longer a threat, girls could "go all the way" if they wanted to without risking their reputations, their future, or even their parents' good will—as long as they covered their tracks and took adequate precautions. As one educator put it, "Middle-class girls no longer lost their virginity and respectability simultaneously."[7] In the process, they gained a measure of personal freedom unheard of for girls in the past outside of the lowest of lower-class circles. They also gained a new measure of responsibility. The combination of reliable birth control and the increasing availability of legal abortions after 1973 brought an end to the shotgun marriages that had forced boys as well as girls to consider the consequences of their actions. Contraception was now the girl's responsibility, and boys no longer felt compelled "to take care of things."[8]

From this point forward, high school students could look at sex through very different eyes. What had once served as an unofficial passage to marriage and adulthood, and all the responsibility that went with them, was now just another part of high school life. Although it was always difficult, when it came to sex, to know how much behavior had actually changed as opposed to attitudes, studies suggested that the shift was profound. In 1973, an estimated 35 percent of high school seniors had lost their virginity; by 1990, 70 percent had—and so had 40 percent of the freshmen! Although pioneer promoters of the teenage market had anticipated the trend with the motto, "They're getting older younger," at the time they had less controversial milestones in mind, like driving, dating, and staying out late. Now, whether adults liked it or not, loss of virginity had been added to the list. According to a 1992 survey by *Sassy* magazine, sixteen was now the appropriate age for teenagers to take the plunge.[9]

The fact that girls were almost as likely as boys to test the sexual waters was probably the most significant aspect of the change. According to a 1988 study, 50 percent of teenage girls (and 27 percent of female fifteen-year-olds) had lost their virginity, as opposed to 60 percent of teenage boys (and 32 percent of male fifteen-year-olds).[10] No longer willing to be the keepers of society's conventions now that they had the chance to expect as much from life as their brothers did, they also refused to suffer a sexual double standard. In fact, by the 1980s they had trouble understanding just how their mothers had survived. "The hypocrisy, and phoniness and pretense—women must have been enraged," a college student said. "My mother says no, she wasn't as 'galled' as I think she was. But if that's the case, they were slaves!"[11] Parents had just as much trouble understanding their liberated daughters, however. A father, distressed by his daughter's behavior, wondered where he had gone wrong. "I talked to her about contraception. I told her no sex before marriage. I tried everything," he told the *Washington Post*. "Her response was, 'Get real, Dad. This is the '90s.'" A sixteen-year-old suburban girl agreed. "Kids are never going to stop having sex," she reported in 1992. "Our parents fought for that right in the '60s. And now it's our reality."[12]

Twenty-five years ago, baby-boomer teenagers would have cheered her defiant directness. Hypocritical parents had neither the right nor the power to set moral standards they could not live up to themselves. As baby-boomer parents, however, they see the issues in a different light. Having exchanged youthful exuberance for middle-aged experience, they now think that their children should slow down. "There's tension between what we did and what we don't want our kids to do," one mother explained. "There's tension between what we did and don't want our kids to know we did."[13] A onetime rebel posed the question on many boomers' minds: Is it hypocritical for a parent who engaged in premarital sex to advise her child not to? Of course not, the experts reply. "There's an important middle ground," a psychiatrist points out. "You might say that even though you felt the same way, now you have a better perspective on the situation and feel you had sex at too young an age." Although boomer teenagers would have hooted at that self-serving explanation, it somehow seems persuasive to them now.[14]

Whether their children will buy it, however, is another question entirely. Many fail to see what all the fuss is about. For instance, a teenager who was grounded after her parents discovered she was no longer a virgin wondered whether they had the right to punish her for that. "I can understand being grounded for sneaking out, but I don't think it's fair that they punished me for having sex just because they believe in abstinence," she wrote to *Seventeen*.[15] A fifteen-year-old boy agreed. "If the time is right and you play it safe, then why shouldn't you [have sex]? If you wait until you are married," he pointed out, "you may only get to have sex with one person and in the long run, you may be upset that you didn't take control of all your options."[16] These matter-of-fact assumptions that teenagers have the right to decide for themselves how and whether they will express their sexuality alarms boomer parents. But it should not, the experts contend. "Many parents who have accepted the fact that their children will make up their own minds when it comes to what they will wear, or how they will spend their money," a psychologist noted, "still insist on controlling their kids' sex lives." They are bound to be disappointed, he added. Boomer parents might now insist that "sex is for adults," as one former rebel told the *New York Times*, but that kind of pronouncement has never held much weight with teenagers determined to go their own way.[17]

As one experienced mother put it, "You can't tell people not to do things they are going to do anyway." The *Ladies' Home Journal* agrees. "Even if you are very much against premarital sex, it's important to remember that you can't keep a tight rein over your child's sexuality," an advice columnist told parents. "You must convey that even if you don't approve of what [your children] are doing, you still love them"—a definite shift from the days when advisors urged parents to keep their standards high and their daughters chaste. The experts' advice fails to address a practical fact of teenage life that many adults find disturbing, though, especially in the context of AIDS. Even if teenagers practice "serial monogamy" and sleep with one "serious date" at a time—the key to "respectable" premarital sex in the middle-class world—the numbers can add up over the course of a high school and college career.[18]

In fact, it is fear of teenage promiscuity more than the fact of sex itself that drives the current interest in teenage private lives. Irresponsible high school students are the new juvenile delinquents, threatening their elders' health and economic well-being with their thoughtless, risky behavior. "Teenagers appear to be starting their sex lives younger, many of them in middle school," the *Washington Post* notes with alarm, "and many are having intercourse with multiple partners before they finish high school." Worse yet, they seem oblivious to the dangers they court. Less than half, apparently, use condoms with any regularity, a blatant denial of sexual reality that results in over 3 million STDs—sexually transmitted diseases—a year.

Approximately 30 percent proceed as if sex were just another form of teenage entertainment like dancing, drinking, or driving. A fourteen-year-old who lost her virginity at age twelve, for instance, admits that she "never really thought about it. It's usually a spur of the moment type of thing. I guess it, like, makes us closer friends," she said, demonstrating what the experts call a "chilling nonchalance" about her sexual behavior. "Really, sex is like a sport, like recreation, like tossing a football," said a seventeen-year-old who has slept with seven "serious" partners (without benefit of a condom) since he lost his virginity at age fourteen. "Sometimes I do wish there was a little more to it," he said.[19]

This startling change in attitude is compounded by a change in family structure that makes it easy for teenagers too young to drive to get off by themselves anyway. In the 1950s, most fourteen-year-olds could expect their mothers (or their grandmothers, or at least their neighbors) to be home during the day; by the 1970s, both parents worked in one out of two families with school-age children; in the 1990s, three out of four do. Newscaster Ted Koppel commented on the change when he hosted a national town meeting in 1995. "The sex drive isn't any stronger now than it was in the 1950s" when he was fourteen. "We certainly wanted to do it. There just didn't seem to be quite as much opportunity," he said, "or public stimulation, or adult understanding."[20]

On all counts he is right. The Carnegie Corporation points out that 30 percent of eighth graders are on their own after school, some as long as five hours a day, which gives them much more private, personal space than their postwar predecessors ever enjoyed. Seventy-five percent of sexually active teenagers cite their home (or their boyfriend's home) as their usual meeting place, since the coast is inevitably clear. "Unsupervised time after school," the *Washington Post* reported in 1992, "is the most common occasion for adolescents to have sexual intercourse, often at a boy's house while his parents are at work."[21]

Public stimulation is also in the air, or rather, on it. According to a Harris poll, the typical teenager watched about 14,000 instances of sexual material on television during the 1987–88 season. Only 165 of these, however, dealt with practical issues like pregnancy, birth control, abortion, or disease.[22] Popular teenage shows like "Beverly Hills 90210" focus on "dating, drinking, sex, broken families, sex, morality, and sex," according to one reporter, and they attract a "teenage" audience as young as eight! An equally young audience can tune into MTV, youth's own cable television station, and watch hours of provocative videos or laugh at "Beavis and Butthead," a show that celebrates mindless behavior and sexual obsession. Direct descendants of *Mad* magazine's Alfred E. Neuman (who charmed earlier generations with his motto "What, me worry?"), Beavis and Butthead are every parent's nightmare. Know-nothing high school students who get high sniffing paint thinner and call adult authority "ass wipe," as *Rolling Stone* puts it, they embody what parents fear might be the teenage creed of the 1990s: "Because they are stupid, they are free." It is no accident, *Rolling Stone* adds, that Beavis and Butthead are latchkey children. Their parents are "otherwise occupied and figure not a whit in their stunningly tasteless activities."[23]

This popular culture of irresponsibility, critics contend, goes hand in hand with a widespread teenage crisis. The entire age group is at risk, or so it seems from the headlines, and sex is only part of the problem. Their SAT scores are falling, they go to college unprepared, they fail to beat the competition in international tests of academic skill. Employers complain that high school students cannot "count, read, write or speak well enough to qualify for entry-level jobs." They are unreliable, always late, and care about nothing except having a good time.[24] Teachers complain that they cannot make students do homework assignments so they have stopped trying. Parents complain about insolent, arrogant teenagers who challenge their authority with the question, "My friends all do it, why can't I?" Apparently convinced that they are the first generation of adults to deal with such unruly children (a notion *their* parents might find amusing), they point out that today's teenagers have changed. "They've lost the cringe factor," one mother laments. "They don't work as hard at pleasing their parents."[25]

In fact, they seem determined to repudiate every value that matters in the adult world, if current styles are any indication. Whether teenagers project themselves as slackers or homeboys (who can be white as well as black), as headbangers, burnouts, gangstas, or just grungy kids, they tend to share a rumpled look that suggests to outsiders that they really don't care. Like their leather-clad predecessors in the 1950s, they can look menacing when they sport tattoos, nipple rings, and satanic flourishes—the mark of heavy metal fans, today's most alienated white suburban youth. In the city, where gangsta rap sets the rebellious beat, their black counterparts wear oversized jeans, wool caps, and very expensive sneakers. Both groups incite panic in the adult world, not because they seem so powerful, but because they seem so disengaged and unable to find their place in life. These teenagers give off an alarming air of futility and despair that is more threatening than teenage arrogance ever was.

For instance, headbangers (or metalheads) have pushed teenage alienation to new heights. The most extreme romanticize suicide, ridicule education, and rely on drugs to give color to their lives, as if the world holds nothing in store for them but disappointment. Apparently convinced that there is nothing they can do to alter their futures, they do not look forward to the "McJobs" they will inevitably hold—low-paid "service" work in fast food joints and convenience stores that will not allow them to live as well as their working-class parents did. The idea that college might open doors to a better life does not seem at all realistic. "Yeah, right. I'll go to college for four years, be bored to death, and come out owing all this money, and then I can get a job that pays less than what some guy pumping gas is making," a boy who got good grades in high school remarked. "They seem convinced there's no point in trying, that maybe *this* is all there is," an adult interpreter explains. "So they get high, they party on, they tattoo and pierce their bodies in a celebration of the moment. They try one last time to stand out in a crowd," she adds, "hoping to be heard once before it's all over."[26]

The teenagers she is talking about are the teenagers at the bottom of the high school heap, dropouts or potential dropouts who are the most likely to bear illegitimate children, get arrested, or live close to—or below—the poverty line. Kids who "fuck off in school [and] have nothing to fall back on."[27] Their counterparts in the inner city are better organized, although they are just as resigned to their fate. Apparently convinced that they will not make it to age thirty, many carve out a risky but lucrative space for themselves in the underground economy of drugs. Others proceed as if life will take care of itself, starting families while they are still in high school, whether they have the resources to raise them or not.

Newspaper headlines give the impression that these extremes define teenage culture, much in the same way that juvenile delinquents in the 1950s and draft-resisting potheads in the 1960s shaped public images, but this is not the case. Like their predecessors, the vast majority are neither reckless nor lost. They do whatever they have to do to get into college, get drunk more often than they get high, manage to avoid pregnancy one way or another, and work at after-school jobs or as community volunteers. Nonetheless, they can still shake adult society at its roots, especially when the styles and attitudes of the disengaged become the emblem of teenage autonomy, by now an almost natural progression that dates back to the rise of rock 'n' roll. Apparently even ambitious college students have been known to show off nose rings, eyebrow rings, nipple rings, belly-button rings—an in-your-face symbol of teenage defiance that rankles parents no end. A sophomore at the University of Virginia considers his lip ring a symbol of personal independence. To his father, however, it is a barbaric—and permanent—reminder of his son's lack of good judgment and his propensity to goof off.[28]

What seems worse, however, is the generational pessimism that often goes along with these styles. Even mainstream teenagers tend to assume that they face more serious problems than any previous group of young people. Moreover, they have apparently internalized the popular notion that teenagers as an age group (whatever their family background or education) are the hapless victims of a stagnant economy and a violent society—a dramatic shift away from the "can-do" idealism of the 1950s and 1960s. A *Washington Post* survey of twelve- to seventeen-year-olds in 1992 found that 60 percent of the respondents thought that the country's best days were behind it. A majority reported that they did

not feel safe in their own high schools, many of which now feature metal detectors and police officers. "You shouldn't have to
worry about getting shot, when you're a kid," a suburban teenager
explained.[29]

"It's much harder to grow up today," a teenager from Los
Angeles told a television interviewer in 1994. Adults "don't realize the problems with drugs and alcohol and gangs. I don't think
they had to deal with it as much when they were younger." A suburban teenager agrees. Although gangs and violence were not a
problem yet at her school, drugs and alcohol were, and parents
were not equipped to handle it. "They never had it as much,
maybe drinking, but not so much drugs," she said. A black
teenager who had already survived a gunshot wound made the
most dramatic case. "They didn't have it as rough as we do,
because back then you'd get into an argument, you'd just fight and
it would be over. . . . Nowadays . . . they argue and they shoot you
and that's it—there's nothing else to talk about." A high school
student put it this way to the New York Times: "I remember when
I was thirteen, I [couldn't] wait until I turned into a teenager.
Except that now I see it's not that fun."[30]

The popularity of this view stuns some observers, who note
that this is the first teenage generation "to live so well and complain so bitterly about it." After all, a third of the age group owns
their own cars (up from 7 percent in 1968), 25 percent have their
own phones, and 50 percent own personal computers. A record 60
percent go to college, where they need an average of sixteen elec-
trical outlets to plug in all their "stuff"—microwaves, computers,
televisions, VCRs, CD players. Yet they take it for granted, a
reporter notes, "that they have it harder than their parents did."[31]

And why on earth not, since that is the message they hear every
day? They have almost no choice but to associate themselves with
disaster, no matter where they fit on the social ladder. They read
about the crisis of premarital sex and illegitimate pregnancy
(despite the fact that adults are more likely to be guilty of this
social crime than teenagers are). They are bombarded with stories
of aggressive, suicidal, or alcoholic teenagers, as if these represented the age group as a whole.[32] They are routinely reminded by
counselors, psychologists, and educators who make their living
from troubled youth that they are more depressed, more cynical,
and more in need of help than previous generations. "They hear

that when they come out of college, there will be no jobs for them," a concerned critic contends. "If they have sex, they're going to die. Between global warming and all the rest . . . do you blame them for feeling bad?" he wanted to know.[33]

Teenagers are also reminded every day that life worked better in the past, when high schools were rigorous, parents attentive, and teenagers respectful of their elders. "In the past," a social scientist attests, "kids knew their place in the larger scheme of things. They had a place in a stable family, a place in a town where people knew them, a sense of place in terms of a life work. Now there aren't any scripts," he points out, and it is up to teenagers themselves to learn to make their own decisions.[34]

This mythical view of an orderly past seems surprisingly compelling, even to boomer parents who grew up in the turbulent 1960s. After a conversation with her teenage daughter about the hard choices high school students have to make today, a boomer parent ended up commiserating "about how difficult decisions are now compared to when society laid down clear rules and expectations." Even that mother was forced to acknowledge that her image of the past was more of a wish for her daughter than a real memory, though. Regardless of their parents' admonitions, she admitted, most of her friends "eventually went out and did what they wanted anyway."[35] No matter what adults now prefer to believe, the record suggests that discretion (not shared values, respect, or obedience) was always the better part of respectability in the teenage world.

No matter what kind of spin adults now put on the good old days, the "rules" they now long for were rules of inequality and social conformity. Did the world really work better when girls had no choice in life but to get married, blacks knew their servile place, and kids who lived outside the charmed circle of upper-middle class life were invisible? Was life really simpler for teenage boys who carried the burden of war in the 1940s, or black teenagers who integrated high schools a decade later? Did the adult world make fewer demands on teenagers who came of age during the Great Depression or kept the home fires burning during the Second World War? If teenagers in the past had less trouble making decisions, it was because they had fewer, not better, choices to make. And if life seems so much harder today, it is because teenagers have such high expectations of what life should bring and almost no tolerance for what the experts call "delayed gratification."

That does not mean they are whiners, and it does not mean that opportunity is there for the asking. There is no denying the fact that teenagers with a talent for schoolwork and a stable family background can move up in the world no matter what their social origins. But there is also no denying that those who lack these basic resources are more or less on their own—as they have been ever since the rise of high schools a century ago. Despite over sixty years of expert consultation and educational reform, we still have a high school system that is better at employing adults than it is at educating the mass of students for either college or "life." And despite—or more likely because—of over sixty years of "sheltering" youth, we have not managed yet to ease their transition to adulthood.

No doubt we never will. But that does not mean adults will stop trying. Whether the current impulse comes from the sense that too many teenagers are at loose ends, or the fact that the teenage population is once again on the rise and will not be ignored, there is a new concern with restructuring teenage life. For instance, high schools are beginning to tighten up the rules again, reinventing dress codes and at least talking about more rigorous course work to lure the best and the brightest back into public schools. At the same time, they are implementing "comprehensive" sex education courses that provide information on "safe" sex, contraception, and abstinence, but also impress upon students the real life burdens that having a child entails.[36] Educators and business representatives are also developing school-to-work apprenticeship programs that put teenagers in touch with adult workers, something after-school jobs in malls and convenience stores often fail to accomplish. "My co-workers were helpful in making my internship a memorable one. I was treated as an adult," a student remarked, "and never expected to do less than the others, which was the best thing they could have done for me," she said.[37]

Whether a strategy of integrating the high school crowd into the adult world of work and sex will produce the kind of teenagers adults believe they want, however, remains to be seen. For no matter how many programs the experts devise, or how many rules adults agree to enforce, it is still up to teenagers themselves to decide who they are, what they want to be, and whether they will cooperate with the adult world to get there. The choices are—and always have been—theirs. The most that adults can do is to see to it that teenagers have good choices to make and real opportunities to gain useful experience, a generational obligation that we have yet to take seriously as a nation.

notes

Introduction "They're Getting Older Younger"

1. "Teens, Here Comes the Biggest Wave Yet," *Business Week* (11 April 1994): 76–86.
2. Richard Gehman, "The Nine Billion Dollars in Hot Little Hands," *Cosmopolitan* 143 (November 1957): 72–78.
3. "Teens, Here Comes the Biggest Wave Yet," p. 76.
4. Joseph F. Kett, *Rites of Passage: Adolescence in America, 1790 to the Present* (New York: Basic Books, 1977), p. 169.
5. "Trust Teena to Bring in Business," *Food Field Reporter* (18 August 1947), clipping in Estelle Ellis Collection, Scrapbook No. 1, National Museum of American History, Smithsonian Institution, Washington, D.C. (hereafter, EE Collection, NMAH.)
6. "Blading, Don't Even Think of It as Roller Skating," *Staten Island Advance*, 4 September 1994, p. F1; "What's Hot What's Not," ibid., 11 July 1994, p. F1; "Meet Me in the Mosh Pit," ibid., 13 March 1994, p. F1; "It's Prom Time," *Santa Fe New Mexican*, 13 May 1995, p. B6.
7. DeNeen L. Brown and Stephen Buckley, "Teens Set to Fight for Right to Party," *Washington Post* (5 March 1993): B1, B4; Jesse Green, "Out and Organized," *New York Times*, 13 July 1993, pp. 1, 7.
8. *Dallas Morning News*, 8 March 1992, cited in Harvey J. Graff, *Conflicting Paths: Growing up in America* (Cambridge: Harvard University Press, 1995), p. 328.
9. Neil Howe, quoted in "Teens, Here Comes the Biggest Wave Yet," p. 78.
10. Here and elsewhere, my discussion of early twentieth-century adolescents is based on Kett, *Rites of Passage*, pp. 144–72, 217–44.
11. U.S. Bureau of the Census, *Historical Statistics of the United States, Colonial Times to 1970*, Bicentennial edition, part 1 (Washington,

D.C.: Government Printing Office, 1975), p. 380. For school attendance rates, see Richard Ugland, "The Adolescent Experience During World War II: Indianapolis as a Case Study" (Ph.D. diss., Indiana University, 1977), 88; David Nasaw, *Schooled to Order: A Social History of Public Schooling in the U.S.* (New York: Oxford University Press, 1979), p. 163.

12. Lawrence A. Cremin, *American Education: The Metropolitan Experience, 1876–1980* (New York: Harper and Row, 1988), p. 546.

13. Alexander Crippen Roberts and Edgar Marian Draper, *Extraclass and Intramural Activities in High School* (Boston: D.C. Heath, 1928), p. 135; Kett, *Rites of Passage*, pp. 234–36; Edward Krug, *The Shaping of the American High School* (Madison: University of Wisconsin Press, 1972), pp. 138–41; David Tyack and Elisabeth Hansot, *Learning Together: A History of Coeducation in American Schools* (New Haven: Yale University Press, 1990), pp. 186–92; Paula Fass, *Outside In: Minorities and the Transformation of American Education* (New York: Oxford University Press, 1989), pp. 74, 77.

14. Promotional material, ca. 1945, Scrapbook No. 1, EE Collection, NMAH.

15. Landon Y. Jones, "1944 to 1984: A Retrospective; How Much Have Teens Changed?" *Seventeen* 43 (September 1984): 163.

16. Laura Blumenfeld, ". . . Connects with Real Life," *Washington Post*, 17 February 1992, p. D5.

17. Catherine S. Manegold, "To Crystal, 12, the Classroom Serves No Purpose," *New York Times*, 8 April 1993, B7.

18. Ed Zwick, quoted in "Teens, Here Comes the Biggest Wave Yet," p. 78.

Chapter One The High School Age

1. "Talking Girl in Film Show Gets Slapped," *Los Angeles Times*, 3 October 1936, p. 9.

2. "What Adolescents Want," *Parents* 7 (December 1932): 14, 39.

3. I. Keith Tyler, *High School Students Talk It Over* (Columbus: Bureau of Educational Research, Ohio State University, 1937), pp. 48–51.

4. Irving King, *The High-School Age* (Indianapolis: Bobbs-Merrill, 1914), pp. 62–64.

5. Joseph F. Kett, *Rites of Passage: Adolescence in America, 1790 to the Present* (New York: Basic Books, 1977), p. 169.

6. Ibid., pp. 234–38; Alexander Crippen Roberts and Edgar Marian Draper, *Extraclass and Intramural Activities in High School* (Boston: D.C. Heath, 1928), pp. 136–40.

7. Kett, *Rites of Passage*, p. 188; David I. Macleod, *Building Character in the American Boy: The Boy Scouts, Y.M.C.A., and Their Forerunners, 1870–1920* (Madison: University of Wisconsin Press, 1983), p. 37.

8. W. Ryland Boorman, *Personality in Its Teens* (New York: Macmillan, 1931), p. 179; Henry James Forman, *Our Movie Made Children* (New York: Macmillan, 1933), p. 165. For a comparison with advice from an earlier day, see "Thou Shalt Not Kiss," Philadelphia *North American*, 27 December 1900, p. 3.

9. [Anti-Cigaret Alliance,] *The Herald* (June 1930), in Records of the Children's Bureau, RG 102, National Archives and Record Administration, Washington, D.C. (hereafter NA).

10. Boorman, *Personality in Its Teens*, p. 172; Tyler, *High School Students Talk It Over*, pp. 46–48, 54.

11. John Modell, *Into One's Own: From Youth to Adulthood in the United States, 1920–1975* (Berkeley: University of California Press, 1989), pp. 85–105; Beth L. Bailey, *From Front Porch to Back Seat: Courtship in Twentieth Century America* (Baltimore: Johns Hopkins University Press, 1988), pp. 28–56; Mary Roberts Rinehart, "If I Had a Daughter," *The Forum* 87 (March 1932): 189.

12. Mary Ellen Chase, "Are Parents Afraid of Their Children?" *Ladies' Home Journal* 50 (March 1937): 60–62.

13. Boorman, *Personality in Its Teens*, p. 48.

14. Tyler, *High School Students Talk It Over*, p. 33; Michael Bernstein, *The Great Depression: Delayed Recovery and Economic Change in America, 1929–1939* (New York: Cambridge University Press, 1987), p. 141n; John Kenneth Galbraith, *A Journey Through Economic Time* (Boston: Houghton Mifflin, 1994), p. 78 ($20,000 is my extrapolation).

15. "Teenage Problems," *Parents* 10 (February 1935): 34.

16. Boorman, *Personality in Its Teens*, p. 48; Tyler, *High School Students Talk It Over*, p. 33.

17. "Teenage Problems," p. 34; "Talking it Over with Aunt Cherry," *Everygirls* 18 (August 1931): 20; "What Adolescents Want," pp. 14, 39.

18. Boorman, *Personality in Its Teens*, pp. 37–38; Dorothy Reed, "Leisure Time of Girls in a 'Little Italy,' A Comparative Study of the Leisure Interests of Adolescent Girls of Foreign Parentage, Living in a Metropolitan Community, to Determine the Presence or Absence of Interest Differences in Relation to Behavior" (Ph.D. diss., Columbia University, 1932), 38; Ruth Cavan, *Building a Girl's Personality* (New York: Abingdon Press, 1932), p. 53.

19. Cavan, *Building a Girl's Personality*, pp. 52–53.

20. David Tyack and Elisabeth Hansot, *Learning Together: A History of Coeducation in American Schools* (New Haven: Yale University Press, 1990), pp. 207–8, 213; Cavan, *Building a Girl's Personality*, pp. 22–23.

21. Reed, "Leisure Time of Girls in a 'Little Italy,'" pp. 31, 50, 52.

22. Ibid., pp. 45, 50.

23. Truman Pierce et al., *White and Negro Schools in the South: An Analysis of Biracial Education* (Englewood Cliffs, N.J.: Prentice-Hall, 1955), pp. 56, 86; Edward Krug, *The Shaping of the American High School* (Madison: University of Wisconsin Press, 1972), p. 126; Doxey A. Wilkerson, *Special Problems of Negro Education* (Washington, D.C.: Government Printing Office, 1939), pp. 38, 52.

24. E. Franklin Frazier, *Negro Youth at the Crossways: Their Personality Development in the Middle States* (Washington, D.C.: American Council on Education, 1940), pp. xvi, xviii, 66, 100, 137–38, 159.

25. Wilkerson, *Special Problems of Negro Education*, pp. 8–9.

26. Alpha Kappa Alpha, "Mississippi Health Project," pamphlet, July 1935, Records of the Children's Bureau, RG 102, NA.

27. "Student Forum," *Scholastic* 30 (20 March 1937): 27.

28. David B. Tyack, Robert Lowe, and Elisabeth Hansot, *Public Schools in Hard Times: The Great Depression and Recent Years* (Cambridge: Harvard University Press, 1984), p. 3.

29. Richard Reiman, "Planning the National Youth Administration: Citizenship and Community in New Deal Thought" (Ph.D. diss., University of Cincinnati, 1984), 137, 222.

30. Tyack and Hansot, *Learning Together*, p. 183.

31. Roberts and Draper, *Extraclass and Intramural Activities*, pp. 137, 147.

Chapter Two Advise and Consent:
Building Adolescent Character

1. Abel Jones Gregg, "Youth's Opportunity," *Parents* 8 (November 1933): 13; James Lincoln Collier, *Benny Goodman and the Swing Era* (New York: Oxford University Press, 1989), p. 193.

2. David I. Macleod, *Building Character in the American Boy: The Boy Scouts, Y.M.C.A., and Their Forerunners, 1870–1920* (Madison: University of Wisconsin Press, 1983), pp. 29–59; Abel Jones Gregg, *Group Leaders and Boy Character* (New York: Association Press, 1927), p. 170; Grace H. Stuff, *How to Plan: A Guide Book for Senior High School Girl Reserves* (New York: Woman Press, 1938), p. 17.

3. Macleod, *Building Character*, p. 293.

4. Ray Sherman, "Learn Good Driving," *American Boy* 110 (June 1936): 26.

5. *Boys' Life* 26 (January 1936): 43 (printing), 50 (bike); *The Open Road for Boys* 12 (January 1930): 33 (Waco Tools); ibid. 12 (February 1930): 35 (radio); "Highway and Byways," *American Boy* 110 (March 1936): 39.

6. Vereen Bell, "The 1936 Graduate Looks for a Job" *American Boy* 110 (June 1936): 5; William Heyliger, "Selling Sunrise," ibid. 110 (September 1936): 5.

7. "Trapped by Glaciers," *The Open Road for Boys* 12 (April 1930): 37; Thomas C. McClary, "Precision in the Air," ibid. 20 (March 1938): 15; "To the Students of American High Schools," *Scholastic* 17 (20 September 1930): 1.

8. Beth Bradford Gilchrist, "You're Only Young Once," *American Girl* 18 (January 1935): 5, 7.

9. "Will You Be Dull at Thirty?" *Everygirls* 19 (October 1931): 13.

10. Ann Warner, "Ups and Down," *American Girl* 13 (January 1930): 9–11, 36–38.

11. Letters to Editor, *American Girl* 13 (March 1930): 5; ibid. 13 (February 1930): 5.

12. Advertisement, *American Girl* 13 (March 1930): 54, 61.

13. Letters to Editor, *American Girl* 13 (June 1930): 7.

14. Virginia Moore, "Brenda Putnam, Sculptor,' *American Girl* 13 (May 1930): 16–17, 43–44; Dorothy Kenyon, "Can Girls Be Lawyers?" ibid. 22 (March 1939): 8–10, 45; Dr. Gulielma F. Alsop, "Women in Medicine and Nursing," ibid. 18 (January 1935): 24–25, 39–40.

15. *American Girl* 13 (June 1930): 7.

16. "Talking It Over with Aunt Cherry," *Everygirls* 18 (March 1931): 16.

17. Ibid. 18 (August 1931): 20 (mothers); ibid. 18 (December 1930): 18 (blind dates and Christmas gifts); ibid. 18 (March 1931): 16 (crushes, nagging); ibid. 18 (April 1931): 18 (using time well); ibid. 18 (August 1931): 20 (cheerfulness).

18. "Be Your Age" *Scholastic* 26 (4 May 1935): 3.

19. Gay Head [pseud. Margaret L. Hauser], "Boy Dates Girl," *Scholastic* 32 (19 February 1938): 36; ibid. 29 (9 January 1937): 23; ibid. 29 (19 September 1936): 24, among others; "Student Forum," ibid. 31 (13 November 1937): 37.

20. "Student Forum," *Scholastic* 28 (1 February 1936): 30.

21. "Classroom Program for This Issue" (teacher's edition), *Scholastic* 30 (3 April 1937): A2.

22. "By Yonder Blessed Moon," *Scholastic* 30 (3 April 1937): 28–29.
23. Aristotle quotation in John Conger, *Adolescence: Generation Under Pressure* (London: Harper and Row, 1979), p. 4
24. "Student Forum," *Scholastic* 29 (10 October 1936): 26.
25. Dr. Winifred Richmond, "When a Boy Gets Interested in Girls," *Parents* 8 (April 1933): 18–19, 45; Elsie Van Orden, "You and Your Son's Best Girl," ibid. 10 (February 1935): 16–17.
26. Van Orden, "You and Your Son's Best Girl," p. 17.
27. "Remote Control," *Ladies' Home Journal* 45 (April 1932): 90.
28. "The Sub-Deb," *Ladies' Home Journal* 56 (December 1939): 6; ibid. 52 (May 1935): 13; ibid. 50 (May 1937): 106; ibid. 52 (April 1935): 90.
29. "The Sub-Deb," *Ladies' Home Journal* 56 (March 1939): 6; ibid. 56 (June 1939): 6.
30. Letters to Editor, *Ladies' Home Journal* 45 (January 1932): 84.
31. "Must I Pet to Be Popular?" *Ladies' Home Journal* 45 (January 1932): 7.
32. Floyd Dell, "Why They Pet," *Parents* 6 (October 1931): 18–19, 60–63; Richmond, "When a Boy Gets Interested in Girls," p. 19.
33. Van Orden, "You and Your Son's Best Girl," pp. 16–17.
34. "Parental Problems," *Parents* 7 (December 1932): 38.
35. "Teenage Problem," *Parents* 12 (January 1937): 30.
36. "The Young Girl and the Cigarette," *Ladies' Home Journal* 45 (January 1932): 21.
37. "The Cosmetic Urge," *Parents* 8 (January 1933): 21.
38. W. Ryland Boorman, *Personality in Its Teens* (New York: Macmillan, 1931), pp. 37, 106.
39. Enid Severy Smith, *A Study of Twenty-five Adolescent Unmarried Mothers in New York City* (New York: Salvation Army Women's Home and Hospital, 1935), pp. 47–48.
40. Ibid., p. 49.
41. Ibid., pp. 50, 52.
42. "My Confession of Summer Madness," *True Confessions* (October 1937): 61; Dorothy Dix, "So You're in Love," *Ladies' Home Journal* 45 (January 1932): 51.

Chapter Three A New Deal for Youth: "Progressive" Education
and the National Youth Administration

1. Steven Mintz, *Domestic Revolutions: A Social History of American Family Life* (New York: Free Press, 1988), p. 139.
2. Abel Jones Gregg, "Youth's Opportunity," *Parents* 8 (November 1933): 13.

3. Ruth Cavan, *The Family and the Depression: A Study of One Hundred Chicago Families* (New York: Arno Press, 1971 [1938]), pp. 175–76.

4. Michael G. Homsay to Beatrice McConnell, 11 January 1936, RG 102, National Archives and Record Administration, Washington, D.C. (hereafter NA).

5. Richard Reiman, "Planning the National Youth Administration: Citizenship and Community in New Deal Thought" (Ph.D. diss., University of Cincinnati, 1984), 7; Betty and Ernest K. Lindley, *A New Deal for Youth, The Story of the National Youth Administration* (New York: Viking Press, 1938), p. 7 (40 percent is my extrapolation).

6. Thomas Minehan, "Boys and Girls on the March," *Parents* 10 (March 1935): 14–15, 70; "Why Girls of Today Leave Home," *Literary Digest* 124 (27 August 1937): 20.

7. H.A.P. Smith to Miss Perkins [n.d., ca. 8 June 1934], RG 102, NA.

8. Herbert R. Packard to K.J. Scudder, 1 December 1931, RG 102, NA; James Mickel Williams, *Human Aspects of Unemployment and Relief, with Special Reference to the Effects of the Depression on Children* (Chapel Hill: University of North Carolina Press, 1933), pp. 84–86, 105–17.

9. "The Effects of the Economic Depression on Children," 31 December 1931, Office of Probation Department, Los Angeles, RG 102, NA.

10. Beatrice McConnell to Katherine Lenroot, 11 June 1935, RG 102, NA; Cavan, *The Family and the Depression*, p. 173.

11. Smith to Perkins [n.d. ca. 8 June 1934].

12. David Tyack, Robert Lowe, and Elisabeth Hansot, *Public Schools in Hard Times: The Great Depression and Recent Years* (Cambridge: Harvard University Press, 1984), p. 38.

13. Lindley, *A New Deal for Youth*, p. 3.

14. Ibid., p. 90.

15. Case Histories, Virginia, Office of the Director, Information Section, RG 119, NA.

16. Success Stories, Office of the Director, Information Section, RG 119, NA.

17. Lindley, *A New Deal for Youth*, p. 195.

18. Anna Laughlin to Brown, 11 June 1936, Executive Director Correspondence, Statistics, Box 1, RG 119, NA; R.R. Jones to S.S. Tucker, 8 February 1936, ibid.

19. Jessie Muse to R.R. Patty, 9 December 1936, ibid.

20. R.E. Rhodes Report, Bemus, N.Y. [n.d.], ibid.

21. Herbert Preston Report, Warsaw N.Y. [n.d]., ibid.; Harry Rude Report, Sodus, New York [n.d.], ibid.; Warren De Jarnett Report, Hamilton, Missouri, 17 February 1936, ibid.

22. Jacob Rone, Individual NYA Stories, Office of the Director, Information Section, RG 119, NA.

23. I. E. Stustman Report, St. Joseph, Missouri, 18 January 1936, Executive Director Correspondence, Statistics, Box 2, RG 119, NA.

24. Cleo Loggins [n.d.], ibid.; NYA Data and Comments, East High School, Des Moines, ibid.

25. Glen Van Gundy [student participant], NYA Data and Comments, East High School, Des Moines, ibid.

26. NYA Data and Comments, East High School, Des Moines, ibid.

27. "Industrial Education" *Scholastic* 26 (23 February 1935): 97–104.

28. Richard Ugland, "The Adolescent Experience During World War II: Indianapolis as a Case Study" (Ph.D. diss., Indiana University, 1977), 88; U.S. Bureau of the Census, *Historical Statistics of the United States, Colonial Times to 1970*, Bicentennial edition, part 1 (Washington, D.C.: Government Printing Office, 1975), p. 379.

Chapter Four Swing Shift: Bobby Soxers Take the Stage

1. "Girls Take Leave of Friends Get Left at Post" *Washington Post*, 5 October 1941, p. 10. For adult beliefs in cultural uplift, see Marion Edman, "Attendance of School Children and Adults at Moving Pictures," *School Review* 48 (December 1940): 753–63; and William G. Brink, "High-School Pupils' Interests in Magazines and Newspapers," *School Review* 48 (January 1940): 40–48.

2. Richard Ugland, "The Adolescent Experience During World War II: Indianapolis as a Case Study" (Ph.D. diss., Indiana University, 1977), 357, n. 26.

3. James Lincoln Collier, *Benny Goodman and the Swing Era* (New York: Oxford University Press, 1989), pp. vii–viii.

4. Ibid., pp. 190–94.

5. Dr. Leslie Hohman, "As the Twig Is Bent," *Ladies' Home Journal* 56 (October 1939): 67.

6. Ugland, "The Adolescent Experience," p. 78.

7. "Sub-Debs—They Live in a Jolly World of Gangs, Games, Gadding, Movies, Malteds, and Music," *Life* 10 (27 January 1941): 75.

8. Ugland, "The Adolescent Experience," pp. 20–21; David B. Tyback, ed., *Turning Points in American Educational History* (Waltham, Mass.: Blaisdell, 1967), p. 360.

9. The *Oxford English Dictionary* credits *Popular Science* (April 1941) with the first use of the term "teenager."

10. See, for instance, "It Was Your Dad's Insurance My Lad!" *Scholastic* 8 (3 April 1926): 29, 32 (Keds), 28 (class rings and pins).
11. "To the Students of American High Schools," *Scholastic* 17 (20 September 1930): 1.
12. "Learning How to Consume," *Scholastic* 26 (9 February 1935): 3.
13. "Do You Dig It?" *Scholastic* 39 (19–24 January 1942): back cover.
14. "No More 'Baby Clothes' for Small Teens," *Calling All Girls* 1 (July 1942): 43.
15. Ugland, "The Adolescent Experience," p. 395.
16. "Tricks for Teens," *Calling All Girls* 5 (January–February 1945): 52; "Date Bait for the Soda Fountain Crowd," ibid. 5 (March 1945): 54; Mary Mattison Eubanks, "First Date," ibid. 1 (June 1942): 16–18.
17. Lawrence A. Cremin, *American Education: The Metropolitan Experience 1876–1980* (New York: Harper and Row, 1988), p. 555; "Sub-Debs," p. 75.
18. "High School Fashions Start in High," *Woman's Home Companion* (September 1941): 59.
19. Marian Stecher, Peggy Davis, and Dorothy Stough, "Here's How, Say the Seniors," *Woman's Home Companion* (September 1941): 70–71; J. Roy Leevy, "Social Competence of High-School Youth," *School Review* 51 (June 1943): 342–47.
20. "The Sub-Deb," *Ladies' Home Journal* 57 (March 1940): 40.
21. Benny Goodman, "Music as You Like It," *Calling All Girls* 1 (February 1942): 20–21; Alice Bar Grayson, "Let's Talk Things Over," ibid. 1 (May 1942): 35; Eleanor Boykin, "Rise to the Occasion," ibid. 1 (March 1942): 10; Thelma Knoles, "What Price Popularity," ibid. 1 (April 1942): 5–8; Nell Giles, "Make up Your Mind About Make-up," ibid. 1 (April 1942): 20–21; John R. Tunis, "Girls in Sports," ibid. 1 (September 1941): 34–36.
22. David M. Considine, *The Cinema of Adolescence* (Jefferson, N.C.: McFarland, 1985), pp. 27–28; Mickey Rooney, *Life Is Too Short* (New York: Villard Books, 1991), p. 112.
23. Rooney, *Life Is Too Short*, pp. 68, 98–99, 114–19; Considine, *The Cinema of Adolescence*, p. 27.
24. "Shirley's a Teener," *Calling All Girls* 1 (February 42): 45–46; Lois C. Eby, *Shirley Temple; The Amazing Story of the Child Actress Who Grew up to Be America's Fairy Princess* (Derby, Conn.: Monarch Books, 1962), pp. 111–12.
25. George J. Sanchez, *Becoming Mexican American: Ethnicity, Culture and Identity in Chicano Los Angeles 1900–1945* (New York: Oxford University Press, 1993), pp. 253–69.
26. Mauricio Mazón, *The Zoot-Suit Riots: The Psychology of Symbolic*

Annihilation (Austin: University of Texas Press, 1984), pp. 2–4; Beatrice Winston Griffith, *American Me* (Westport, Conn.: Greenwood Press, 1973 [1948]), pp. 55–59.

27. Griffith, *American Me*, pp. 46–47.
28. Mazón, *The Zoot-Suit Riots*, p. 63; Griffith, *American Me*, p. 47; Sanchez, *Becoming Mexican American*, p. 265.
29. Griffith, *American Me*, pp. 76–77.
30. Ibid., pp. 41, 50–51.
31. Sanchez, *Becoming Mexican American*, pp. 257–60; Griffith, *American Me*, pp. 153–69.
32. Irving Whitman to Louis Varrachione, 9 November 1942, Records of the Director, Letters Received from NYA Youth and Their Parents, Records of the National Youth Administration, RG 119, National Archives and Records Administration, Washington, D.C.

Chapter Five Andy Hardy Goes to War: Soldiers, Defense Workers, "V-Girls," and Zoot Suiters

1. Richard Ugland, "The Adolescent Experience During World War II: Indianapolis as a Case Study" (Ph.D. diss., Indiana University, 1977), 37–38, 53, for student indifference to current events; Student letters "How to Aid National Defense," 7 May 1941, Summaries of Data on Place of NYA Youth in Defense Work, Box 1, Records of the National Youth Administration, RG 119, National Archives and Records Administration, Washington, D.C. (hereafter NA).
2. Ugland, "The Adolescent Experience," pp. 67–68.
3. Ibid., pp. 61, 160; John Modell, *Into One's Own: From Youth to Adulthood in the United States 1920–1975* (Berkeley: University of California Press, 1989), p. 166.
4. Valene Olson to Mr. Mahoney, 5 November 1942, Director's Divisional File, Box 5, RG 119, NA; Calvin Graham obituary, *New York Times*, 9 November 1992, p. B4.
5. John Morton Blum, *V Was for Victory: Politics and American Culture During World War II* (New York: Harcourt Brace Jovanovich, 1976), pp. 55–59.
6. Army Air Forces recruiting ad in *Boys' Life* 34 (January 1944): 19.
7. Roger Tuttrup interview, in Studs Terkel, *The Good War: An Oral History of World War II* (New York: Pantheon, 1984), p. 174.
8. Robert Rasmus interview, in ibid., p. 38.
9. Private Shelley Rosenblatt to Varrichione [n.d.], Records of the Director, Letters Received from NYA Youth and Their Parents (hereafter Letters from NYA Youth), RG 119, NA.

10. Tuttrup interview, p. 174; Private Rudy Festa to family, 7 May 1944, in my possession.

11. Ugland, "The Adolescent Experience," p. 160; Modell, *Into One's Own*, p. 166; James Early to Leon J. Kowal, 27 April 1942, Director's Divisional File, Box 1, RG 119, NA.

12. Mrs. J. Moscatello to Varrichione, 3 March 1943, Letters from NYA Youth, RG 119, NA.

13. Mrs. Sara Stack to Varrichione, 10 January 1943, ibid.; Mrs. J. Schwartzman to Varrichione, 3 February 1943, ibid.

14. Mrs. Blanchette to Varrichione, 17 March 1942, ibid.; Aubry H. Carter to Varrichione, 1 March 1943, ibid.

15. Edith Ray to Varrichione, 2 April 1943, ibid.

16. Daniel Parent to Varrichione, 15 March 1943, ibid.

17. Thomas Casey to Thomas J. Fox, 30 January 1943, Director's Divisional File, Box 5, RG 119, NA; Coburn Allen to Margaret Griffin, 24 October 1942, ibid.

18. Howard Walpin to Varrichione, 7 January 1943, Letters from NYA Youth, RG 119, NA.

19. Private Shelley Rosenblatt to Varrichione [n.d.], ibid.; Sidney Rubinstein to Varrichione, 2 May 1943, ibid.

20. Pauline Gage Report, California State Advisory Meeting, 14 March 1942, Form Replies Establishing the Value of Local Programs, Box 1, RG 119, NA; Muriel Myer to NYA, 16 March 1943, Letters from NYA Youth, ibid.; Edna Hutchins to NYA, 15 March 1943, ibid.; Mary Rich to NYA, 15 March 1943, ibid.; Mrs. Gunna Anderson to NYA, 12 February 1943, ibid.; Judy Fraser to NYA, 10 January 1943, ibid.

21. Curley Alevy to Hank, 7 January 1942, Letters from NYA Youth, RG 119, NA.

22. Valene Olsen to Mr. Mahoney, 5 November 1942, Director's Divisional Files, Box 5, RG 119, NA; Robert Steiner to Margaret Griffin, 8 January 1943, ibid.; Steiner to May Risher, 12 February 1943, ibid.

23. Eleanor Wilson to Miss Diggs, 21 November 1942, Director's Divisional File, Box 2, RG 119, NA.

24. [Della Montoya] to dear sister, 3 February 1943, Director's Divisional File, Box 5, RG 119, NA; Della Montoya to Daddy and Mother, 1 February 1943, ibid.; Douglas A. Doyle to Steiner, 13 March 1943, ibid.

25. Marie Lane to Frischknect, 16 February 1943, ibid.

26. Valene Olsen to Mr. Mahoney, 5 November 1942, ibid.; Robert Steiner to Margaret Griffin, 8 January 1943, ibid.; Steiner to May Risher, 12 February 1943, ibid.

27. Dorothy Aaronson to NYA, 24 February 1943, Letters from NYA Youth, RG 119, NA.
28. Bessie Holmes to NYA, 18 February 1943, ibid.
29. Norman V. Carlisle, "Are Your Courses 'On the Beam,'" *Scholastic* 41 (2–7 November 1942): 27.
30. Ugland, "The Adolescent Experience," p. 49.
31. Ibid., p. 158.
32. Richard Ugland, "'Education for Victory': HS Victory Corps and Curricular Adaptation During WWII," *Journal of Education Quarterly* 19 (Winter 1979): 435–51; Carlisle, "Are Your Courses 'On the Beam,'" p. 27.
33. Gay Head [pseud. Margaret L. Hauser], "Boy Dates Girl: On the Assembly Line," *Scholastic* 41 (26–31 October 1942): 31.
34. Ugland, "'Education for Victory,'" pp. 435–51.
35. Richard Ugland, "Viewpoints and Morale of Urban High School Students During World War II—Indianapolis as a Case Study," *Indiana Magazine of History* 77 (June 1981): 161; Peter A. Bertocci, "The Moral Outlook of the Adolescent in War Time," *Mental Hygiene* 28 (July 1944): 356–57.
36. Ronald Lippitt and Alvin Zander, "A Study of Boy Attitudes Toward Participation in the War Effort," *Journal of Social Psychology* 17 (1943): 309–25; Caroline B. Zachry, "The Adolescent and His Problems Today," in *The Family in a World at War*, ed. Sidonie Gruenberg (New York: Harper, 1942), p. 219.
37. Dolores Duckett and Sylvia Jacobs, "We 'Took It' in Hawaii," *Calling All Girls* 1 (April 1942): 9; Beryl Williams, "Navy Girl," ibid. 1 (June 1942): 33; Margaret E. Jessup, "Girls Can Help Win War," ibid. 1 (March 1942): inside front cover.
38. Ugland, "The Adolescent Experience," pp. 67–68.
39. Jean Bartlett interview, in Terkel, *The Good War*, p. 244.
40. Ibid.
41. Reaction to *Life* magazine article [nd], Social Protection Division, Box 9, Records of the Office of Community War Services, RG 215, NA; *Reader's Digest*, cited in Greater Little Rock Chamber of Commerce VD Public Information Program [nd], Community File Alabama to California, Box 1, ibid.
42. Ugland, "The Adolescent Experience," p. 219; Pete Daniel, "Southern Reactions to World War II," *Journal of American History* 77 (December 1990): 908; Max Lerner, *Public Journal: Marginal Notes on Wartime America* (New York: Viking Press, 1945), p. 17.
43. Ugland, "The Adolescent Experience," p. 219; Edwin J. Cooley to Thomas Devine (Los Angeles), 21 January 1946, Social Protection Division, Community File Alabama to California, RG

215, NA; *Washington Post*, 6 May 1946; Charles Taft, "Juvenile Delinquency and Its Relation to the War Effort," 9 July 1943, Records Relating to Juvenile Delinquency, Box 1, ibid.

44. Reaction to *Life* magazine article, Social Protection Division, Box 9, RG 215, NA.

45. Greater Little Rock Chamber of Commerce VD Public Information Program.

46. Reaction to *Life* magazine article.

47. Allan M. Brandt, *No Magic Bullet: A Social History of Venereal Disease in the United States Since 1880* (New York: Oxford University Press, 1985), p. 164; Charles Livermore to Thomas Devine, Report on Enlisting Labor's Support, 23 August 1945, Social Protection Division, Box 6, RG 215, NA.

48. Dr. Leslie Hohman, "As the Twig Is Bent," *Ladies' Home Journal* 58 (March 1941): 138; Major George Leibig and Captain Granville Larimore, "A Study of Factors Allied with Venereal Disease," Social Protection Division, Box 9, Records of the Office of Community War Services, RG 215, NA; George E. Gardner, "Sex Behavior of Adolescents in Wartime," *Annals of the American Academy of Politics and Social Science* 236 (November 1944): 60–66; "Boys and Sex: Report of Glenn V. Ramsey Study, Indiana University," *Time* 42 (27 September 1943): 75–76.

49. Aimee Zellmer, PTA Social Hygiene Chairman, "Sex Hygiene in a World at War," radio script, 20 April 1942, Social Protection Division, Box 9, RG 215, NA.

50. Manuel P. Servin, ed., *An Awakened Minority: The Mexican Americans* (Beverly Hills, Calif.: Glencoe Press, 1970), p. 119.

51. Griffith, *American Me*, p. 23; *Herald Express*, 8 June 1943, p. B-2, cited in Servin, *An Awakened Minority*, p. 120.

52. Servin, *An Awakened Minority*, p. 140.

53. Louis Levitan to Margaret Griffin, 20 February 1943, Director's Divisional File, Box 5, RG 119, NA. For the black experience, see Anthony Tucker statement, Unionville, Conn., 9 February 1943, Letters Received from NYA Youth, ibid.

54. Mazón, *The Zoot-Suit Riots*, p. 63.

Chapter Six Do You Know Where Your Children Are?:
Juvenile Delinquency, Teen Canteens, and
Democratic Solutions

1. Richard M. Ugland, "The Adolescent Experience During World War II: Indianapolis as a Case Study" (Ph.D. diss., Indiana University, 1977), 224, 225.

2. Ibid., pp. 228, 262, 264.

3. Ibid., p. 228.

4. Ibid., p. 259.

5. Mrs. Winifred Ferguson to Elliot Ness, 27 October 1943, Social Protection Division, Box 9, Records of the Office of Community War Services, RG 215, National Archives and Records Administration, Washington, D.C. (hereafter NA); Charles Livermore to Thomas Divine, 23 August 1945, Report on Enlisting Labor's Support, Box 6, ibid.

6. Ugland, "The Adolescent Experience," pp. 260–61.

7. Ibid., p. 243.

8. Ibid., pp. 271–74.

9. Ibid., pp. 271–75; Letters to Editor, *Seventeen* 3 (4 November 1944): 4.

10. McCloskey Meeting of Regional Recreation Representatives, 28–30 May 1943, Recreation Division, Youth Problems, Box 1, RG 215, NA.

11. C. D. Van Orsdel, Defense Council of Dade County, Fla., 29 November 1943; Dolly Glazier, Home and Community Service, St. Petersburg, Fla., 29 November 1943; Curtis Hixon, Mayor of Tampa, 27 November 1943; G. W. Waterbury, Oswego Chamber of Commerce, Oswego, N.Y., 26 November 1943; Congressional Hearing Material, all in Recreation Division, Youth Problems, Box 1, RG 215, NA.

12. Ugland, "The Adolescent Experience," pp. 295–97.

13. E. P. Grise, Executive Secretary, Public Welfare Board, Charleston, S.C., Congressional Hearings, 27 November 1943, Recreation Division, Youth Problems, Box 1, RG 215, NA.

14. Helen D. Pigeon, "Effects of War Conditions on Children and Adolescents in the City of Hartford, Ct." [n.d.], Recreation Division, Juvenile Delinquency, Box 1, RG 215, NA; Charles Taft, "Juvenile Delinquency and Its Relation to the War Effort," 9 July 1943, ibid.; O. B. McRae [Athens, Ga.], Playground and Recreation Board, Congressional Hearings, 27 November 1943, Youth Problems, Box 1, ibid.

15. Mark McCloskey statement, Meeting of Regional Representatives, 28–30 May 1943, Records Relating to Youth Problems, Box 1, RG 215, NA.

16. Ugland, "The Adolescent Experience," pp. 313–14, 324; "Teen Town at Jacksonville" *Seventeen* 4 (March 45): 26, 159.

17. Ugland, "The Adolescent Experience," p. 331; "Teen Town at Jacksonville," pp. 26, 159; "*Seventeen* Drops in on a Teen Canteen," *Seventeen* 3 (October 1944): 92.

18. "*Seventeen* Drops in on a Teen Canteen," p. 92.
19. Grace Morgan Smith to E. Ward Cole, 23 August 1944, Recreation Division, Director's Office, Box 14, RG 215, NA.
20. August B. Hollingshead, *Elmtown's Youth and Elmtown Revisited* (New York: Wiley, 1975 [1949]), p. 173. The research for this book was done in 1941.
21. Ibid., p. 175.
22. Annual Convention File 1944, NAACP Papers, Group I, Manuscript Division, Library of Congress, Washington, D.C. (hereafter LC).
23. "Teen Canteens," *Seventeen* (April 1945): 168; Indianapolis Report, n.d. [ca. October 1943], and Marshalltown, Iowa, Report, 4 October 1943, Annual Activities of Youth Council Reports, NAACP Papers, Group II-E, Box 1, LC.
24. "And a Child Shall Lead Them," *Ebony* 1 (December 1945): 28.
25. Ibid.
26. Barbara Gair, "What Kind of World Do You Want?" *Seventeen* 4 (February 1945): 60–61, 138, 158; Alice Beaton, "I'm Not Prejudiced But," ibid. 4 (May 1945): 34–35, 128; "The World Is Yours," ibid. 4 (April 1945): 58–59, 139.
27. Editorial, *Seventeen* 3 (September 1944): 33.
28. "Straw Vote," *Seventeen* 3 (October 1944): 10–11.
29. "A Code for Everyday Living," *Seventeen* 4 (April 1945): 65, 159.
30. "Jobs Have No Gender," *Seventeen* 4 (April 1945): 18, 159.
31. "How to Swing a Canteen," *Seventeen* 3 (December 1944): 70–71, 86; Alice Beaton, "For Seniors Only," ibid. 3 (September 1944): 60–61; "Why Finish High School?" ibid. 3 (September 1944): 76, 87; "Stardust or Indigestion?" ibid. 4 (April 1945): 97, 130.
32. Letters to Editor, *Seventeen* 3 (November 1944): 4; Phyllis Quinlin to Editor [n.d., ca. 1945], in Scrapbook No. 2, Estelle Ellis Collection, National Museum of American History, Smithsonian Institution, Washington, D.C.
33. Letters to Editor, *Seventeen* 4 (January 1945): 4.
34. Mark McCloskey, "Youth's New World," Speech delivered 20 April 1945, Recreation Division, Records Relating to Youth Problems, RG 215, NA.
35. Ibid.
36. Ugland, "The Adolescent Experience," p. 346; Ernest Groves and Gladys Hoagland Groves, "Social Background of Wartime Adolescents," *Annals of the American Academy of Politics and Social Science* 236 (November 1944): 26–32; Lester D. Crow and Alice Crow, *Our Teen-Age Boys and Girls: Suggestions for Parents, Teachers*

and Other Youth Leaders (Freeport, N.Y.: Books for Libraries Press, 1969 [1945]), pp. 354–55.

Chapter Seven The Advertising Age: *Seventeen,* Eugene Gilbert, and
 the Rise of the Teenage Market

1. Betty Cavanna, *Going on Sixteen* (New York: Scholastic Book Services, 1962 [Westminster Press, 1946]).
2. Maureen Daly, ed., *Profile of Youth* (Philadelphia: Lippincott, 1951), p. 8.
3. American Forum of the Air, 13 November 1945, "Are We Facing a Moral Breakdown in America," Records of the Office of Community War Services, Social Protection Division, 1941–46, Box 9, RG 215, National Archives and Record Administration, Washington, D.C. (hereafter NA).
4. "Choosing a Career," pamphlet, Estelle Ellis Collection, Scrapbook No. 2, National Museum of American History, Smithsonian Institution, Washington, D.C. (hereafter EE Collection, NMAH).
5. Susan M. Jackson "History of the Junior Novel in the United States 1870–1980" (Ph.D. diss., University of North Carolina Library School, 1986), 32, 155, 259.
6. Jessie Bernard, "Teen-Age Culture: An Overview," *Annals of the American Academy of Politics and Social Science* (November 1961): 2–5.
7. Vance Packard, "How Does Your Income Compare with Others," *Collier's* 138 (23 November 1956): 54–59; Harold F. Clark, "Education and the American Economy in 1960," *NEA Journal* 44 (May 1955): 293; Landon Y. Jones, *Great Expectations: America and the Baby Boom Generation* (New York: Coward McCann and Geoghegan, 1980), p. 40.
8. Mary Beth Norton, et al, *A People and a Nation*, vol. 2 (Boston: Houghton Mifflin, 1982), p. 880; Kenneth Jackson, *Crabgrass Frontier: The Suburbanization of the United States* (New York: Oxford University Press, 1985), p. 233.
9. Joseph M. Hawes and N. Ray Hiner, *American Childhood: A Research Guide and Historical Handbook* (Westport, Conn.: Greenwood Press, 1985), p. 558.
10. Irwin Porges, "Your Teenager Is Big Business" *American Mercury* 87 (July 1958): 94–96.
11. "Teen Canteen," *Variety* 162 (8 May 1946): 34.
12. Estelle Ellis interview, 26 December 1993.

13. Letters to Editor, *Seventeen* 3 (November 1944): 4.
14. Promotion Circulars, Scrapbook No. 1, EE Collection, NMAH.
15. Ibid.
16. Clipping, "*Seventeen:* A Unique Case Study," *Tide: News Magazine of Advertising and Marketing* (15 April 1945), in Scrapbook No. 2, EE Collection, NMAH.
17. Benson and Benson, Inc., *Life with Teena; A Seventeen Magazine Survey of Subscribers and Their Mothers* (Princeton, N.J.: Opinion Research, 1945), pp. 20–28; Clipping, *Women's Wear Daily* (August 1946), Scrapbook No. 1, EE Collection, NMAH.
18. Promotion material [n.d.], Scrapbook Nos. 1, 2, EE Collection, NMAH.
19. Promotion material, Bill Rosen to E. Rubenstein, 1 October 1946, Scrapbook No. 2, EE Collection, NMAH.
20. *Life with Teena*, pp. 26, 82.
21. Promotion material ca. 1945, Scrapbook No. 1, EE Collection, NMAH.
22. Ellis interview; "*Seventeen:* A Unique Case Study," *Tide* (4 April 1945), Scrapbook No. 2, EE Collection, NMAH.
23. Letters to Editor, *Seventeen* 3 (November 1944): 4.
24. Ellis interview.
25. Tie-up kit, EE Collection, NMAH.
26. Ellis interview; Clipping, "Why Snub 8 Million Customers?" *Cosmetics and Toiletries* (August 1949), Scrapbook No. 2, EE Collection, NMAH; "Beaux Catcher," *Seventeen* 4 (October 1945): 36; "Flame-Glo," ibid. 9 (September 1950): 216; "Chen Nu," ibid. 4 (September 1945): inside cover.
27. Clipping, *Printer's Ink* (March 1948), in Scrapbook No. 1, EE Collection, NMAH; ads in *Seventeen* 9 (December 1950): 9, 24.
28. Clipping, *Hollywood Reporter* (17 November 1948), Scrapbook No. 1, EE Collection, NMAH; "*Seventeen* Gets Them Young," ibid.
29. Bill Rosen Memo, 20 October 1948, Scrapbook No. 2, EE Collection, NMAH; Pillsbury ad, *Seventeen* 9 (September 1950): 179; Sure-Jell ad, ibid. (September 1950): 178.
30. "Why Don't Parents Grow Up?" *Seventeen* 3 (December 1944): 94–95.
31. "Why Don't Parents Grow Up?" *Seventeen* 3 (September 1944): 12, 87; ibid. 3 (October 1944): 12–13; ibid. 3 (December 1944): 94–95; ibid. 9 (March 1950): 31–32; "For Seniors Only," ibid. 9 (February 1950): 72.
32. James Burkhart Gilbert, *A Cycle of Outrage: America's Reaction to*

the Juvenile Delinquent in the 1950s (New York: Oxford University Press, 1986), pp. 205–7; Ron Goulart, *The Assault on Childhood* (London: Gollancz 1970), pp. 138–40.

33. Cited in Richard M. Ugland, "The Adolescent Experience During World War II: Indianapolis as a Case Study" (Ph.D. diss., Indiana University, 1977), p. 394.

34. Gilbert, *Cycle of Outrage*, pp. 205–7.

35. Ugland, "The Adolescent Experience," p. 395; Gilbert, *Cycle of Outrage*, pp. 205–7; *Advertising Age* (1 November 1948): 18.

36. Gilbert, *Cycle of Outrage*, pp. 205–7; *Advertising Age* (1 November 1948): 18.

37. Eugene Gilbert, "Everybody Talks About Youth Advertising . . . ," *Advertising Age* (26 February 1951): 1; "Accentuate the Youthful," *Variety* 162 (6 February 1946): 35; "Teenage Party," ibid. 160 (14 November 1945): 36; "Teentimers Band Tie Up," ibid. 160 (21 November 1945): 34; "Macy's Quiz Teen Show," ibid. 176 (16 November 1949): 50; "NBC Also Joins in Sat. Sweepstakes," ibid. 167 (11 June 1947): 24; "Teen Town," ibid. 162 (24 April 1946): 30.

38. Rosamond du Jardin, *Double Date* (Philadelphia: Lippincott, 1952); Mary Stolz, *The Seagulls Woke Me* (New York: Scholastic Book Services, 1970 [Harper and Row, 1951]).

39. Anne Emery, *Sorority Girl* (Philadelphia: Westminster Press, 1952).

40. Daly, *Profile of Youth*, p. 14.

41. Ibid., pp. 27–31.

42. Ibid., pp. 27–32, 40, 155.

43. Olga Druce, "Kid Shows," *Variety* 167 (9 July 1947): 33; NAB Code, ibid. 168 (17 September 1947): 28; "Six Times a Week Banned by NBC," ibid. 176 (26 October 1949): 1, 79.

44. *Advertising Age* (6 September 1954): 1; ibid. (11 October 1954): 50.

45. Maureen Daly, *Seventeenth Summer* (New York: Dodd Mead, 1942), p. 66.

46. Ibid., pp. 171–72.

47. Emery, *Sorority Girl*, pp. 65, 163.

48. Gilbert, "Everybody Talks About Youth Advertising," p. 1; "Admen Don't Impress Teenagers with Brand Names," *Advertising Age* (13 September 1954): 85.

49. Nelson George, *The Death of Rhythm and Blues* (New York: Obelisk/Dutton, 1989 [1988]), pp. 24–26, 46–51.

Chapter Eight Great Balls of Fire: Rhythm and Blues,
Rock 'n' Roll, and the Devil's Music

1. Alex Haley, ed., *The Autobiography of Malcolm X* (New York: Grove Press, 1977 [1964]), pp. 58–59.
2. Charlie Gillett, *The Sound of the City: The Rise of Rock and Roll* (New York: Pantheon, 1983 [1970]), p. 135.
3. Ibid., p. 10.
4. Nick Tosches, *Unsung Heroes of Rock 'n' Roll: The Birth of Rock in the Wild Years Before Elvis* (New York: Harmony Books, 1991 [1984]), p. 7. Gillett, *Sound of the City*, p. 3.
5. George, *The Death of Rhythm and Blues*, pp. 27–28.
6. John Jackson, *Big Beat Heat: Alan Freed and the Early Years of Rock and Roll* (New York: Schirmer Books, 1991), p. 40; Gillett, *The Sound of the City*, p. 39; Ed Ward, et al., *Rock of Ages: The Rolling Stone History of Rock & Roll* (New York: Rolling Stone Press, 1986), pp. 68–69; George, *The Death of Rhythm and Blues*, p. 45
7. Ward, *Rock of Ages*, pp. 68–69.
8. Jackson, *Big Beat Heat*, pp. 10–11.
9. Ibid., pp. 23–25.
10. Ibid., pp. 30–31.
11. Freed 1956 interview, cited in Gillett, *The Sound of the City*, p. 13.
12. Jackson, *Big Beat Heat*, pp. 42–43.
13. Ibid., p. 44.
14. Ibid., pp. 3–5.
15. Ibid., p. 5.
16. Ward, *Rock of Ages*, pp. 70, 85.
17. Jackson, *Big Beat Heat*, pp. 58–60.
18. Ibid., pp. 58–61.
19. Ibid., p. 64; Ward, *Rock of Ages*, pp. 89–93; Herm Schoenfeld, "R&B Big Beat in Pop Biz," *Variety* 197 (19 January 1955): 49.
20. Schoenfeld, "R&B Big Beat in Pop Biz," p. 54.
21. "Dr. Jive's Rhythm & Blues Troup Hits Swinging Beat at Apollo B.O.," *Variety* 199 (24 August 1955): 65.
22. Review of Frank Sinatra performance, Paramount Theater, New York, *Variety* 160 (14 November 1945): 49.
23. "Dr. Jive's R&B Troupe," p. 65.
24. "R&B Best Thing That's Happened in Disk Biz in Years: Bob Theil," *Variety* 197 (23 February 1955): 43.
25. "A Warning to the Music Business," *Variety* 197 (23 February 1955): 2; "Leer-ics Part II," ibid. 197 (2 March 1955): 49; "Leer-ics Part III," ibid. 198 (9 March 1955): 49; Ward, *Rock of Ages*, pp. 90–91.

26. "Dr. Jive's R&B Troupe," p. 65.
27. Gillett, *The Sound of the City*, pp. 20–21.
28. Ibid., pp. 17–26; H. Kandy Rohde, ed., *The Gold of Rock and Roll* (New York: Arbor House, 1970), p. 16; Jeff Greenfield, *No Peace No Place: Excavations Along the Generational Fault* (Garden City, N.Y.: Doubleday, 1973), p. 60.
29. Conversation with Jim Linear, Southern Historical Association Annual Meeting, Atlanta, October 1992.
30. William Graebner, *Coming of Age in Buffalo: Youth and Authority in the Postwar Era* (Philadelphia: Temple University Press, 1990), p. 5.
31. Ward, *Rock of Ages*, p. 129; "R&B Cracking Racial Barriers in Southwest," *Variety* 199 (6 July 1955): 43; Jackson, *Big Beat Heat*, pp. 95–96. "Nigger music" phrase was quoted in a newsclip included in "Biography: Elvis Aaron Presley," television program, Arts & Entertainment, 8 February 1995.
32. Jackson, *Big Beat Heat*, p. 98.
33. "British Rock 'n' Rollers Just as Rowdy as in U.S.," *Variety* 204 (5 September 1956): 2.
34. Patricia Jobe Pierce, *The Ultimate Elvis: Elvis Presley Day by Day* (New York: Simon and Schuster, 1994), p. 26.
35. Ibid., p. 55; George, *The Death of Rhythm and Blues*, p. 63.
36. Phillips made the statement on "Elvis: The Great Performances," a television program produced by Priscilla Presley, the Family Channel, 21 October 1995; the question of his popularity was discussed on "Biography: Elvis Aaron Presley."
37. Quoted in "Elvis: The Great Performances."
38. "The Impact of Elvis Presley," *Life* 41 (27 August 1956): 101–9.
39. Ward, *Rock of Ages*, p. 121.
40. "The Impact of Elvis Presley," pp. 101–9; marijuana rumor cited in "Hy Gardiner Calling" segment, in "Biography: Elvis Aaron Presley;" Pierce, *The Ultimate Elvis*, p. 123.
41. "The Impact of Elvis Presley," pp. 101–9.
42. Marvin Newman and Jerry Leviton, "Rock 'n' Roll Battle: Boone vs. Presley," *Collier's* 138 (26 October 1956): 109–11.
43. Letters to the Editor, *Collier's* 138 (7 December 1956): 16–17.
44. Rohde, *The Gold of Rock and Roll*, pp. 43, 69.
45. Ward, *Rock of Ages*, p. 121.
46. Ed Sullivan segment, on "Elvis: The Great Performances."
47. Cited in "Biography: Elvis Aaron Presley."
48. Rohde, *The Gold of Rock and Roll*, pp. 56–59; Ward, *Rock of Ages*, pp. 130–31.
49. Eugene Gilbert, *Advertising and Marketing to Young People* (Pleasantville, N.Y.: Printers' Ink Books, 1957), p. 286.

50. Greenfield, *No Peace No Place*, p. 29.
51. Ibid., p. 52.
52. Ward, *Rock of Ages*, p. 88.
53. Michael Shore and Dick Clark, *The History of American Bandstand: It's Got a Great Beat and You Can Dance to It* (New York: Ballantine Books, 1985), p. 8.
54. Ibid., p. 10.
55. George, *The Death of Rhythm and Blues*, p. 91.

Chapter Nine Stairway to Heaven:
               The Real Life Business of Rock 'n' Roll

1. Arthur Whitman, "How a Teen-Age Singing Idol is Made," *Cosmopolitan* 149 (November 1960): 68, 70.
2. Mark Ribowsky, *He's A Rebel: The Truth About Phil Spector, Rock and Roll's Legendary Madman* (New York: Dutton, 1989), pp. 36–39.
3. "Tweedle Dee Girl," *Ebony* 11 (April 1956): 106–8.
4. Ronnie Spector, *Be My Baby: How I Survived Mascara, Miniskirts, and Madness, or My Life as a Fabulous Ronette* (New York: Harmony Books, 1990), pp. 10, 13.
5. Ibid., pp. 16–17, 22.
6. J. Randy Taraborrelli, *Call Her Miss Ross: The Unauthorized Biography of Diana Ross* (New York: Birch Lane Press, 1989), p. 36.
7. Ibid., p. 32.
8. Raynoma Gordy Singleton, *Berry, Me, and Motown: The Untold Story* (Chicago: Contemporary Books, 1990), p. 14.
9. Taraborrelli, *Call Her Miss Ross*, p. 69.
10. Ibid., p. 24; Singleton, *Berry, Me, and Motown*, pp. 84–87.
11. Singleton, *Berry, Me, and Motown*, pp. 79, 84–87; Taraborrelli, *Call Her Miss Ross*, pp. 60–61.
12. Singleton, *Berry, Me, and Motown*, pp. 113–14.
13. Spector, *Be My Baby*, p. 37.
14. Ibid., pp. 24–25.
15. Dorothy Wade and Justine Picardie, *Music Man: Ahmet Ertegun, Atlantic Records, and the Triumph of Rock 'n' Roll* (New York: Norton, 1990), pp. 71–75.
16. "FEP Law Opens Way for Negro Jobs in NY Banks," *Ebony* 7 (December 1951): 16; "Democracy Comes to Washington," ibid. 10 (February 1956): 18–20; "Society Achievement Supplants Ancestry as Yardsticks of Social Status," ibid. 2 (May 1947); "Is the Urban League Dying?," ibid. 7 (May 1952): 118.
17. Taraborrelli, *Call Her Miss Ross*, pp. 39–42.

18. Ibid., pp. 55–56.
19. Ibid., pp. 31, 41–42.
20. Ibid., p. 56.
21. Joseph Himes, "Negro Teenage Culture," *Annals of the American Academy of Politics and Social Science* 338 (November 1961): 95–97.
22. Taraborrelli, *Call Her Miss Ross*, pp. 44, 52–53.
23. Spector, *Be My Baby*, p. 28.
24. Ibid., pp. 34–36.
25. Ibid., p. 30.
26. Ibid., pp. 31–32.
27. Taraborrelli, *Call Her Miss Ross*, pp. 76–77.
28. Ibid., pp. 76–77.
29. Ed Ward, et al., *Rock of Ages: The Rolling Stone History of Rock & Roll* (New York: Rolling Stone Press, 1986), p. 129; "R&B Cracking Racial Barriers in Southwest," *Variety* 199 (6 July 1955): 43; John Jackson, *Big Beat Heat: Alan Freed and the Early Years of Rock and Roll* (New York: Schirmer Books, 1991), pp. 95–96; "That Rhythm, Those Blues," episode of "The American Experience," PBS, 6 December 1988.

Chapter Ten The Perils of Prosperity: Teenage Rebels,
Teenage Sex, and the Communist Menace

1. "Teenage Singers," *Cosmopolitan* 149 (October 1960): 72; George Marek, "It Isn't All Junk," *Good Housekeeping* 143 (October 1956): 228–31; Barbara Schwarz, "Pop Music and Me," *Seventeen* 17 (January 1958): 37.
2. Jeff Greenfield, *No Peace No Place: Excavations Along the Generational Fault* (Garden City, N.Y.: Doubleday, 1973), p. 37; Donald Katz, *Home Fires: An Intimate Portrait of One Middle-Class Family in Postwar America* (New York: HarperCollins, 1992), p. 93.
3. Grace and Fred M. Hechinger, *Teen-Age Tyranny* (New York: William Morrow, 1963), pp. 110–11, 116–17. See also Edgar Z. Friedenberg, *The Vanishing Adolescent* (Boston: Beacon Hill Press, 1959); Dorothy Thompson, "Are Our Teenagers So Dumb?" *Ladies' Home Journal* 74 (November 1957): 11, 118–19; George Benson King, "Fan-Club Swindle," *Good Housekeeping* 143 (November 1956): 80–81, 221–23.
4. William Graebner, *Coming of Age in Buffalo: Youth and Authority in the Postwar Era* (Philadelphia: Temple University Press, 1990), pp. 52–58, 91; Maureen Daly, ed., *Profile of Youth* (Philadelphia: Lippincott, 1951), pp. 49–51.

5. Graebner, *Coming of Age in Buffalo*, p. 58.
6. "Teenage Sex Hysteria," *Science Newsletter* 67 (1 January 1955): 4.
7. Graebner, *Coming of Age in Buffalo*, p. 89.
8. Ibid., p. 90.
9. Abigail Heath, "I'm Fed up with Teenagers," *McCall's* 80 (January 1953): 28–31, 116.
10. James B. Gilbert, *A Cycle of Outrage: America's Reaction to the Juvenile Delinquent in the 1950s* (New York: Oxford University Press, 1986), pp. 15–18, 72.
11. Milton L. Barron, "The Delinquent: Society or the Juvenile?" *Nation* 178 (5 June 1954): 482–84.
12. Gilbert, *A Cycle of Outrage*, pp. 184–85; Thomas Doherty, *Teenagers and Teenpics: The Juvenilization of American Movies in the 1950s* (Boston: Unwin Hyman, 1988), pp. 134–35.
13. Hy Hollinger, "Handling Rowdies," *Variety* 199 (10 August 1955): 4.
14. Ezra Bowen, ed., *This Fabulous Century: 1950–1960*, vol. 4 (New York: Time-Life Books, 1970), p. 234.
15. Gilbert, *A Cycle of Outrage*, p. 68.
16. Bowen, *This Fabulous Century: 1950–1960*, p. 234.
17. John Logley, "The Young Rebels," *Commonweal* 66 (13 September 1957): 593.
18. Heath, "I'm Fed Up with Teenagers," pp. 28–31, 116; Sumner Ahlbum, "Are You Afraid of Your Teenager?" *Cosmopolitan* 143 (November 1957): 41–45.
19. Gilbert, *A Cycle of Outrage*, pp. 15–18, 72.
20. Graebner, *Coming of Age in Buffalo*, p. 102.
21. Gilbert, *A Cycle of Outrage*, pp. 15–18, 72.
22. Schwarz, "Pop Music and Me," p. 37.
23. Robert Hampel, *The Last Little Citadel: American High Schools Since 1940* (Boston: Houghton Mifflin, 1986), p. 50.
24. James B. Lane, ed., *Steel Shavings: Rah Rahs and Rebel Rousers: Relationships Between the Sexes in the Calumet Region During the Teen Years of the 1950s*, vol. 23 (Valpariso, Ind.: Indiana University Northwest, 1994), p. 45.
25. Ibid., pp. 48–49.
26. Ibid., pp. 45–50.
27. Richard M. Ugland, "The Adolescent Experience During World War II: Indianapolis as a Case Study" (Ph.D. diss., Indiana University, 1977), p. 78.
28. Lane, *Steel Shavings*, p. 48
29. Ibid., pp. 48–49.
30. Ibid., p. 64.

31. Daly, *Profile of Youth*, pp. 152–53; Lane, *Steel Shavings*, p. 86.
32. Linda Wagner-Martin, *Sylvia Plath: A Biography* (New York: Simon and Schuster, 1987), p. 57. Quotations cited in Frances McCullough, ed., *The Journals of Sylvia Plath* (New York: Dial Press, 1982), pp. 9, 15.
33. Evelyn Mills Duvall, "Are They Too Young for Love?" *National Parent-Teacher* 48 (March 1954): 4–6; Dorothy Baruch, "A Frank Talk with Parents of Teenagers," *Parents* 28 (October 1953): 52, 108–10.
34. Thompson, "Are Our Teenagers So Dumb?" pp. 11, 118–19.
35. Lane, *Steel Shavings*, p. 69; Ira L. Reiss, "Sexual Codes in Teen-Age Culture," *Annals of the American Academy of Politics and Social Science* 338 (November 1961): 54–55.
36. Lane, *Steel Shavings*, pp. 34, 86.
37. "Most Child Brides Already Pregnant When They Marry," *Ebony* 8 (March 1953): 25–27, 30; "Young U.S. Adults Marry Considerably Later, Live with Parents Longer Than Counterparts in the 1960s," *Family Planning Perspectives* 20 (May/June 1988): 144; "What Should a Girl Do About College?" *Changing Times* 16 (April 1962): 35–38.
38. "What Girls Think About Sex," *Seventeen* 18 (July 1959): 75–77, 98; David Riesman, "Permissiveness and Sex Roles," *Marriage and Family Living* 21 (August 1959): 212–13.
39. Riesman, "Permissiveness and Sex Roles," pp. 212–13.
40. "Crisis in Education," *Life* 44 (24 March 1958): 25–34; Hampel, *The Last Little Citadel*, p. 58; Frederic Morton, "The Teenager Here and Abroad," *Holiday* 23 (September 1958): 48, 85–89.
41. Hampel, *The Last Little Citadel*, pp. 59–60, 65–66.
42. H. Kandy Rohde, ed. *The Gold of Rock and Roll 1955–1967* (New York: Arbor House, 1970), p. 65.
43. Hampel, *The Last Little Citadel*, p. 64.
44. Susan J. Douglas, *Where the Girls Are: Growing up Female with the Mass Media* (New York: Times Books, 1994), p. 22.
45. "Fight Over Aid to Schools," *Changing Times* 19 (February 1965): 43–46; Joel Spring, *The Sorting Machine: National Educational Policy Since 1945* (New York: David McKay, 1976), pp. 34, 49, 90–91; Kenneth T. Jackson, *Crabgrass Frontier: The Suburbanization of the United States* (New York: Oxford University Press, 1985), pp. 289–90.
46. J. D. Salinger, *The Catcher in the Rye* (New York: Bantam Books, 1967 [1951]).
47. Greenfield, *No Peace No Place*, p. 119.
48. Ibid., pp. 116–19.

Chapter Eleven The Content of Their Character:
Black Teenagers and Civil Rights in the South

1. Richard Gehman, "The Nine Billion Dollars in Hot Little Hands," *Cosmopolitan* 143 (November 1957): 72–78; Frederic Morton, "The Teenager Here and Abroad," *Holiday* 23 (September 1958): 48, 85–89; Eugene Gilbert, *Advertising and Marketing to Young People* (Pleasantville, N.Y.: Printers' Ink Books, 1957), pp. 64–65, 158; "You're Out of Business Unless You Get the Teens," *Variety* 197 (9 March 1955): 1.
2. "Negroes Aren't Getting TV Break Sez Council," *Variety* 199 (17 August 1955): 2; Ella Taylor, *Prime-Time Families: Television Culture in Postwar America* (Berkeley: University of California Press, 1989), p. 26.
3. Kenneth T. Jackson, *Crabgrass Frontier: The Suburbanization of the United States* (New York: Oxford University Press, 1985), pp. 289–90.
4. August Meier and Elliott Rudwick, *From Plantation to Ghetto: An Interpretive History of American Negroes* (New York: Hill and Wang 1966), pp. 274–76; Stephen J. Whitfield, *A Death in the Delta: The Story of Emmett Till* (New York: Free Press, 1988), p. 9.
5. Anne Moody, *Coming of Age in Mississippi* (New York: Dell, 1968), p. 125.
6. Melton A. McLaurin, *Separate Pasts* (Athens: University of Georgia Press, 1987), p. 14.
7. Ellen Levine, *Freedom's Children: Young Civil Rights Activists Tell Their Own Stories* (New York: Putnam, 1993), p. 16.
8. Claudette Colvin interview, in Levine, *Freedom's Children*, p. 20.
9. Ibid., p. 25.
10. James Roberson interview, in Levine, *Freedom's Children*, p. 7.
11. Pete Daniel, *Standing at the Crossroads* (New York: Hill and Wang, 1986), p. 164.
12. Levine, *Freedom's Children*, pp. 32–33.
13. Ricky Shuttlesworth interview, in Levine, *Freedom's Children*, p. 66.
14. Gwen Patton interview, in Levine, *Freedom's Children*, p. 41.
15. George McMillan, "The Ordeal of Bobby Cain," *Collier's* 138 (23 November 1956): 68–69.
16. Shuttlesworth interview, pp. 37–38.
17. Myrna Carter, James Roberson interviews, in Levine, *Freedom's Children*, pp. 39–40.
18. David Halberstam, *The Fifties* (New York: Villard Books, 1993), p. 688.

19. Ernest Green interview, in Levine, *Freedom's Children*, pp. 45–46.
20. Elizabeth Huckaby, *Crisis at Central High Little Rock 1957–58* (Baton Rouge: Louisiana State University Press, 1980), pp. 54–55; Halberstam, *The Fifties*, pp. 688–89.
21. Green interview, p. 46.
22. Huckaby, *Crisis at Central High*, pp. 86–91.
23. Ibid., p. 103.
24. Ibid., pp. 151, 157
25. Green interview, p. 47; Halberstam, *The Fifties*, p. 680.
26. Green interview, p. 49.
27. Henry J. Abraham, "School Desegregation in the South," *Current History* 41 (August 1961): 94–96.
28. Delores Boyd interview, in Levine, *Freedom's Children*, p. 54.
29. Todd Gitlin, *The Sixties: Years of Hope Days of Rage* (New York: Bantam Books, 1987), pp. 82–85.
30. Shuttlesworth interview, p. 59.
31. Frances Foster, Barbara Howard, and Gladis Williams interviews, in Levine, *Freedom's Children*, pp. 60–61, 66, 69.
32. Cyrill Levitt, *Children of Privilege: Student Revolt in the Sixties: A Study of Student Movements in Canada, the United States and West Germany* (Toronto: University of Toronto Press, 1984), p. 77.
33. Donald Katz, *Home Fires: An Intimate Portrait of One Middle-Class Family in Postwar America* (New York: HarperCollins, 1992), p. 153.
34. Thelma Eubanks interview, in Levine, *Freedom's Children*, p. 94.
35. Gitlin, *The Sixties*, p. 163.
36. Ibid., p. 104.

Chapter Twelve A Hard Day's Night: Beatles, Boomers, and the Bomb

1. Rachel Goodman, "The Day the King of Swing Met the Beatles," *Esquire* 64 (July 1965): 53, 110–11.
2. Ibid.
3. Steve Vogel, "Why Astrid Kirchherr Believes in Yesterday," *Washington Post*, 12 June 1994, Section G, pp. 8–9.
4. Goodman, "The Day the King of Swing Met the Beatles."
5. Ibid., p. 53; "Double Your Money Double Your Fun," *PTA Magazine* 59 (October 1964): 23.
6. James Lincoln Collier, *Benny Goodman and the Swing Era* (New York: Oxford University Press, 1989), p. 193.
7. Diana Ravitch, *The Troubled Crusade: American Education 1945–1980* (New York: Basic Books, 1983), p. 322.
8. Steve McConnell interview, in Studs Terkel, *The Good War: An*

Oral History of World War Two (New York: Pantheon Books, 1984), p. 581; Landon Y. Jones, *Great Expectations: America and the Baby Boom Generation* (New York: Coward McCann and Geoghegan, 1980), pp. 68, 82.

9. Jones, *Great Expectations*, pp. 50, 68, 73.

10. Arthur Whitman, "How a Teen-Age Singing Idol Is Made," *Cosmopolitan* 149 (October 1960): 72; Carol and Harry Smallenburg, "Our Hard-Pressed Teenagers," *PTA Magazine* 59 (February 1965): 35; "Teenage Tycoons," ibid., p. 9; Joseph M. Hawes and N. Ray Hiner, *American Childhood: A Research Guide and Historical Handbook* (Westport, Conn.: Greenwood Press, 1985), p. 588.

11. "Students: On the Fringe of a Golden Era," *Time* 85 (29 January 1965): 56–59, cited in Michael Medved and David Wallechinsky, *What Really Happened to the Class of '65?* (New York: Random House 1976), p. 115; Finding Aid 1961, "Now It's Pepsi for Those Who Think Young," Pepsi Generation Collection, National Museum of American History, Smithsonian Institution, Washington, D.C.; Grace and Fred Hechinger, "In the Time It Takes You to Read This the Teen-Ager Has Spent $2378.22," *Esquire* 64 (July 1965): 67–68, 113.

12. H. Kandy Rohde, ed., *The Gold of Rock 'n' Roll 1955–1967* (New York: Arbor House, 1970), pp. 191–92; Nick Tosches, *Unsung Heroes of Rock 'n' Roll: The Birth of Rock in the Wild Years Before Elvis* (New York: Harmony Books, 1991 [1984]), pp. 148–49.

13. Elaine Dundy, "The Image in the Marketplace," *Esquire* 64 (July 1965): 115.

14. Susan J. Douglas, *Where the Girls Are: Growing up Female with the Mass Media* (New York: Times Books, 1994), pp. 116–17; Dundy "The Image in the Marketplace," p. 115.

15. Donald Katz, *Home Fires: An Intimate Portrait of One Middle-Class Family in Postwar America* (New York: HarperCollins, 1992), p. 180; Medved and Wallechinsky, *What Really Happened to the Class of '65?*, p. 48.

16. "Beatles' Quickie 2-Wk. U.S. Tour Flips Their Cap LP Past 2,000,000 Mark," *Variety* 234 (26 February 1964): 65; "Promoters Fears About Economics of the Beatle," ibid. 234 (12 February 1964): 1, 87; "Beatles' $40,000 (60%) for 2 Nites at Tennis Stadium," ibid. 234 (15 April 1964): 53; "Fear Aping of Salary Levels," ibid. 236 (2 September 1964): 49, 52.

17. Jones, *Great Expectations*, p. 74.

18. Grace and Fred M. Hechinger, *Teen-age Tyranny* (New York: Morrow, 1963), p. 210.

19. "Kids 'Won't Speak to Me' So Grandmas Get Up $50 for Beatles' CP Benefit," *Variety* 236 (9 September 1964): 1, 62.

20. "Rolling Stones Gather 5G Loss for Promoter Pazdur in Anti-Beat Cleve," *Variety* 236 (11 November 1964): 57.

21. Bill Greeley, "Demos & GOP Pose Headaches," *Variety* 236 (30 September 1964): 31.

22. "Wild Fans of the Beatles a Shocker Even to Long-Memory Sophisticates," *Variety* 236 (30 September 1964): 2, 53.

23. "Beatles' Paul McCartney Bum Raps U.S. Cops," *Variety* 236 (9 September 1964): 2, 18; Lary Solloway, "Jaded Miami Beach Takes Beatles in Stride," ibid. 233 (19 February 1964): 49; Michael S. Willis, "Lo! The Beatles Descend from Sky for Apotheosis in Frisco," ibid. 236 (26 August 1964): 45; Sanford Markey, "Beatles Rap Cleveland Cops for Stopping Show," ibid. 236 (23 September 1964): 85.

24. "Grown-Ups a Go-Go," *Esquire* 64 (July 1965): 41; "Surrey Sound Has Thin B.O. Fringe as Beatles Top Minets in Hub 'Contest,' " *Variety* 236 (16 September 1964): 51.

25. "Beatles Batter All B.O. Records," *Variety* 236 (2 September 1964): 41, 47.

26. Katz, *Home Fires*, p. 181.

27. "Religioso Slants in Beatles 'Rebellion'?" *Variety* 234 (4 March 1964): 55.

28. Katz, *Home Fires*, pp. 148–49.

29. Ad "Nice Girls Finish First," *Variety* 233 (15 January 1964): 37.

30. "The Last Word," *Esquire* 64 (July 1965): 100.

31. Jack Shepherd, "Are You a Teen-Ager? Yeah I'm Afraid So," *Look* 30 (20 September 1966): 44; "I Could Never Join Mainstream Society Now," *Newsweek* 67 (21 March 1966): 70.

Chapter Thirteen Lies My Father Told Me:
                 Berkeley, Vietnam, and the Generation Gap

1. "College Enrollment Trends," *School and Society* 90 (13 January 1962): 4; "What Should a Girl Do About College?" *Changing Times* 16 (April 1962): 35–38; "What's Going On in Schools and Colleges," ibid., 16 (September 1962): 43; Susan J. Douglas, *Where the Girls Are: Growing up Female with the Mass Media* (New York: Times Books, 1994), p. 142; August Meier and Elliott Rudwick, *From Plantation to Ghetto: An Interpretive History of American Negroes* (New York: Hill and Wang, 1966), p. 322.

2. "What's Going On in Schools and Colleges," pp. 43–44; Todd

Gitlin, *The Sixties: Years of Hope Days of Rage* (New York: Bantam Books, 1987), pp. 1–3, 88.

3. Ibid., pp. 67–69, 87, 90–91.
4. Donald Katz, *Home Fires: An Intimate Portrait of One Middle-Class Family in Postwar America* (New York: HarperCollins, 1992), p. 168.
5. Gitlin, *The Sixties*, p. 27; "What's Going On in Schools and Colleges," p. 43; Katz, *Home Fires*, p. 167.
6. James Miller, *Democracy Is in the Streets* (New York: Simon and Schuster 1987), p. 44; Katz, *Home Fires*, p. 151.
7. Cyrill Levitt, *Children of Privilege: Student Revolt in the Sixties: A Study of Student Movements in Canada, the United States and West Germany* (Toronto: University of Toronto Press, 1984), pp. 30–34, 74–75; Logan Wilson, "Is the College Student Becoming a 'Forgotten Man'?" *School and Society* 93 (6 February 1965): 81; Landon Y. Jones, *Great Expectations: America and the Baby Boom Generation* (New York: Coward McCann and Geoghegan, 1980), p. 92.
8. Nathan Glazer, *Remembering the Answers: Essays on the American Student Revolt* (New York: Basic Books, 1970), pp. 79–83; Rushian Neil Reynolds, "The Characterization of American Student Dissent in Selected General Circulation Magazines" (Ph.D. diss., Florida State University, 1970), 42.
9. Gitlin, *The Sixties*, p. 163; Glazer, *Remembering the Answers*, p. 81.
10. Gitlin, *The Sixties*, p. 291.
11. Glazer, *Remembering the Answers*, p. 85.
12. "Education in 1965," *School and Society* 93 (25 December 1965): 491–92; Miller, *Democracy Is in the Streets*, p. 223.
13. Glazer, *Remembering the Answers*, p. 227n.
14. Paul Woodring, "The Editor's Bookshelf," *Saturday Review* (11 September 1965): 77.
15. Reynolds, "The Characterization of American Student Dissent," pp. 94, 146.
16. Wilson, "Is the College Student Becoming a 'Forgotten Man'?" pp. 78–80; Art Buchwald, "Anatomy of a Revolt," *School and Society* 93 (16 October 1965): 371 [originally published in the *Washington Post*, 22 April 1965]; Victor A. Rapport, "Some Ways Toward Campus Peace," *School and Society* 93 (Summer 1965): 296–97; Woodring, "The Editor's Bookshelf," p. 77.
17. Margaret L. Habein, *Spotlight on the College Student* (Washington, D.C.: American Council on Education, 1959), pp. 6–7; Rapport, "Some Ways Toward Campus Peace," pp. 296–97.
18. Woodring, "The Editor's Bookshelf," p. 77.

19. Wilson, "Is the College Student Becoming a 'Forgotten Man'?" pp. 78–80; Miller, *Democracy Is in the Streets*, p. 223.
20. Draft calls in Jones, *Great Expectations*, p. 92; and "Doubling the Draft," *Life* 59 (20 August 1965): 24.
21. Katz, *Home Fires*, p. 208.
22. John D. Marciano, "An Analysis of the Students for a Democratic Society (SDS) at Cornell University" (Ed.D. diss., State University of New York at Buffalo, 1969), 42.
23. Harrison E. Salisbury, ed., *Vietnam Reconsidered: Lessons from a War* (New York: Harper and Row, 1984), p. 72.
24. Douglas, *Where the Girls Are*, p. 150.
25. Katz, *Home Fires*, p. 208.
26. Dr. Martin Luther King Jr. segment, on "LBJ: Part 2," episode of "The American Experience," PBS, 2 October 1991.
27. "The Hullabaloo Is Old Hat to Hershey," *Life* 59 (20 August 1965): 29.
28. "Military Service: The Choices," *Changing Times* 16 (February 1962): 43.
29. John Modell, *Into One's Own: From Youth to Adulthood in the United States 1920–1975* (Berkeley: University of California Press, 1989), p. 324; troop figures from Mary Beth Norton, et al., *A People and a Nation: A History of the United States*, vol. 2 (Boston: Houghton Mifflin, 1982), p. 907.
30. Michael Medved and David Wallechinsky, *What Really Happened to the Class of '65?* (New York: Random House, 1976), p. 104.
31. "Conscientious Objector," *Look* 30 (20 September 1966): 67.
32. Miller, *Democracy Is in the Streets*, p. 251.
33. "The Hullabaloo Is Old Hat," p. 29.
34. Lawrence M. Baskir and William A. Strauss, *Chance and Circumstance: The Draft, the War, and the Vietnam Generation* (New York: Knopf, 1978), p. 25.
35. Glazer, *Remembering the Answers*, p. 10.
36. Tim O'Brien, *If I Die in a Combat Zone, Box Me up and Ship Me Home* (New York: Delacorte Press, 1973), p. 20.
37. Marciano, "An Analysis of the Students for a Democratic Society," p. 75; Baskir and Strauss, *Chance and Circumstance*, p. 68.
38. Gitlin, *The Sixties*, p. 254; Marciano, "An Analysis of the Students for a Democratic Society," pp. 32–33.
39. Gitlin, *The Sixties*, pp. 247, 285–86, 307; Norton, *A People and a Nation*, p. 944.
40. "Cheerleader," *Look* 30 (20 September 1966): 88.
41. Reynolds, "The Characterization of American Student Dissent," p. 129.

42. Nicholas Katzenbach interview, on "LBJ: Part 4," episode of "The American Experience," PBS, 2 October 1991.

43. Medved and Wallechinsky, *What Really Happened to the Class of '65?*, p. 273.

44. Ibid., pp. 274–75.

45. Ibid., p. 198.

46. Baskir and Strauss, *Chance and Circumstance*, p. 34.

47. Ray Raphael, *The Men from the Boys: Rites of Passage in Male America* (Lincoln: University of Nebraska Press, 1988), pp. 147, 151.

48. Norton, *A People and a Nation*, p. 942; Baskir and Strauss, *Chance and Circumstance*, pp. 34, 87; Gitlin, *The Sixties*, p. 291.

49. Baskir and Strauss, *Chance and Circumstance*, pp. 3, 9, 36; Gitlin, *The Sixties*, p. 412; Clancy Sigal, "Desertion as a Form of Resistance," in Salisbury, *Vietnam Reconsidered*, p. 68.

50. Baskir and Strauss, *Chance and Circumstance*, p. 254.

51. Ibid., pp. 6, 248.

52. Ibid., pp. 248–49.

53. Ibid., p. 7.

54. Medved and Wallechinsky, *What Really Happened to the Class of '65?*, p. 44.

Chapter Fourteen Up the Down Staircase:
Sex, Drugs, and Rock 'n' Roll

1. Lillian Roxon, *Rock Encyclopedia* (New York: Grosset and Dunlap, 1969), p. 158; Todd Gitlin, *The Sixties: Years of Hope Years of Rage* (New York: Bantam Books, 1987), pp. 196–97.

2. Roxon, *Rock Encyclopedia*, p. 422.

3. Ed Ward, et al., *Rock of Ages: The Rolling Stone History of Rock & Roll* (New York: Simon and Schuster, 1986), p. 285.

4. Mary Stolz, *A Love or a Season* (New York: Harper and Row, 1964), p. 192.

5. "TV's 'Mainstream of Morality,'" *Variety* 236 (23 September 1964): 80.

6. Robert L. Hampel, *The Last Little Citadel: American High Schools Since 1940* (Boston: Houghton Mifflin, 1986), p. 86.

7. Ibid., pp. 94–95.

8. Ibid., p. 86.

9. James B. Lane, ed., *Steel Shavings: Rah Rahs and Rebel Rousers: Relationships Between the Sexes in the Calumet Region During the Teen Years of the 1950s*, vol. 23 (Valpariso, Ind.: Indiana University Northwest, 1994), p. 26.

10. Jack Shepherd, "Are You a Teenager? Yeah I'm Afraid So," *Look* 30 (20 September 1966): 40

11. "Big Sprout-Out of Male Mop Tops," *Life* 59 (30 July 1965): 56–58.

12. Steve Vogel, "Why Astrid Kirchherr Believes in Yesterday," *Washington Post*, 12 June 1994, p. G8.

13. Shepherd, "Are You a Teenager?" p. 48; "Big Sprout-Out of Male Mop Tops," pp. 56–58.

14. Daniel Sugerman, *Wonderland Avenue: Tales of Glamour and Excess* (New York: William Morrow, 1989), p. 160; Michael Medved and David Wallechinsky, *What Really Happened to the Class of '65?* (New York: Random House, 1976), pp. 97, 100.

15. John P. Sisk, "The Fear of the Young," *Catholic World* 208 (November 1968): 680–84.

16. Ibid., pp. 680–84; "Stop Giving in to the Kids," *America* 115 (15 October 1966): 478.

17. Dorothy Waleski, "Regulating Student Dress," *NEA Journal* 55 (April 1966): 12–14.

18. Ibid., pp. 12–14.

19. Figures from "Education in 1965," *School and Society* 93 (25 December 1965): 491–92; Landon Y. Jones, *Great Expectations: America and the Baby Boom Generation* (New York: Coward McCann and Geoghegan, 1980), p. 302; *Seventeen* and *Senior Scholastic*, cited in Waleski, "Regulating Student Dress," pp. 12–14.

20. Stephen Birmingham, "American Youth: A Generation Under the Gun," *Holiday* 37 (March 1965): 44–60, 137–43. Quotation is on p. 44.

21. "Sometimes I Feel Like Dropping Out," *Newsweek* 67 (21 March 1966): 67. The teenager was Jan Smithers, who later went on to star in the television show "WKRP in Cincinnati."

22. Letters to Editor, *America* 115 (26 November 1966): 685–87; "I Could Never Join Mainstream Society Now," *Newsweek* 67 (21 March 1966): 70.

23. "Unisex," *Newsweek* 67 (14 February 1966): 59; Letters to Editor, ibid. 67 (28 February 1966): 2–4.

24. "Today's Rebellious Generation," *America* 115 (17 September 1966): 271; Letters to Editor, ibid. 115 (26 November 1966): 685–87.

25. "Sometimes I Feel Like Dropping Out," pp. 66–67.

26. Shepherd, "Are You a Teen-ager?" pp. 44–47.

27. Gregory Corso, "Life Death and Dancing: A Buffalo Shindig," *Esquire* (July 1965): 35; Shepherd, "Are You a Teen-ager?" p. 48.

28. "The Teen-agers," *Newsweek* 67 (21 March 1966): 60.

29. Ibid.

30. Catherine S. Chilman, *Adolescent Sexuality in a Changing American Society: Social and Psychological Perspectives* (Washington, D.C.: Government Printing Office, 1978), p. 113; Sandra Hofferth, et al., "Long Term Trends in Premarital Sexual Activity," *Family Planning Perspectives* 19 (March/April 1987): 46–53; Reiss and Gebhard are quoted in "The Teen-Agers," p. 60.

31. Cecile Landau, *Growing up in the '60s* (London: McDonald Optima, 1991), p. 73.

32. Medved and Wallechinsky, *What Really Happened to the Class of '65?*, p. 209; Landau, *Growing up in the '60s*, p. 73.

33. Susan J. Douglas, *Where the Girls Are: Growing up Female with the Mass Media* (New York: Times Books, 1994), p. 142.

34. Ibid., pp. 66, 70.

35. Chilman, *Adolescent Sexuality in a Changing American Society*, p. 113; Medved and Wallechinsky, *What Really Happened to the Class of '65?*, p. 137; Gitlin, *The Sixties*, p. 353.

36. Landau, *Growing up in the '60s*, pp. 86–87.

37. Medved and Wallechinsky, *What Really Happened to the Class of '65?*, p. 140

38. Landau, *Growing up in the '60s*, pp. 76–77.

39. Medved and Wallechinsky, *What Really Happened to the Class of '65?*, pp. 159, 184, 253.

40. Gitlin, *The Sixties*, p. 201.

41. "Kooks at Dr. Timothy Leary's Weekly 'Psychedelic Celebrations' in N.Y.," *Variety* 245 (23 November 1966): 59.

42. This comment was made to me by a former Berkeley student who prefers to remain anonymous.

43. Hampel, *The Last Little Citadel*, p. 89.

44. Landau, *Growing up in the '60s*, pp. 76–77.

45. Barbara Goldfarb, Northwood High School, Silver Spring, Maryland, in Diane Divoky, *How Old Will You Be in 1984? Expressions of Student Outrage from the High School Free Press* (New York: Discus Books, 1969), p. 26.

46. Joyce Maynard, *Looking Back: A Chronicle of Growing up Old in the Sixties* (Garden City, N.Y.: Doubleday, 1973), pp. 133–36.

47. Sugerman, *Wonderland Avenue*, p. 106.

48. Ibid., pp. 103–4.

49. Abigail Heath, "I'm Fed Up with Teenagers," *McCall's* 80 (January 1953): 28–31, 116.

50. Normon Solomon, Montgomery Blair High School, Silver Spring, Maryland, in Divoky, *How Old Will You Be in 1984?*, pp. 213–14.

51. Jon Grell, High School Independent Press Service [HIPS], New York City, in Divoky, *How Old Will You Be in 1984?*, p. 145; "US," Ann Arbor High School, Michigan, in ibid. p. 144; introduction [n.p.].

52. Grell, p. 146.

53. "Links," Madison, Wisconsin, in Divoky, *How Old Will You Be?*, pp. 118–19; Charlotte Massey and Jerry Michelson, Ann Arbor High School, Michigan, in ibid., p. 149.

54. "Open Door," Milwaukee, Wisconsin, in Divoky, *How Old Will You Be?*, p. 32; "The Issue" Framingham High School, Massachusetts, in ibid., p. 159.

55. HIPS, p. 39.

56. Hampel, *The Last Little Citadel*, p. 95.

57. Ibid., pp. 119, 122–24, 129–30.

58. Howard Swerdloff, "Life in These United States," in Divoky, *How Old Will You Be?*, p. 291.

59. Marybeth Norton et al., *A People and a Nation: A History of the United States*, vol. 2 (Boston: Houghton Mifflin, 1982), p. 947.

60. Gitlin, *The Sixties*, p. 411; James Miller, *Democracy Is in the Streets* (New York; Simon and Schuster, 1987), p. 320.

61. Gitlin, *The Sixties*, p. 417.

62. Cyril Levitt, *Children of Privilege: Student Revolt in the Sixties* (Toronto: University of Toronto Press, 1984), pp. 184–85.

63. Hampel, *The Last Little Citadel*, p. 105.

64. Ibid., p. 125.

65. Medved and Wallechinsky, *What Really Happened to the Class of '65?*, p. 100.

66. Ibid., pp. 100, 170.

Conclusion   Back to the Future

1. Carol Lawson, "A Bedtime Story That's Different," *New York Times*, 4 April 1991, pp. C1, C8.

2. Ibid., p. C8.

3. Mary Stolz, *A Love or a Season* (New York: Harper and Row, 1964 [1954]), dust jacket cover.

4. Mary Stolz, *Two by Two* (Boston: Houghton Mifflin, 1954), p. 238.

5. Mary S. Calderone, M.D., "Adolescent Sexual Behavior," *PTA Magazine* 59 (September 1964): 4–7.

6. Ibid.; Seymour M. Farber, M.D., and Roger Wilson, M.D., eds., *Teenage Marriage and Divorce* (Berkeley: Diablo Press, 1967), pref-

ace, p. 14; Catherine S. Chilman, *Adolescent Sexuality in a Chang-ing American Society: Social and Psychological Perspectives* (Washing-ton, D.C.: Government Printing Office, 1978), pp. 195–96.

7. Robert L. Hampel, *The Last Little Citadel: American High Schools Since 1940* (Boston: Houghton Mifflin, 1986), p. 89.

8. Susan Moore and Doreen Rosenthal, *Sexuality in Adolescence* (London: Routledge, 1993), p. 127.

9. Estelle Ellis coined the phrase cited in Kelly Schrum, " 'Teena Means Business': *Seventeen* Magazine and the Emerging Image of the Teenage Girl 1944–1950," seminar paper, The Johns Hopkins University Department of History, March 1995, p. 7; Chilman, *Adolescent Sexuality in a Changing American Society*, p. 113; Stephen Buckley and Debbi Wilgoren, "Young and Experienced," *Washington Post*, 24 April 1994, pp. A1, A8; "You Can't Make This Stuff Up," *Sassy* 4 (October 1992): 63.

10. "Teenagers and Sex," *Ladies' Home Journal* 110 (January 1993): 76–78.

11. Robert Coles and Geoffrey Stokes, *Sex and the American Teenager* (New York: Harper and Row, 1985), p. 5.

12. Chilman, *Adolescent Sexuality in a Changing American Society*, p. 113; Buckley and Wilgoren, "Young and Experienced," pp. A1, A8; "Virginity," *Seventeen* 53 (June 1994): 117. According to the Alan Guttmacher Institute, the number of sexually active teenagers increased 63 percent between 1968 and 1988. See "Teenagers and Sex," pp. 76–78. Quotation is from Laura Blu-menfeld, ". . . Connects with Real Life," *Washington Post*, 17 Feb-ruary 1992, p. D5.

13. Susan Cohen, "Baby Boomerang," *Washington Post Magazine* (24 July 1994): 5.

14. "Teenagers and Sex," pp. 76–78.

15. "Sex and Body," *Seventeen* 52 (November 1993): 96.

16. "Saying No to Sex," *Staten Island Advance*, 27 February 1994, p. F1.

17. "Teenagers and Sex," pp. 76–78; Ellen Hopkins, "Sex Is for Adults," *New York Times*, 26 December 1992, p. 21.

18. Lawson, "A Bedtime Story That's Different," pp. C1, C8; "Teenagers and Sex," pp. 76–78.

19. Buckley and Wilgoren, "Young and Experienced," pp. A1, A8; Moore and Rosenthal, *Sexuality in Adolescence*, pp. 17–20; Barbara Vobejda, "Teens Improve on Prevention of Pregnancy," *Washing-ton Post*, 7 June 1994, pp. A1, A9; ABC News Broadcast Town Meeting on Teenage Sex, "Nightline," 17 February 1995.

20. ABC News Broadcast Town Meeting on Teenage Sex.

21. Barbara Vobejda, "Home Alone Glued to the TV," *Washington Post*, 10 December 1992, p. A3.

22. Jon Nordheimer, "For Lovers No. 1 Activity These Days Is Worrying," *New York Times*, 12 February 1992, pp. C1, C10.

23. "Teens, Here Comes the Biggest Wave Yet," *Business Week* (11 April 1994): 77; Vobejda, "Home Alone Glued to the TV," p. A3; Charles M. Young, "Beavis and Butthead," *Rolling Stone* (19 August 1993), pp. 43, 50, 87.

24. "Entry Level Skills in Short Supply," *Staten Island Advance*, 20 March 1994, p. A7; Thomas J. Lueck, "Health Care Keeps Rank as Job Leader," *New York Times*, 25 May 1993, p. B2; Donna Gaines, *Teenage Wasteland: Suburbia's Dead End Kids* (New York: Pantheon Books, 1991), p. 157.

25. Cohen, "Baby Boomerang," p. 5.

26. Gaines, *Teenage Wasteland*, pp. 154, 158, 202, 238.

27. Ibid., p. 157.

28. Debra Tortora, "Ouch! Body Piercing," *Staten Island Advance*, 19 December 1993, p. F1; Laura Blumenfeld, "Holier Than Thou," *Washington Post*, 7 February 1993, pp. F1, F6.

29. Laura Sessions Stepp, "When Life's the Pits," *Washington Post*, 12 January 1993, p. B5.

30. CBS News Broadcast "This Morning," 11 July 1994; "On Turning 13: Reports from the Front Lines," *New York Times*, 28 February 1993, section 4, p. 2.

31. Christopher Georges, "The Boring Twenties," *Washington Post*, 12 September 1993, p. C1.

32. For instance, "On the Rocks: Is Your Child Drinking Behind Your Back?" *Family Circle* 107 (5 April 1994): 81; "The Rise of Teenage Gambling," *Chicago Times*, 25 February 1991, p. 78; Judy Mann, "AIDS and the Teenage Girl," *Washington Post*, 4 August 1993, p. E5; Steve Twomey, "Indiscretions That Are Not So Youthful," ibid., 6 December 1993, pp. B1, B3; Jerry Kreitzer, *The Peer Partners Handbook: Helping Your Friends Live Free from Violence, Drug Use, Teen Pregnancy, and Suicide* (Barrytown, N.Y.: Station Hill Press, 1995). For a different view, see Laura Sessions Stepp, "Positively Teens: The Rebellious Kid Is the Exception Not the Rule," *Washington Post*, 28 March 1995, p. E5.

33. Arthur Kropp, in Stepp, "When Life's the Pits," p. B5.

34. Ibid.; Bob Herbert, "Listen to the Children," *New York Times*, 27 June 1993, p. 15.

35. Cohen, "Baby Boomerang," p. 5

36. Earl Ubell, "Sex Education Programs That Work—and Some

That Don't," *Parade* (12 February 1995): 20; "Saying No to Sex," *Staten Island Advance*, 27 February 1994, p. F1; "High-Tech Dolls Simulate What Drugs Do to Infants," *Santa Fe New Mexican*, 8 April 1995, p. A1.

37. "For One Teen," *Staten Island Advance*, 10 October 1993, p. F3; "Maine's Month-Old Youth Apprenticeships Show How a National Plan Might Work," *Chronicle of Higher Education* (31 March 1991): A20.

index